T0301625

Fighting Working Poverty in Post-industrial Economies

Causes, Trade-offs and Policy Solutions

Eric Crettaz

Lecturer, Centre for the Understanding of Social Processes, University of Neuchâtel, Switzerland

Edward Elgar

Cheltenham, UK • Northampton, MA, USA

Published by
Edward Elgar Publishing Limited
The Lypiatts
15 Lansdown Road
Cheltenham
Glos GL50 2JA
UK

Edward Elgar Publishing, Inc.
William Pratt House
9 Dewey Court
Northampton
Massachusetts 01060
USA

A catalogue record for this book is available from the British Library

Library of Congress Control Number: 2011931012

ISBN 978 0 85793 487 1

Typeset by Columns Design XML Ltd, Reading
Printed and bound by MPG Books Group, UK

Contents

Acknowledgements

I have greatly benefitted from the critical spirit and the valuable comments of many outstanding researchers. I am particularly grateful to Giuliano Bonoli, Yves Flückiger, Nils Soguel and François-Xavier Merrien.

I would also like to thank the European Network of Excellence Reconciling Work and Welfare in Europe (RECWOWE, Framework Programme 6), especially for funding the short-term scientific mission I carried out at the University of Oviedo, Spain, in the spring of 2009. I would like to warmly thank Rodolfo Gutiérrez, Ana Guillén, Marta Ibáñez and Sergio González for the invaluable scientific discussions we had, as well as for their friendliness during my stay in Oviedo. Thank you very much to all the members of the task 'Working poverty in the European Union, a comparative approach' of RECWOWE, especially Rodolfo Gutiérrez, Neil Fraser and Ramón Peña-Casas.

I am very grateful to the University of Neuchâtel, Switzerland, for its financial support to this project, and to Janine Dahinden, Christian Suter and Cédric Jacot for their trust and support. I would also like to thank Kimberly Way for her commitment to the language editing of the manuscript.

Last but certainly not least, I am very grateful to Anne for her great support and her amazing patience throughout the intensive phases of the publication process. This book is dedicated to her and to my parents.

1. The dilemmas and puzzles of the fight against working poverty

Why do we need to study working poverty in post-industrial countries? It would certainly make sense to be concerned about the situation of those who work in developing countries' informal economy and who are never sure if they will 'make it until the next day'. Similarly, it makes obvious sense to analyse the most severe forms of deprivation, especially homelessness, in high-income countries. But in today's advanced economies, we may be puzzled to find that a person holding a job – sometimes a full-time job – has to endure poverty. The puzzle is particularly striking given the development of dual earnership and the expansion of the welfare state in recent decades; and yet, working poverty has been 'rediscovered' in recent years and is perceived to be a growing problem. This book deals with the apparent paradox of the re-emergence of working poverty in post-industrial economies and contributes to the identification of potential solutions.

As will be shown, low wages and income poverty follow partly independent logics, which are mainly due to the two above mentioned phenomena, namely the development of the welfare state, on the one hand, and the increasing share of dual-earner families, on the other hand. In countries in which this dual-earner household type is widespread and has set the norm in terms of consumption and living standards, living in a single-earner family becomes a disadvantage. As a result, there is no compelling reason why workers, even full-time year-round workers, should escape (relative) poverty. Moreover, the effectiveness of work as an antidote to poverty depends on the amount of work performed. Working only few hours per week cannot be expected to protect someone from poverty.

Working poverty constitutes a puzzle worth studying in the sense that work constitutes for most of us a guarantee of a poverty-free existence. However, the metamorphoses of the labour markets in post-industrial economies have led to a growing relative disadvantage for certain subgroups of the labour force, and it is fundamental to understand these changes.

1.1 RESEARCH QUESTIONS

Trade-offs and tensions are at the heart of the present work. This is, indeed, one of the most striking features of the fight against poverty among the working-age population. On the one hand, by imposing strong labour market protections and high labour costs in the form of non-wage costs (mainly social security contributions), some policies may increase the difficulty disadvantaged adults have in finding a job or workers in keeping theirs, thereby replacing working poverty by unemployment and inactivity. On the other hand, maximizing labour force participation by reducing employment protection and lowering benefits can lead to skyrocketing inequalities, with many unemployed persons and welfare recipients thrown into poverty. As a matter of fact, it could be said that the working poor, as well as policymakers, are held hostage by the situation.

The central goal of this book is to identify policy mixes that both limit the incidence of poverty among the workforce and enable an employment-friendly environment. Put differently, my objective is to identify social policy interventions that support low-income workers and largely limit collateral damages in terms of employment, taking into account the fact that there are also many tensions at the household level, between labour market participation, earning levels, family formation and fertility.

More specifically, the main questions I want to answer are the following:

- Are there different types of working poverty, depending on its causes?
- To what extent do working poverty mechanisms differ across welfare regimes, and how do they translate into differences in terms of the size and composition of the working poor population?
- What specific policy tools have a positive antipoverty impact? What is their impact on employment? In which context do they work?
- How are these policy tools organized in real welfare states and what is their impact?

1.2 ANALYTICAL APPROACH AND METHODOLOGY

How is it possible to identify policy mixes that can ease the tension between working poverty and unemployment, that is, between the quality and the quantity of jobs available?

After a brief summary of the main economic and sociodemographic determinants of working poverty in post-industrial economies, I devote more attention to public policy factors. They seem to have a pervasive impact; hence, it is fundamental to review the social policy literature in order to identify public policy instruments that seem to work in specific socio-economic contexts and to ask whether these policies are 'exportable' or not. The main instruments I have been able to identify are minimum wages, tax credits for workers, family cash benefits and childcare policies.

Moreover, I also identify the three mechanisms through which economic, sociodemographic and public policy factors have a direct bearing on households, namely: low wage rates; low labour force attachment expressed as a percentage of full participation; and high needs given the household's earning potential (mainly the number of children per working-age adult, as well as the increase in needs after a divorce). This allows understanding as to why the size and composition of the working poor population differs across countries, and shows that there are various groups of poor workers who are in different situations. At this stage, I will show that there are various types of working poverty and that failing to acknowledge these contrasting situations can only obscure the debates on how to fight working poverty.

The chapter devoted to public policy factors (Chapter 4) is concluded by a reflection on welfare regimes; these regimes are defined by the role that markets, the government and families play in the provision of (material) well-being. Markets are the main income source of most households: the labour market, financial markets, the housing market and so on. The welfare state can provide disadvantaged individuals and households with cash benefits in the event of job loss, of disability, of sickness, of the death of the main wage earner, and can provide the population with services (for example subsidized childcare centres, job search coaching with public employment services, courses for lowly qualified workers, social housing, to name a few examples), as well as serving the population by improving infrastructures (hospitals, road networks, public transportation, university campuses and so on). Finally, money and time are redistributed within families; some household members may reduce their labour market partici-pation in order to take care of young children or an elderly family member, the main contributors to the household's income can be more or less generous with family members who do not earn their living, parents can support their adult children financially and offer them free lodging while middle-aged children can support their elderly parents.

This interplay of the government with markets and families defines a welfare regime. Researchers argue about the best typology of welfare regimes that should be used in comparative analyses, and Esping-Andersen's (1990) famous triptych – social-democratic, liberal[1] and conservative corpo-ratist welfare regimes – has been criticized on many grounds. Feminist authors blame it for failing to account for gender issues, as countries that promote a dual-earner model and those who promote single earnership are often classified in the same cluster. Other authors propose typologies based on other indicators, specific social policies for instance; finally, others have advocated the addition of clusters of countries, mainly Mediterranean, Southern European countries and the Antipodes.

In the present work, I show that the social policy literature allows the identification of three approaches to the fight against working poverty, namely minimum wages, social transfers and an employment-maximizing strategy. Each approach can be broken down into two subcategories: minimum wages can be either legally enforced or collectively bargained; social transfers can either constitute a substitution income for persons who cannot earn a living or a complementing income for working households; and the employment-maximization strategy can be either based on incentives and productivity-enhancing measures or on coercion. This allows me to conclude that a four-cluster typology is the most appropriate for the analysis of policies that are aimed at combating working poverty: social-democratic, 'liberal', conservative corporatist and Southern European welfare regimes.

After the identification of promising social policy instruments and the definition of a welfare regime typology, the first prong of my empirical work consists of a research synthesis that goes beyond the traditional literature reviews, namely a meta-analysis – in the form of a weighted vote-counting procedure accompanied by statistical tests – of particular social policy tools in their 'natural' social, political and institutional environment in the recent past (namely articles published in the twenty-first century). The main objective is to assess both antipoverty and employment effects. After a systematic selection of articles through scientific search engines allowing the collection of regression and simulation results, I assess whether researchers were able to reach a consensus as to the efficiency or inefficiency of a measure, and if not, if the majority of articles conclude that a given policy has positive or negative effects and if these effects are significant, depending on the methodology used and the population studied. In addition to general conclusions, in order to take the 'real world' of social policy into account, results are then broken down by welfare regimes. This first empirical contribution enables the following questions to be answered: which policy instruments are effective in which context, and for whom?

In the real world of social policies, however, single policy tools are intertwined in a complex set of other social policies and labour market regulations, and their efficiency also depends on the sociodemographic composition of the labour force and on the state of the economy (for instance, the American Earned Income Tax Credit was strongly expanded at a time when the US experienced one of the most prosperous decades of its history). Hence, the second prong of my empirical strategy consists of an analysis of existing welfare regimes, by using the above mentioned typology (liberal, social-democratic, conservative corporatist and Southern European), which is based on the main social policy tools and labour market regulations that have an impact on the extent of working poverty and the relative size of various risk groups. The US, Sweden, Germany and Spain epitomize these four welfare state clusters.

This approach accounts for the fact that various social policy instruments do not work independently, but interact with each other; it also includes a reflection on recent shocks to these welfare systems and the ways in which welfare regimes reacted to these exogenous shocks. Empirically, the relative weight of each working poverty mechanism in each welfare regime is assessed, as well as the composition of the working poor population, the latter being a consequence of the former. Robustness checks are carried out based on various poverty indicators and thresholds. This second empirical contribution enables the following questions to be answered: what kind/s of working poverty is/are generated in which welfare regime, and why?

The combination of the two prongs will allow the identification of the policy mix that works in certain welfare regimes, and the reasons for this efficiency. At the very end of the present work, I analyse the ability of each welfare regime to overcome the trade-off between working poverty and employment performance, based on the empirical results provided throughout this book. Most countries do not seem to be in a situation to overcome the tension between the quality and the quantity of jobs. However, Scandinavian countries combine low working poor rates, low unemployment and high employment rates. The present work provides explanations as to why the social-democratic welfare regime appears to be better equipped to face the challenges posed by post-industrial mutations in general and working poverty in particular, as well as the very specific conditions under which this model functions that make it difficult to export. I also provide some elements as to the main characteristics this trade-off has in the other three welfare regimes.

However, it is not possible to do what is described in the previous paragraphs right away, because there is a big problem with the definition of working poverty in post-industrial economies. Until recently, there was a definitional 'chaos' characterized by arbitrariness, which is probably attributable to the fact that conceptual reflections were largely missing. First, it is complex to set a poverty line, a task that has kept social scientists busy ever since the first poverty reports were published at the end of the nineteenth century. Usually, social policy research is based on a monetary poverty line and the headcount ratio (the number of poor persons divided by the size of the population), but other monetary thresholds, other poverty indicators and different approaches (non-monetary and subjective indicators) have been proposed. There is no consensus among poverty researchers to which is the best way to measure poverty; however, for national studies, I advocate the use of thresholds derived from social policy entitlement thresholds. For comparative studies, it can be useful to rely on official definitions, in order to increase the comparability of different studies. More problematic in my view is the fact of setting an arbitrary threshold in terms of number of hours per week or months per year to define who is 'working'. I advocate the use of an encompassing definition, combined with a typological approach to the definition, rather than excluding groups of disadvantaged workers from the outset.

Regarding the empirical part of the present work, other approaches would have been conceivable, in particular meta-regression techniques in order to quantify the employment and antipoverty impact of each policy. Microsimulation methods that allow the checking of the impact of the introduction of a new policy mix, or the reform of an existing one, would have in a given country, would also be an option.

Developing meta-regression models would indeed be the next step to take after the meta-analysis carried out in the present work, once a particular set of policies is deemed to be potentially efficient in a given context, in order to further the understanding of its impact. In this case, it would be necessary to enlarge the pool of estimates at disposal, for instance by extending the period of time considered for the selection process; indeed, meta-regression, as any other econometric technique, requires a minimum number of observations in order to carry out reliable analyses. It is probably advisable to have at least 100 estimates to be able to draw reliable conclusions. Moreover, meta-regression requires the use of a common metric for all results, which is far from evident when generalized linear models are used (logit, probit and so on). This approach necessitates a considerable amount of empirical work; hence, this kind of approach usually focuses on a specific policy in a specific subset of countries (with comparable institutional and economic environments), whereas my perspective is broader in scope as I aim to identify various policy mixes that seem to work in various institutional contexts, without attempting to accurately assess the magnitude of their effect. Another type of meta-regression is conceivable; it does not attempt to calculate a 'grand mean effect size', but focuses on the predictors of a positive or negative impact on employment and poverty (see for example Kluve, 2006). This kind of calculation would be possible with the data provided in this book.

With regards to microsimulation, this method necessitates a focus on one country and requires detailed knowledge of its fiscal system, labour market regulations and welfare state. In the case of countries with federal institutions, a microsimulation at the national level can become extremely tricky. This type of empirical work should only come after a careful examination of the interplay of the national context and social policy instruments, a stage that is sometimes skipped in the literature, with authors directly assessing whether a specific social policy measure would reduce working poverty without any adjustment of the parameters of this measure to the sociodemographic reality of the country in which the simulation is carried out. This methodological device should, indeed, represent the final step in a comprehensive approach of the analysis of policies that allow for the combating of working poverty in a specific country.

1.3 THE MAIN ARGUMENTS OF THIS BOOK

Throughout this book, I develop an understanding of the problematic of working poverty in post-industrial economies that is structured by three main arguments. These arguments were not determined from the outset; they progressively emerged as the conceptual and empirical work went forward.

- *There is no such thing as 'the working poor'; there are (at least) three types of working poverty.* Conceptual reflections about the definition of 'the working poor' and estimations of the size of various risk groups led to an analysis of working poverty mechanisms, which in turn led to the conclusion that there are at least three types of working poverty: some workers are poor because they are badly paid; others could escape poverty should they work more hours but they cannot; while a third group of poor workers are in a difficult situation because of their household's needs.
- *Different welfare regimes generate different types of working poverty.* After having identified different types of working poverty, and because it is a well-known finding that the socio-economic composition of the working poor population varies across welfare regimes, I investigated the impact of welfare regimes on the three working poverty mechanisms I had identified and came to the conclusion that welfare regimes have, indeed, a pervasive impact on these mechanisms.
- *There is no 'one-size-fits-all' policy mix. Each regime must find its own combination of policies.* As the relative weight of the three mechanisms leading to working poverty varies widely across welfare regimes, a logical consequence is that it is impossible to determine a

single policy mix that would have the same efficiency in each regime. This logical conclusion was confirmed by the meta-analyses I carried out, especially when results were broken down by welfare regime.

1.4   ANALYTICAL LIMITS

In what follows, this book does not evaluate the impact of two important potential solutions to the working poverty problem. A first option would be to combat in-work poverty by promoting a general upgrading of skill level. Low-skilled workers have experienced an increasing disadvantage in post-industrial labour markets characterized by the growing importance of computerized processes and of interactions with other persons (in the service sector), requiring a higher educational level and better 'social skills'. This goal, however noble and advisable it may be, pertains to a completely different field of public policy, as well as to a different type of knowledge and strand of literature, than the policies analysed in the present work. Another option would be to put more emphasis on active labour market policies targeted at non-working partners of poor workers, in order to enhance households' earnings and financial autonomy. This would go, however, far beyond the scope of the present work, and would constitute a research topic of its own.

Another limitation needs to be highlighted. In the empirical part of the present work, monetary definitions of poverty have been used. In fact, it has proved impossible to find any evaluation using non-monetary poverty indicators for the meta-analysis. However, as will be analysed below, some researchers have advocated the use of non-monetary indicators to measure poverty as they perceive them to be more revealing and more accurate depictions of the living conditions of disadvantaged families (Ferro Luzzi et al., 2008; Suter and Paris, 2002). These indicators usually take the form of direct measures of living conditions (whether or not respondents possess certain goods) combined with 'subjective' indicators, for example asking respondents why they do not possess a specific good (is it due to lacking financial resources or is it a choice?). Other scholars have proposed the use of purely subjective indicators such as the degree of satisfaction with family income or the level of income deemed absolutely necessary to 'make ends meet' (van Praag et al., 1980).

Whereas I agree with the idea that non-monetary indicators can provide a more accurate account of living conditions than income, especially for some sub-groups of the population whose financial situation is very diffi-cult to assess (Antille et al., 1997), it also needs to be said that for the social policy objectives outlined above, monetary indicators appear to be more useful, as the vast majority of social and labour market-related benefits are monetary (minimum wages, tax credits and allowances, child allowances, family benefits, as well as all 'passive' benefits related to disability, old age, sickness, unemployment, widowhood and so on) or consist in near-cash benefits (food stamps, housing subsidies, childcare vouchers and so on). This is the reason why a monetary definition of poverty is used in the present work, and the robustness of the findings is checked by using various indicators of the financial situation and various poverty indicators.

Last but not least, in this work I analyse the formal labour market and legally earned incomes. Bourgois, an American anthropologist, lived during his fieldwork in an East Harlem neighbourhood dubbed El Barrio and noted that, according to official statistics, his neighbours should have been homeless and starving, but the majority were not, which indicated the presence of an underground economy that had a major impact on living conditions. A part of this economy consisted of informal but non-criminal activities, such as curbside car repairing and baby-sitting; but the cocaine-, crack- and heroin-related activities seemed to be the only equal-opportunity activities in this neighbourhood (Bourgois, 2003). Interestingly, all drug dealers working in the crack selling network Bourgois observed had previously had legal jobs in the formal labour market (messenger or mail room clerk, janitor assistant, photocopier-servicer and other service-sector entry-level occupations) and started working at a very young age. More surprisingly, some of them had not completely withdrawn from the legal, just-above-minimum-wage labour market. Bourgois met a female drug dealer who, in order to make ends meet and bring up her children, had to combine legal low-wage employment, welfare benefits (welfare gave this lone mother at the time of the interview US$53 per week only) and drug selling. According to Bourgois (2003: 92),

> [street dealers'] income is almost never as consistently high as they report it to be … According to my calculations, [the dealers Bourgois befriended] averaged slightly less than double the minimum wage – between seven and eight dollars an hour … it took me several years to realize how inconsistent and meager crack income can be.

The situation of disadvantaged people earning meagre incomes from legal jobs as well as from underground, illegal activities is certainly very interesting and of paramount importance. Probably, workers holding undeclared jobs are disproportionately affected by poverty. More generally, the underground economy is a non-negligible reality in social policy analysis, as it allows some employers and employees to circumvent labour market regulations and taxes. Nonetheless, I focus in the present work on the situation of legally employed persons, in order to avoid confusions between various important social phenomena, each one requiring different social (as well as educational, housing and judicial) policies.

NOTE

1. The word 'liberal' is polysemantic: Esping-Andersen's (1990) use is very different from that of American conservatives who blame 'liberal' policies for the behaviours they generate and the 'liberal' politicians who implemented them. Esping-Andersen's use of the term refers to a welfare regime that mainly relies on market mechanisms, while public policies compensate for market failures and provide help to the poorest members of society. In what follows, the expression 'liberal welfare regime' refers to Esping-Andersen's phraseology, while 'neoliberal' refers to the belief that free-operating markets and the leanest possible welfare state is the only way to achieve well-being for all.

2. Arbitrary definitions, official definitions and useful typologies

When defining working poverty, obviously, two definitional issues need to be dealt with: how to define poverty and, perhaps more importantly, how to define work and where to set a threshold in terms of the amount of work performed.

2.1 WHAT IS 'POVERTY' IN RICH COUNTRIES?

Ongoing controversies and hard-fought debates have taken place ever since the founding fathers of applied poverty research released their first reports (Booth, 1888; Rowntree, 1901 [1980]), and it seems that the worst forms of poverty have virtually been eradicated in rich countries. Some may even think that poverty no longer exists in post-industrial economies, whereas this opinion is probably not dominant. In 1989, former British Prime Minister Margaret Thatcher said to *The Guardian* that 'Poverty no longer exists in Britain, only inequality' (quoted in Atkinson, 1998: 45). But is it really true that poverty has disappeared in rich countries? As indicated above, the most extreme forms of poverty have been virtually eradicated. However financial hardship is a pressing problem for many workers in post-industrial countries, as is shown in this book. Atkinson gave a convincing answer: 'I would certainly agree that the problems of the Sahel are more pressing than those addressed in [his book *Poverty in Europe*] ... but poverty within rich countries may legitimately come next on our list of concerns' (Atkinson, 1998: 1).

It should be noted that the definition and the measurement of poverty will not be my main focus. A vast literature already exists and I do not wish to review it extensively; however, the main debates and indicators will be presented briefly.

2.2   ABSOLUTE VS RELATIVE POVERTY

Seebohm Rowntree's seminal work, which was carried out in the city of York, is the most famous example of an absolute poverty measurement method (Rowntree, 1901 [1980]). He consulted American nutritionists and collected data pertaining to the cost of basic food items available to working class families. He determined a bundle of absolutely necessary goods that allowed people to satisfy their basic needs; if these were not met, people faced 'primary poverty'. Rowntree's original poverty line was based on the following diet presented in Table 2.1.

Table 2.1 Basic diet for a man, 1899

	Breakfast	Dinner	Supper
Sunday	Bread, 8 oz Margarine, ½ oz Tea, 1 pt	Boiled bacon, 3 oz Pease pudding, 12 oz	Bread, 8 oz Margarine, ½ oz Cocoa, 1 pt
Monday	Bread, 8 oz Porridge, 1 ½ pts	Potatoes with milk, 24 oz Bread, 2 oz Cheese, 2 oz	Bread, 8 oz Vegetable broth, 1 pt Cheese, 2 oz
Tuesday	Porridge, 1 ½ pts Skim milk, 1 pt	Vegetable broth, 1 pt Bread, 4 oz Cheese, 2 oz Dumpling, 8 oz	Bread, 4 oz Porridge, 1 ½ pts

Source: Glennerster et al. (2004), Box 2, p. 34.

The cost of clothing, rent, light and fuel was added to these prices. All in all, the poverty line for a couple and three children aged three, six and eight was, at 2000 prices, £53.10 in 1899.

Rowntree carried out two more studies in York in 1936 and 1950, which showed that 'primary' poverty amounted to 9.9 per cent at the end of the nineteenth century, 3.9 per cent in the 1930s, despite the Great Depression, and had virtually been eradicated in 1950 (Atkinson, 1989), which was largely attributable to the development of the welfare state (Piachaud and Webb, 2004).

Indeed, the nature and implications of poverty have changed in advanced economies. Paugam (2005), among other researchers, has shown that poverty in pre-industrial Europe was an 'integrated' poverty, characterized by the fact that there was a large number of poor people who did not differ much from the rest of the population and led a socially integrated life. In post-industrial Europe, high unemployment countries such as France are characterized by 'social exclusion'. The long-term unemployed accumulate social disadvantages that are associated with a degradation of family and friendship ties. Another form can also be found in post-industrial countries, namely a 'marginal' poverty that is typical of low unemployment countries such as in Scandinavia where this minority can be perceived as a residual category, and the degree of stigmatization can be high (Bergmark, 2000).

Given this evolution of 'poverty', many researchers who analyse the situation in high-income countries define a 'sociocultural' subsistence level which encompasses more than basic goods. The idea is that an individual is poor compared to the average living standard of the society he or she lives in. This is a *relative* definition of poverty that takes into account the fact that society imposes needs and expectations as to what is necessary to live a decent life (Townsend, 1974), that is, that human needs are socially constructed. Townsend insisted on what he called relative deprivation, which he defined as 'the absence or inadequacy of those diets, amenities, standards, services and activities which are common or customary in society' (Townsend, 1979: 915). Bourdieu (1993) noted that the modern form of poverty seems very relative compared to the worst forms of material hardship; however, it can hurt people inasmuch as it is a 'misery of position'. Industrialized societies have been very good at reducing extreme poverty, but through a process of differentiation, they multiplied social spaces, which favoured the development of this 'relative misery' (Bourdieu, 1993).

Sen has summarized this tension by asking whether one should define a threshold below which people are absolutely impoverished or a level that reflects some kind of average living standard. He underlined, however, that there is an irreducible core of absolute deprivation, that is, starvation, malnutrition and other forms of harsh deprivation, in the notion of poverty (Sen, 1981). Sen's view that poverty is an absolute notion in the space of capabilities, but usually takes a relative form in terms of commodities, appears to be the most satisfying answer to the conceptual problem posed by the changing nature of poverty as the level of economic development increases (Sen, 1983).

It is extremely important to underline the fact that relative and absolute poverty are not synonymous of relative and absolute poverty lines. It is conceivable to define a level of poverty related to the customary living standard in a given society at a given time by using an absolute poverty line, that is, fixed in real terms in order to observe the evolution of a given living standard throughout a certain period.

2.3 INCOME, LIVING CONDITIONS AND PERCEPTIONS OF ONE'S FINANCIAL SITUATION

Most studies rely on household income as a poverty yardstick. Many scholars, however, have questioned the relevance of income to account for someone's well-being. Other monetary indicators are conceivable, such as consumption levels. It is noteworthy that the correlation between income and consumption levels is not necessarily very high (Headey et al., 2009). Debts and indebtedness can also be interesting for poverty analysis and Eurostat has included debt indicators in its Survey on Income and Living Conditions (European Commission, 2006). Wealth is also an important monetary indicator; the problem is, however, that the vast majority of surveys do not include questions pertaining to wealth.

Some researchers criticize monetary indicators in general and advocate a direct (and mostly multidimensional) measure of poverty, which consists of assessing actual living conditions, by measuring the possession of con-sumption goods and the access to services. Indeed, in many countries, the relationship between income and living conditions is surprisingly weak (Halleröd, 2006; Mayer, 1995; Nolan, 1998). This is due, among other things, to the fact that income measures usually do not take into account disparities in wealth and credit. Moreover, it is very difficult to adjust income for family size, and there is no agreement among researchers as to which equivalence scale is the most appropriate, and non-monetary indica-tors have the massive advantage that they do not require the use of an equivalence scale.

Townsend was one of the first scholars to promote this direct approach of poverty based on a predefined array of goods and services, and calcu-lated an additive deprivation index (Townsend, 1979). Mack and Lansley have improved Townsend's method by using opinion polls to determine what goods and services are deemed to be absolutely necessary by a majority of respondents and by asking respondents who did not possess a given item whether this was so because they did not want it or because they could not afford it (Halleröd, 2006; Leu et al., 1997; Mack and Lansley, 1985). Recently, social scientists and economists have further refined this method (Andress and Lipsmeier, 1995; Ferro Luzzi et al., 2008; Halleröd, 1994; Suter and Paris, 2002).

It should be noted, however, that the direct measurement of living conditions also has drawbacks. International comparisons of living conditions are difficult to carry out, because there is no such thing as a consensus regarding the items that should be included in questionnaires; moreover, the importance of each item may vary from one country to another. The approach advocated by Mack and Lansley (1985) postulates that it is possible to distinguish when people choose not to have a good from when they cannot afford it. This is indeed much more complex than it appears at first thought, as disadvantaged social groups tend to adjust their preferences to their monetary resources (Halleröd, 2006). Bourdieu demonstrated more than 30 years ago that one of the main characteristics of the members of the working class was the tendency to make a virtue of necessity, by adjusting their expectations and their judgements to their material, social and cultural situation (Bourdieu, 1979).

Regardless of these drawbacks, non-monetary indicators are valuable and are particularly useful in the case of population groups for which it is difficult to calculate disposable income, such as self-employed workers in general and farmers in particular (Crettaz and Forney, 2010; The Canberra Group, 2001).

Another approach is based on subjective indicators. Respondents are asked to indicate a minimum level of income they deem necessary to 'make ends meet', or to say if their household income is sufficient in order to meet certain needs, or if they are satisfied with their income/consumption level. The economists of the Leyden School have advocated the use of such indicators to define poverty lines (Falter, 2006; Strengmann-Kuhn, 2003; van Praag and Ferrer-i-Carbonell, 2008; van Praag et al., 1980).

In fact, a review of the literature on working poverty reveals that subjective indicators have hardly ever been used. It should be noted that these subjective thresholds may 'overestimate' poverty, as it seems that they yield high poverty rates (Citro and Michael, 1995; Strengmann-Kuhn, 2003). This approach may also overestimate the well-being of population groups who have lived on a low income for a long time. In order to reduce the subjective feeling of deprivation, long-term disadvantaged persons tend to, subconsciously, lower their expectations and adjust their satisfaction to their income level (Crettaz and Forney, 2010; Halleröd, 2006), which is confirmed by ethnographic evidence in the case of small farmers (Droz, 1998).

2.4 POVERTY LINES

The US official poverty threshold is the best-known example of an *absolute poverty threshold*. Since the mid-1960s, the US Census Bureau has been publishing poverty rates based on the following approach:

$$\text{Poverty line} = H \cdot \vec{P}^T \cdot \vec{X}$$

where $\vec{P}^T$ is a vector of prices, $\vec{X}$ is an array of foods and H is a multiplier. The Orshansky[1] multiplier equals 3, because consumption surveys carried out in the 1960s by the US Department of Agriculture had established that low-income households spent about one-third of their income to meet their alimentary needs. This kind of indicator, as already mentioned, should not necessarily be an indicator of extreme poverty, depending on the multiplier. The 'Orshansky poverty line' has been subject to criticism in recent years (Citro and Michael, 1995) because it is no longer in line with today's US average living standards, amongst other reasons.

Relative poverty lines rest upon median or mean household income. The most common poverty lines are 50 and 60 per cent of median income. American researchers sometimes use 40 per cent as a threshold, as this roughly corresponds to the level of the official poverty line (Kamerman, 1995; Smeeding, 2005). Interestingly, in the first half of the twentieth century, Rowntree's poverty lines amounted to 30–35 per cent of weekly disposable income per capita, and around 40 per cent in the second half of the twentieth century (Piachaud and Webb, 2004).

Relative poverty indicators should only be used to compare countries with *similar* standards of living. Eurostat notes, for instance, that some of the lowest at-risk-of-poverty rates in the European Union are found in the Czech Republic and Hungary, whereas median income in these countries (adjusted for the cost of living) is significantly lower than the EU-25 median income (Eurostat, 2005). In addition, relative thresholds are sometimes criticized for being mainly inequality indicators (Ravallion, 2003); indeed, they are strongly correlated to income inequality indicators such as the Gini coefficient. Interestingly, an absolute approach tends to show a decline in overall poverty rates in OECD countries between the mid-1980s and 2000, while relative indicators lead to the opposite conclusion for most countries (Whiteford and Adema, 2007).

The advantage of relative poverty lines is that they facilitate international comparisons, which probably explains why they are used by Eurostat, the OECD and other international organizations. Another way to proceed to international comparisons is to define a basket of goods and services and calculate its cost in a given country, and to use purchasing power parities (PPP) to account for differences in the cost of living and exchange rates across countries. As a rule of thumb it can be said that the use of relative poverty lines 'disadvantages' countries with high median incomes and large income inequalities, such as the US, whereas the use of absolute poverty lines adjusted with PPP tends to 'disadvantage' countries in which many services are provided for free or at a very low cost by the state, such as Sweden.

In order to compare the income of households of different size and composition, an *equivalence scale* is used to transform household disposable income into a theoretical one called 'equivalized' income. Usually, equivalence scales are either derived from consumption surveys or they rely on social security experts' opinions. However, they can also be derived from opinion surveys in the case of subjective equivalence scales (Atkinson, 1998; Jäntti and Danziger, 2000).

An equivalence scale ascribes a specific weight to each household member in order to account for economies of scale. There is no agreement among researchers as to the choice of an equivalence scale; Table 2.2 shows the most widely used scales.

Table 2.2 Various equivalence scales found in the poverty literature

	Square root	Modified OECD	McClements	Orshansky	Canadian LICOs
Single adult	1	1	1	1	1
Lone parent, 1 child	1.41	1.3–1.5	1.33–1.52	1.33	1.22
Lone parent, 2 children	1.73	1.6–2	1.66–2.05	1.55	1.52
Couple, no children	1.41	1.5	1.64	1.29	1.22
Couple, 1 child	1.73	1.8–2	1.97–2.16	1.55	1.52
Couple, 2 children	2	2.1–2.5	2.3–2.69	1.95	1.89

Source: Whiteford and Adema (2007).

The choice of an equivalence scale can, obviously, have an impact on the identification of risk groups, as each equivalence scale ascribes a different weight to adults and children. These scales, however, are not the only existing scales. Some researchers advocate the use of subjective indicators, such as the 'minimum income question' – respondents are asked what amount of money is necessary so that their household can make ends meet – or an income satisfaction question (Falter, 2006). The results obtained are at odds with the equivalence scales used in comparative poverty research, showing that families with, say, three children hardly have higher needs than families with one child. In the case of Switzerland, for instance, results are completely different from those derived from consumption data (Gerfin et al., 2009).

Even though consumption partly reflects preferences and not only needs, this gap remains to be explained, as it is quite unlikely that parents develop luxury tastes once they have a second or a third child. Indeed, answers to the income satisfaction question and the minimum income question may instead reflect the fact that parents have lowered their expectations rather than the well-being of their children. In addition, it seems unlikely that having three children or more has nearly zero impact on needs.

These findings raise important scientific questions, though: how can the extra needs associated with the birth of a child be measured, as consumption patterns do not only reflect needs, but they also reflect preferences? How large is the bias generated by the use of the same equivalence scale in different countries in comparative research, as it is very unlikely that economies of scale and the cost of having children are identical across countries? Until now, no satisfying answer has been provided, and the use of standard equivalence scales in comparative social policy research remains one of the main weaknesses of this approach. In this context, non-monetary poverty indicators, such as those mentioned above, could prove helpful, as they do not require the use of an equivalence scale.

These findings also raise interesting political and normative questions: to what extent should a welfare state help parents who have made the decision to have a large number of children, given that children cannot be held responsible for their parents' choice? To what extent is the number of children the result of a 'choice'? The latter question raises another one: do all women have an easy and informed access to contraception?

2.5 THE INCIDENCE, DEPTH AND SEVERITY OF POVERTY

The poverty rate (or headcount ratio) is by far the most widely used poverty indicator; it is the number of poor persons divided by the size of the population and measures the incidence of poverty. The poverty gap aims at measuring the intensity or depth of poverty, that is, how poor disadvantaged households are. It is based on the difference between the poverty line and each household income:

$$pg = \frac{1}{N_p} \sum_{i=1}^{N_p} \frac{(pl - x_i)}{pl}$$

where N_p is the number of poor people, pl the poverty line and x_i the i-th observation of disposable income among the poor population. However, some consider that this indicator is the *income gap*, whereas the *poverty gap* is defined as:

$$\frac{1}{N} \sum_{i=1}^{N_p} \frac{(pl - x_i)}{pl}$$

with N being the population size, and the non-poor have zero income gap. This definition means than the poverty gap is the product of the headcount ratio and the income gap. *The squared poverty gap* is an indicator of the severity of poverty and is defined as follows:

$$spg = \frac{1}{N} \sum_{i=1}^{N_p} \left[\frac{(pl - x_i)}{pl} \right]^2$$

In Chapter 7, the poverty gap is calculated as the product of the poverty rate and the income gap expressed in per cent of the poverty line.

In some of the evaluations meta-analysed in Chapter 6, another poverty indicator is used, namely the FGT index; it allows us to take into account various aspects of poverty and is defined as follows (Foster et al., 1984):

$$FGT = \frac{1}{N_p} \sum_{i=1}^{N_p} \left(\frac{pl - x_i}{pl} \right)^\alpha$$

The higher the α, the greater the weight ascribed to the poorest people; it is an aversion coefficient. If $\alpha = 0$, the FGT index is the headcount ratio, if $\alpha = 1$, it is the poverty gap (Heinrich, 2003), and if $\alpha = 2$, the FGT index measures the severity of poverty.

2.6 POVERTY INDICATORS USED IN THIS BOOK

In this book, I rely exclusively on monetary indicators and mainly on the headcount ratio. However, in Chapter 7, consumption poverty lines are also defined, and both the headcount ratio and the poverty gap are calculated. In addition, two types of relative poverty lines are used whenever possible, namely 50 and 60 per cent of median disposable income. I make use of the dominant type of equivalence scales, that is, consumption-based and expert scales, which are overwhelmingly found in the social policy literature. In my view, the fact that parents are able to lower their expectations after having chosen to have many children does not say much about the well-being of their children.

Whereas direct poverty measurements are scientifically very relevant tools that allow a more subtle understanding of deprivation in post-industrial societies (Ferro Luzzi et al., 2008), they are rarely found in the social policy literature, for reasons already mentioned. It is probably advisable for future research on social policy topics to use these indicators more systematically, in order to get a less abstract picture of the situation of disadvantaged social groups. As to subjective indicators in general, it is probably fair to say that they seem to be of little use for most social policy analyses, as welfare benefits are not attributed to families or individuals because they feel poor but because their income is too low (Halleröd, 2006). However, subjective factors are necessary to understand specific phenomena; they are decisive, for instance, to explain the non-take-up of welfare benefits, as feelings of shame and stigma appear to play a significant role (Leu et al., 1997; Strengmann-Kuhn, 2003; Van Oorschot, 1991).

2.7 DEFINING LABOUR MARKET PARTICIPATION: WHO IS 'WORKING'?

Regarding labour market participation, I can rely on existing scholarship to a much lesser extent, as most of the literature on working poverty uses an arbitrarily set minimum number of hours or months worked, ranging from one hour of work in a reference week (usually the week prior to the

interview) to full-time year-round labour market participation. As a consequence, there may be a group of persons who hold a job at the time of the
interview but are not considered to be 'working'.

Table 2.3 shows the absence of consensus among researchers and in
official statistics, as well as the systematic use of arbitrary thresholds.

Table 2.3 Definitions of 'working poor'

Country	Source	Work definition	Poverty threshold
EU	Eurostat	Employed at least 15 hours/ most frequent activity status in the last year New indicator: in-work at-risk-of-poverty rate: individuals classified as employed (according to their most frequent activity status)	Low-income threshold: less than 60% of the median equivalized household income (relative monetary poverty) At risk of poverty: individuals living in a household with an equivalized disposable income below 60% of the median
France	INSEE/ Academics/ National Action Plan for Social Inclusion 2001–2003/2003–2005	Individuals who have spent at least six months of the year on the labour market (working or searching for a job)/working at least six months/have had a job for at least one month during a year	Low-income threshold: less than 50% (60%–70% occasionally) of the median equivalized household income (relative monetary poverty)
Belgium	National Action Plan for Social Inclusion	Individuals who have spent at least six months of the year on the labour market (working or searching for a job)/working at least six months	Low-income threshold: less than 60% of the median equivalized household income (relative monetary poverty)
Switzer-land	Swiss Federal Statistical Office/ Academics	All 'active' individuals, regardless of the number of hours they work/all individuals working full-time (that is 36 hours or more weekly/at least one individual having a lucrative activity for at least 40 hours per week (one full-time job) New indicator: individuals who work and live in a household in which the overall volume of work (of all members) amounts to at least 36 hours per week	Administrative flat rates of social security modified (monetary administrative poverty)

Table 2.3 continued

Country	Source	Work definition	Poverty threshold
US	US Census Bureau (USCB)	Total hours worked by family members greater than or equal to 1750 hours (44 weeks)	Federal poverty line (absolute monetary poverty)
	US Bureau of Labor Statistics (USBLS)	Individuals who have spent at least six months (27 weeks) of the year on the labour market (working or searching for a job)	Federal poverty line (absolute monetary poverty)
	US researchers in general	Adults working, on average, at least half time (approximately 1000 hours)/definition of USCB and USBLS (see above)	Less than 125%–150%–200% of Federal poverty line (absolute monetary poverty)
Canada	National Council of Welfare (NCW)	More than 50% of total family income come from wages, salaries or self-employment	Statistics Canada's Low-income cutoffs (LICOs) (absolute monetary poverty)
	Canadian Council on Social Development (CCSD)	Adult members have, between them, at least 49 weeks of either full-time (at least 30 hours per week) or part-time work	CCSD relative low-income threshold (relative monetary poverty)
	Canadian Policy Research Networks (CPRN)	Full-time, year round	Relative low-income threshold; less than CAN$20,000 per year (relative monetary poverty)
Australia	Social Policy Research Centre	All 'active' individuals, regardless of the number of hours they work	Henderson absolute poverty line (absolute monetary poverty)

Source: based on Peña-Casas and Latta (2004), modified and completed for this book.

I feel that setting an arbitrary threshold is unsatisfactory, and would like to propose an alternative solution. My conception rests upon the International Labour Organization's definition of employment: those who work at least an hour during a reference week are deemed to be employed.

Contrary to many authors, I suggest that *there is no such thing as 'the working poor'*, as this label characterizes various groups of disadvantaged workers who are in different situations that require different policy interventions. The approach I advocate relies on a very encompassing definition of 'working', so that no poor adult who participates in the labour market is left out of the analysis, whatever his or her degree of labour force attachment.

The goal is, then, to identify multiple types of working poverty according to the main mechanisms that have caused it, as will be analysed in depth in subsequent chapters: low labour force attachment, low earnings per unit of time and higher needs due to household size and composition. This classification appears to provide useful information for social policy purposes, as it allows the following question to be answered: which types of working poverty are mostly found in which welfare regime?

Apart from its use for comparative social policy analysis, my approach can also be useful for national analyses. If large data-sets are available, which is more likely to be the case in national than in international data-sets, it is possible to draw detailed typologies of poor workers, by defining various levels of labour force attachment, child-per-working-age-adult ratios and earning levels, which are, as will be analysed at great length below, the three immediate causes of working poverty. At that stage, setting arbitrary thresholds is no longer a problem, as no group of disadvantaged workers has been ignored from the outset. Moreover, it is also possible to use cluster analysis in order to identify sub-groups of poor workers without setting arbitrary thresholds: in so doing, it is possible to let 'the case define the concept' (Becker, 1998). This kind of approach may allow a fine tuning of social policy interventions and a more appropriate allocation of resources, by defining various categories of poor workers who are characterized by the separate intervention their poverty requires. I get back to this point in the conclusion of this book.

The approach I advocate, based on a very encompassing definition of work, however, also has some drawbacks. First, the situation of poor workers who have a very loose connection to the labour market, either because they are unemployed most of the time or not able to work more than a few hours, probably requires policy interventions that differ fundamentally from those analysed in the present work. For instance, for this sub-group of poor workers, vocational training, counselling and in some instances health-related interventions, if these workers have a condition preventing them from increasing their labour force participation, could prove much more useful than, say, minimum wages or tax credits. Second, a researcher is always dependent, one way or another, on the indicators and findings other researchers produce, especially in the field of comparative social policy analysis. In this regard, official definitions appear to play a decisive role: as will become obvious in the following chapters, many American scholars use the US official poverty definition and European researchers increasingly use Eurostat's definition of 'in-work poverty'. I have shown above that any definition of working poverty implies a certain degree of arbitrariness; hence, using an official definition has the advantage of limiting each researcher's subjectivity and facilitates comparisons (Fraser et al., 2011).

All in all, even if I think that my approach might be more relevant by not excluding sub-groups of workers from the outset, in order to obtain more accurate and detailed results, I also think that comparative analyses using official indicators have important advantages.

NOTE

1. Mollie Orshansky (1915–2006) was an American economist and statistician who worked for the Social Security Administration and developed the official poverty line in the mid-1960s.

3. The three mechanisms that lead to working poverty

After having dealt with definitional aspects, I can now turn to the main driving factors of poverty among workers in post-industrial economies, in order to understand the roots of the problem. The present chapter regards socio-economic factors, while Chapter 4 will analyse public policy factors.

The main contribution of this chapter is to present, in a systematic and summarized fashion, findings derived from a large body of literature in the fields of economic sciences and sociology, pertaining to a broad spectrum of topics such as low-wage employment, overall poverty, income inequality and unemployment, in order to identify the main working poverty factors.

Perhaps more importantly, whereas the poverty literature identifies a myriad of risk factors and of at-risk groups, I have been able to single out three immediate causes of working poverty, which are the channels through which all poverty factors identified in the literature have a direct bearing on working households. The existence of these three mechanisms confirms the necessity of distinguishing various groups within the working poor. In this chapter, I argue that there is no such thing as 'the working poor', but different groups of poor workers who experience very different situations.

3.1 ECONOMIC FACTORS

Most of the explanations provided below pertain to low-wage employment and income inequality, as the working poverty literature was until recently quite limited. I hereby present a wide variety of factors, which range from business-cycle related factors, to structural transitions in the labour market, as well as macrosocial changes.

3.1.1 General Framework

According to Nobel laureate Krugman (1990), there are three roots of welfare:

- productivity growth;
- income distribution;
- and unemployment.

'If these things are satisfactory, not much else can go wrong, while if they are not, nothing can go right' (Krugman, 1990: 7), and productivity is probably the most influential factor. Obviously, working poverty is directly linked to the first two roots of welfare. Hence, in order to explain working poverty, the main factors found in the literature that affect productivity and the income distribution[1] must be accounted for:

- the impact of business cycles and economic growth;
- the transition from an industrial to a post-industrial economy, in which service employment becomes overwhelmingly important;
- technological changes, which might improve productivity but also affect the labour demand, especially if these changes are skill-biased;
- globalization and the import of manufactured goods from developing countries.

3.1.2 The Interplay of Economic Growth, Unemployment and Poverty

It is noteworthy that findings regarding the impact of economic growth on working poverty seem to depend on the kind of poverty measure used:

> Roughly speaking, the more 'relative' your poverty measure, the less impact economic growth will have on its value. If the poverty line is proportional to mean income then it behaves a lot like a measure of inequality ... This method can show rising poverty even when the standards of living of the poor have in fact risen (Ravallion, 2003: 4).

Indeed, the correlation coefficients between poverty defined as an income lower than 60 per cent of median equivalized income and the Gini coefficient, on the one hand, and the top-to-bottom-quintile ratio, on the other hand, amount to $r = 0.847$ and 0.909 respectively (own calculations based on figures for the EU-25 in 2007, obtained from Eurostat's website).

Nonetheless, economic growth seems to be a prerequisite to fight poverty (Stiglitz, 2002) even though not sufficient. But once a certain level of economic development has been achieved, the relationship between poverty and economic growth might be more complex and blurred. In the US, an inequality upswing despite positive economic growth took place, a fact sometimes dubbed the 'great U-turn' (Moller et al., 2003; Nielsen and Alderson, 2002). During the period 1983–90 there was a recovery which led to an increase in average wages in the US; however, the increase in inequality kept poverty rates above the levels achieved during the 1970s (Gottschalk and Joyce, 1995). However, the 1990s in the US told another story, because sustained economic growth contributed to a decrease in poverty.

Temporary and contingent work increased rapidly in the US and Europe, especially during the generalized downturn in the 1980s (see for example McFate, 1995a; Paugam, 1996). Standing notices that unemployment can also have an impact on workers because it exerts a downward pressure on wages (Standing, 1995). Hence, unemployment can have an indirect impact on working poverty, because fixed-term contracts and temp agency work become more prevalent and make a direct impact because of downward pressures on wages (Levitan and Shapiro, 1988).

Danziger and Gottschalk (1996) provide decisive evidence on the interplay of economic growth, income inequality and poverty in the US. A long-term perspective is possible because income data has been collected for about 60 years in the US; moreover, there is an official poverty line that was implemented in the mid-1960s (for previous years the poverty threshold can be deflated with a price index). Simulating various situations if each factor had remained unchanged (counterfactuals), Danziger and Gottschalk were able to decompose the impact of various factors on the poverty rate (see Table 3.1).

Table 3.1 Decomposition of percentage-point change in the poverty rate for all persons, 1949–1969 and 1973–1991

	1949–1969	1973–1991
(1) Actual change in poverty rate	**–25.7**	**1.8**
% point change owing to:		
(2) Economic changes	**–26.9**	**–0.1**
(a) Growth in mean adjusted income	–21.4	–2.1
(b) Change in income inequality	–5.5	2.0
(3) Demographic changes	**1.2**	**2.0**
(a) Race/ethnic composition	0.6	0.7
(b) Family structure composition	0.7	1.6
(c) Interaction	–0.1	–0.3

Source: Danziger and Gottschalk (1996), Table 5.3, p. 102.

The economic growth massively reduced poverty between 1949 and 1969. At the end of the 1960s James Tobin forecasted that poverty would be eliminated by 1980 (Danziger and Gottschalk, 1996). At the beginning of the 1980s, however, the unemployment rate exceeded 10 per cent for the first time since the Great Depression due to a severe recession that ended in November 1982; then, the economy entered a relatively strong recovery that lasted until 1990; nonetheless, the poverty rate hardly decreased. It is very striking that the inequality upswing that took place in the 1980s nearly cancelled the positive impact of economic growth. Put differently, 'stimulating economic growth and avoiding recessions are necessary, but not sufficient solutions to America's poverty problem' (Danziger and Gottschalk, 1996: 10).

Likewise, Heinrich notes that economic growth has a positive impact on incomes, but it is also likely to exacerbate income inequality, which might imply that there is a trade-off between inequality and economic growth (Heinrich, 2003). Heinrich's estimates show that, in the mid-1990s, Sweden had virtually the same inequality-growth trade-off index[2] as the US, whereas Sweden is known for its low relative poverty rate, which leads him to conclude that 'There can be no sustained reduction in poverty without income redistribution' (Heinrich, 2003: 1). The poverty measure used by Heinrich is relative (50 per cent of median income) and is, hence, strongly correlated with income inequality measures, so that his conclusion applies to relative poverty, while Danziger and Gottschalk's conclusion is valid for poverty measured with an absolute threshold.

Ravallion (2007) notes that, in the case of developing countries, and contrary to what is often stated, the evolution of income inequality also matters. He established a formula that accounts for the combined impact of the economic growth and income inequality:

Rate of change in poverty = *Constant* · (1 – *inequality index*)$^\theta$ · *growth rate*,

with $\theta \geq 1$

This formula models the empirically observed interplay of these three factors, and underlines the fact that an increase in inequality reduces the antipoverty impact of economic growth (Ravallion, 2007).

In summary, the interplay of economic growth and (working) poverty is complex. First, the above considerations depend on the degree of economic development of the society under analysis. Second, conclusions may depend on the kind of poverty indicators used, absolute poverty rates being more responsive to economic growth. Third, the antipoverty impact of economic growth can be offset, at least partly, by increases in income inequality. Hence, income redistribution by the tax and benefits system must play a fundamental role. Obviously, the causal links between business cycles, economic development and poverty would deserve a more in-depth analysis; however, I think it is safe to conclude that economic growth is a necessary but not sufficient condition in the fight against working poverty.

3.1.3 Productivity and the Cost-disease Problem of Post-industrial Societies

Wilson notes that in the US during the industrial era plenty of blue-collar jobs were available to workers with little formal education, but this is no longer the case, and most unskilled jobs are now found in the service sector, especially in personal services (Wilson, 1996). Many factory workers were forced to become, in popular terms, 'hamburger flippers' (Gottschalk and Joyce, 1995). In today's labour markets high school drop-outs cannot find the same type of stable and relatively well-paid jobs anymore (Bourgois, 2003), and the service sector is typified by lower than average wages and a higher level of inequality (Nielsen and Alderson, 2002). Likewise, in the UK, 1.5 million jobs were lost in the manufacturing sector between September 1979 and December 1982, a fall of 22 per cent (Pahl and Wallace, 1985).

This decline in industrial employment went hand-in-hand with productivity declines (McFate, 1995a). Gershuny noted in 1985 that in the UK, Belgium, France, West Germany, the Netherlands and Italy, productivity growth for market and non-market services were below average (Gershuny, 1985). In fact, there is a 'cost-disease' problem in post-industrial economies, because for some service jobs, it is hardly possible to improve productivity. As prices rise, even at a reasonable rate, workers in the service sector will ask for pay raises in order to maintain their purchasing power. In the long run, these workers could be priced out of the market or earn declining real wages. This cost-disease problem was first brought to the forefront by Baumol (Baumol et al., 1990); the lower end of the service sector may be particularly affected (Esping-Andersen, 1999).

In addition, a whole range of public services has developed, notably non-market services such as education, health and welfare, which pose a budgetary problem to governments (Gershuny, 1985) due to this 'cost disease'.

Boyer and Durand (1998) relativize the cost-disease problem, however, as some service sector industries are able to keep on improving their productivity (such as transportation and health services). The computer and telecom sectors, for instance, have been able to strongly increase productivity (Merrien, 2002). Moreover, some industrial sectors also experienced declining productivity levels, which can be attributed to the very principles of the rationalization of industrial production in the Taylorian–Fordist system, which had been pushed too far and led to an underutilization of an increasingly blocked capital, slow reactions to market fluctuations, difficulties to diversify production, neglect of quality and a decreasing interest of workers in their job. The growing share of supervisors among the personnel also slowed down productivity growth (Boyer and Durand, 1998).

Wood also relativizes the impact of deindustrialization on earnings inequality. Shifts in the sectoral composition of the labour market have played an important role, but most of the rise occurred *within* industries and occupations (Wood, 1994). Actually, the scope and the causes of the productivity slowdown are controversial, but according to Wood, it does not simply reflect the shift of employment from manufacturing to lower-productivity services.

3.1.4   The Evolution of the Occupational Composition of the Labour Force

Switching to a sociological approach of these topics, based on socio-occupational categories and social mobility, it appears that the Fordist manual worker had a very predictable, stable and flat career profile and was condemned to a predetermined 'class destiny'. In post-industrial economies, on the contrary, the bottom is not hermetically closed; yet, the mobility prospects are not necessarily large for many low-skilled workers (Erikson and Goldthorpe, 1992; Esping-Andersen, 1993). With the decline of the Fordist model, there has been an increase in the share of professionals, on the one hand, and of lower-end service occupations, on the other hand (Esping-Andersen, 1993). In this context, education and social skills have an increasing impact on class outcomes (Bourgois, 2003; Esping-Andersen, 1993), and human capital has become the 'hegemonic determinant of life-chances' (Esping-Andersen, 1993: 234). For instance, in the European Union, high-skill jobs account for two-thirds of net employment creation since the mid-1990s (Hemerijck, 2002).

Beside low-skilled service sector employees, another category situated at the bottom of post-industrial societies has drawn researchers' attention, namely the 'outsider population' excluded from the labour market (Castel, 1995; Paugam, 1996; Wilson, 1996). In fact, there may be a trade-off between 'accepting a larger outsider population or, alternatively, a large service proletariat' (Esping-Andersen, 1993: 28). In the present work, however, I focus on disadvantaged workers, even though this topic cannot be completely disconnected from the 'underclass' problem – many members of the underclass being former low-wage workers (Bourgois, 2003) – but this marginalized group of the population probably requires social policy interventions that are very different from those aiming at alleviating working poverty.

The next section identifies the main economic factors that explain this growing disadvantage of unskilled workers, furthering the reflection on productivity presented above; more precisely, the question is: is the growing disadvantage of low-skilled workers in post-industrial economies mainly due to endogenous or exogenous economic mutations?

3.1.5   Globalization vs Skill-biased Technological Changes: Which Factor Explains the Plight of Unskilled Workers?

While the import of manufactures from the 'South' was negligible in the 1950s, they had risen to US$250 billion by 1990. The share of manufacturing in total employment in the South increased from 6 per cent in 1950 to 13 per cent in 1990, with a particularly sharp increase in the 1980s. Conversely, in the North, this share declined from almost 30 per cent at the end of the 1960s to 21 per cent by 1990 (Wood, 1994). International transport and telecommunications have become quicker and less expensive, while import restrictions and tariffs have been reduced (Wood, 1994). Low-skilled jobs can be easily transferred to emergent countries (Levitan and Shapiro, 1988), and the unskilled have suffered disproportionately from structural changes, as the least skill-intensive manufacturing industries have been declining due to imports from the South (Glyn and Salverda, 2000).

However, 'although there is little dispute about the *pattern* of the impact on the composition of labour demand, there is a lot of disagreement about its *magnitude*' (Wood, 1994: 8, original emphasis). According to Wood's estimates, trade with the South reduced the demand for unskilled workers relative to skilled workers in the North by approximately 20 per cent (Wood, 1994). As a consequence, the skill differentials in relative wages widened and were strongest in the UK and the US. Where institutional forces resisted this widening in wage differentials, they generated surpluses of unskilled labour. These factors contributed to greater income inequality; according to Wood, this was mainly due to the increase in North–South trade, but also to the spread of new technology based on microprocessors (Wood, 1994). Some support for Wood's view can be found: Nielsen and Alderson note that their empirical analyses show that direct investment and North–South trade have had a strong impact on income inequality (Nielsen and Alderson, 2002). Moreover, part of the impact of technological changes may have been caused by North–South trade, because industrial sectors invest in technology to counter the import of manufactures from the South, a phenomenon dubbed 'defensive innovation' (Wood, 1994).

However, many researchers have doubted the importance Wood attributes to international trade and capital flows. Krugman thinks that the US trade deficit does not have a decisive influence on the well-being of US workers (Krugman, 1990). Imports from developing countries only amount to a small share of OECD countries' GDP; furthermore, OECD exports to these emerging economies have grown in line with imports (OECD, 1997). The bulk of trade occurs between OECD countries: for instance, the share of the EU trade with non-EU countries is less than 10 per cent, most of which is with North America and the Antipodes (Esping-Andersen, 1999).

Other factors have been brought to the forefront, for instance macroeconomic policies in the 1980s aiming to stop inflation (Krugman, 1990; Wood, 1994). Many authors also point to skill-biased technological changes in developed economies (Esping-Andersen, 1999; Gregory and Machin, 2000; McFate, 1995a), especially computer-operated machine tools and information highways (Wilson, 1996). By the mid-1990s, 46.8 per cent of the EU's workforce were in jobs involving the use of a computer or automated equipment (Gallie, 2002). In addition, a new production model has been developed that is based on just-in-time production and aims at increasing quality at a constant price. This system requires more polyvalent and more skilled workers than traditional mass production (Boyer and Durand, 1998). A reinforcing problem for low-skilled workers is that it is mainly young and highly educated employees who benefit from in-career training provided by employers. Many low-skilled workers are, hence, caught in a 'skills trap' (Gallie, 2002).

In summary, most unskilled workers in high-income countries are facing more difficult times today than they did 40 years ago. The 'golden age' of the Fordist model provided these workers with relatively well-paid jobs in the manufacturing industry, while today they face a higher risk of being low-paid, poor and unemployed. To a certain extent, this might be due to the rise of emerging economies, because low-skilled jobs are being exported; however, endogenous changes within post-industrial economies, especially skill-biased technological changes, are more likely to be the main culprits. As Gottschalk and Joyce (1995: 217) put it, 'While there is still no "smoking gun" to explain the rise in inequality in ... industrialized countries ... both international competition and technological change played a role'.

Regarding the earnings inequality upswing, complementary explanations are conceivable. First, a shift in behavioural pay norms occurred, from a traditional model with relatively low-wage differentials for equally qualified workers to a model in which many more workers are paid on the basis of their productivity, with a switch from hierarchical pay to rent-sharing, with employees paid like 'salesmen' rather than on fixed-salary scales. The second model is the 'superstar theory' underlining an increase in superstar wages resulting from the expansion of technology and trade: some employees perform much better and get much better wages. In fact, in order to explain changes in top earnings, Atkinson (2008) suggests combining both theories.

3.2   SOCIODEMOGRAPHIC FACTORS

Now that the main economic factors that have an impact on working poverty have been briefly discussed, sociodemographic factors need to be analysed, as they may have played a very important role. In the US, for instance, from the 1970s onwards, demographic changes have had the same impact on poverty as the income inequality upswing (see Table 3.1 above).

3.2.1   Changing Families: Declining Stability and Single Parenthood

From the 1960s onwards, women have become economically more independent and the adult population in general less devoted to the traditional model of an everlasting relationship; in most countries divorce rates have doubled (Esping-Andersen, 1999; Kamerman, 1995). The rising labour force participation of married women has been the most dramatic change in gender roles during the last decades. Combined with the enormous increase in the divorce rate, this led to a massive increase in the share of female-headed single-parent households; for instance, in the US, they have more than doubled in number between 1970 and the mid-1990s (Kamerman, 1995).

The poverty risk associated with lone parenthood is systematically put forth by poverty researchers in all post-industrial countries, due to the fact that in the aftermath of a divorce there is a significant increase in needs. The two resulting households (usually a father who lives alone and a mother who lives with the children) have greater needs, because many economies of scale are no longer possible. Moreover, parents' earnings remain rather stable in the short run, which obviously leads to a problematic situation.

Indeed, needs increase 'overnight' by one-quarter to one-third following a divorce. For instance, in the US, 30 per cent more income is required to maintain the pre-divorce standard of living (Kamerman, 1995). In the case of Switzerland, needs are evaluated to increase by 33.6 per cent (Swiss Conference of Welfare Institutions, 2003). Moreover, married fathers contribute 20 to 25 per cent of their income to support their children, while this share amounts to less than 10 per cent for divorced fathers (McLanahan and Garfinkel, 1995).

A growing number of children live in lone-parent households and experience poverty. In fact, according to Sawhill and Thomas (2001), the increase in single-parent families explains all of the increase in child poverty since the 1970s in the US. Moreover, single-headed households also suffer longer poverty spells (Oxley et al., 2000).

As will be shown below, single-parent families run a much higher risk of working poverty in the US, Germany and Spain, whereas their over-representation among the working poor is more limited in Sweden. There are significant differences, too, in the labour force participation rate of single mothers across countries and poverty is lowest in countries with a high maternal employment rate. In Sweden, a very high proportion of lone mothers are in the labour force, which is usually attributed to generous childcare policies. Likewise, in France in 1992, 82 per cent of lone mothers worked; this high participation rate can be attributed, at least partly, to the very good childcare services provided by the state (Martin, 1996). In the US and the UK, single mothers' employment rate has been a central policy concern in the recent past, which led to far-reaching reforms that also aimed at decreasing poverty among single mothers (McLanahan and Garfinkel, 1995). I get back to this very important topic in Chapters 6 and 7.

Kamerman summarizes these facts in terms of policy implications: 'the ultimate question for all industrialized countries is: what policy package reduces the risk of poverty for mother-only families and their children and simultaneously provides working mothers with assistance in easing the time pressures and stresses that labor force participation generates?' (Kamerman, 1995: 253). This is particularly true because the traditional welfare state was based on the male-breadwinner–housewife model; it was, hence, not at all conceived to support lone mothers (Esping-Andersen, 1999; Heclo, 1995).

Though the employment of lone mothers is a central policy concern, it is noteworthy, as will be shown below, that maternal employment in general matters a great deal when it comes to fighting working poverty and child poverty.

3.2.2   Social Endogamy and Female Labour Force Participation

'Assortative mating' (Becker, 1981) and 'class homogamy'[3] (Erikson and Goldthorpe, 1992) refer to the fact that individuals tend to marry people with similar social backgrounds and educational levels. The fact that most couples are made up of persons with similar social position and status affects income inequality, work opportunities, as well as the transmission of cultural and economic inequalities to the next generation, as more and more women have entered the labour market in advanced economies and invested in human capital.

People with a low educational attainment are worse off today, in relative terms, than during the post-war boom. As they tend to marry persons with similar educational levels, and because they have a much higher likelihood of being unemployed or trapped in low-pay/no-pay cycles, the absence of work tends to be more and more concentrated. In the UK for instance, the share of two-earner households grew from 54 to 62 per cent between 1983 and 1994, while workless households grew from 6 to 19 per cent, and similar trends are observed in Belgium, France and Germany (Esping-Andersen, 2002b).

Moreover, the same mechanism has a negative impact on household income. Female labour participation has inflated the bottom of the earnings distribution, as women have lower average earnings; in addition, due to assortative mating, it has amplified the advantage of high-income households and the disadvantage of low-income households when both spouses work (Crompton and Brockmann, 2006; Esping-Andersen, 1993). For instance, between 1979 and 1997, social endogamy accounts for 13 per cent of the rise in household income inequality in the US (Kenworthy, 2004).

3.2.3 Risks Have Shifted Towards Young Adults

In societies in which skills and education have become hegemonic determinants of life-chances (Esping-Andersen, 1993), employment opportunities are scarcer, jobless households and single-parent families are more widespread, while pension systems efficiently fight poverty among elderly households, a logical consequence is that many risks have shifted towards young adults and especially towards young parents: 'youth and young families are being disproportionally bombarded from all sides with risks of poverty, low income, [and] unemployment' (Esping-Andersen, 1999: 167). Lawson and Wilson (1995), likewise, note that the poverty risk has grown disproportionately among young and prime-aged workers. Chapter 7 will show that the median working poor is in his or her thirties in all countries analysed.

In what follows, I analyse the interplay of economic and sociodemographic factors and the channels through which they have a direct impact on households. This will allow me to confirm my initial idea: there are different groups of disadvantaged workers who have ended up in relative poverty because of different mechanisms. This is the object of the next section.

3.3   THE THREE WORKING POVERTY MECHANISMS

Apart from its ability to synthesize and organize findings stemming from a plethoric literature in the fields of social and economic sciences, the main contribution of this chapter is the following: on the basis of the literature on the working poor and low-wage workers, I conclude that there are basically three working poverty mechanisms that can be identified: low earnings, low labour force attachment and high needs (especially a high number of dependants), relative to national averages. Working poverty can only be the consequence of one or more of these three factors.

Hence, while the poverty literature identifies a myriad of risk factors and categories of disadvantaged workers, these three mechanisms are the channels through which economic and sociodemographic factors have a direct bearing on working households. Public policy factors, the object of the next chapter, also have an impact on each working poverty mechanism, which I now describe:

- *Low hourly earnings*. The most intuitive mechanism leading to working poverty is the fact of being badly paid. Although several researchers have pointed out that low wages alone are seldom the cause of working poverty (Andress and Lohmann, 2008; Nolan and Marx, 2000; Peña-Casas and Latta, 2004; Strengmann-Kuhn, 2003), few will object to the fact that being paid a low wage vastly increases the risk of ending up in working poverty.
- *Low labour force attachment.* This mechanism is proteiform and hits underemployed and intermittent workers, as well as persons – usually women – who cannot or are not willing to work more due the presence of children in the household. The rise in double-earnership observed in most OECD countries puts families with a non-working spouse in a relatively more difficult situation than during the post-war years, when single-earnership was the norm.
- *High needs, especially a large number of dependent children in the household.* Most studies show that having many children can lead to poverty. As already discussed in Chapter 2, the conclusions drawn depend in part on the equivalence scale used; however, evidence derived from opinion questions must be interpreted with caution, as they may reflect parents' adaptive preferences (Halleröd, 2006) rather than children's living conditions. It is fundamental to note that the same number of children is more likely to lead to poverty for one-parent families than for two-parent families. In fact, after a breakup or a divorce, even just two children may become problematic, because

the needs of the two resulting households increase significantly, as already discussed. What matters, as a result, is not the absolute number of children in a household, but rather the ratio of children to adults.

Each mechanism can be seen as a necessary but not sufficient condition; that is, the working poor will have at least one of the features described above; however, none of these factors necessarily leads to working poverty. The accumulation of these mechanisms will increase the likelihood of being working poor.

Why focus on mechanisms? As will be shown in Chapter 7, the relative weight of each mechanism varies across welfare regimes. This is the reason why the composition of the working poor population varies significantly from one country to another. This will reinforce the first main conclusion drawn in Chapter 2: analysing working poverty as a single category is not the best approach for social policy analysis; a typological approach is probably more useful. Moreover, focusing on the relative weight of the three working poverty mechanisms allows identifying policy mixes that appear to efficiently combat various forms of working poverty.

3.4 CONCLUSIONS

A review of the literature that analyses the impact of economic factors on disadvantaged workers points us in an important direction: the impact of the transition to a service economy and the growing disadvantage of unskilled workers vary considerably across post-industrial nations, because of institutional differences, as underlined by many authors. Similar conclusions apply to the review of the literature devoted to the sociodemographic changes that have characterized post-industrial countries: divorce rates have skyrocketed and poverty risks increasingly hit younger persons; however, outcomes vary largely from one country to another, which most authors attribute to public policy factors.

In summary, it appears that public policy factors play a very significant role in shaping the income distribution and labour market participation of various groups, especially labour market regulations and welfare state benefits and services. These factors are the object of the next chapter. Moreover, these policy factors affect the relative weight each of the three immediate causes of working poverty have in each welfare regime, and, as a consequence, the relative size of each sub-group of poor workers. This point will be clearly demonstrated in Chapter 7.

NOTES

1. As discussed in this chapter, the third root of welfare, namely the unemployment rate, also has a non-negligible impact on workers, because it exerts downward pressure on wages.
2. IGTI= $\frac{\delta\mu}{\delta G}\frac{G}{\mu}$ with μ the mean income and G the Gini coefficient.
3. 'Assortative mating' may be perceived as having a biological connotation, which is unfortunate, as we are dealing with a social phenomenon. 'Class homogamy' is also problematic, because it refers to an existing class structure, which is a contentious issue. I prefer the more neutral expression 'social endogamy'.

4. Potential solutions: minimum wages, social transfers and childcare policy

As indicated in Chapter 3, pervasive socio-economic factors have been affecting the living and working conditions in post-industrial economies; these structural changes vary in terms of degree and timing, but are broadly the same in all countries. Due to institutional factors, however, the practical challenges these countries face vary significantly. In some countries, these socio-economic changes translated into a strong income inequality upswing, while in other countries unemployment rates shot up. In further nations, the main problem consisted in the explosion of public expenditure and deficit.

This 'trilemma' of post-industrial societies – that is, the impossibility to achieve income equality, employment growth and budgetary restraint simultaneously – leads governments to choose among three alternatives. They can promote freely operating markets and budgetary restraint, which eventually leads to an increase in earnings inequality (in the US for instance, workers lacking college education had their real wages reduced by 15 per cent during the 1980s) (Hemerijck, 2002); whilst other, mostly Christian democratic administrations promote budgetary restraint and income equality, at the expense of employment growth, by reducing labour supply (Germany being a typical example until recently). Another option has been chosen by social-democratic governments in Nordic countries: they tend to prefer a combination of jobs for all through public employment and income equality, which leads to higher taxes or deficits, which in turn can lead to a growing division between private-sector and public-sector employees (Iversen and Wren, 1998).

Blank et al. (1999) state that policymakers have long struggled to achieve these three goals: that is, raise the living standards, encourage work and keep government costs low. The conflict between these goals can be described as the 'iron triangle' of welfare reform (Blank et al., 1999). Likewise, Esping-Andersen (1993) thinks that three outcomes are possible: first, mass unemployment; second, the lower end of the service sector expands thanks to low wages; and third, service jobs are promoted via the creation of public employment.

In the present chapter, I first identify the main approaches that underpin the fight against working poverty in post-industrial countries – whether or not it was their primary objective when they were implemented – namely minimum wages, social transfers and policies aiming at the maximization of labour market participation. The role these policies play in each welfare regime reflects the approach to the trilemma policymakers have chosen. For each approach I present the expected employment and antipoverty effects based on the literature; these hypotheses will be tested in the chapter devoted to the meta-analysis of various social policy instruments.

4.1   MINIMUM WAGES

Minimum wages are traditional tools in the fight against poverty, and are usually the first issue that comes to mind when working poverty is discussed. Minimum wages are either set through collective agreements or legislation. The effects of the minimum wage will obviously depend on the level at which it is set, and large variations exist across countries.

Statutory or quasi-statutory minimum wages exist in 21 OECD countries. In order to compare the level of the minimum wage across countries, one can use purchasing power parities (PPP) in order to account for exchange rates and differences in the cost of living; it is also possible to express the minimum wage in relation to the average. In 2005, the *after-tax* value of legal minimum wages ranges from 60 per cent of net average wage (for a full-time worker) in Ireland and France, to around 55 per cent in the UK, slightly more than 50 per cent in Australia, 50 per cent in New Zealand, to about 40 per cent in Spain and slightly less than 40 per cent in the US and approximately 30 per cent in Japan. In US$ at 2005 PPP, the country ranking is affected: the UK and Australia are on top of the ranking with slightly more than US$7; France at around US$7; and Japan, Spain and the US in the same ballpark, with an after-tax minimum wage slightly higher than US$4 (Immervoll, 2007).

Two of the four countries I analyse in Chapters 5 and 7 have legal minimum wages, namely the US and Spain. In the US, the gross minimum wage has decreased between 2000 and 2005, from US$5.85 to US$5.15 at 2005 market exchange rates and constant prices (which represents a decline from 39 to 35 per cent of gross average wages), but there has been an increase in the recent past, from US$5.85 in 2007 to US$7.25 in 2009. In addition, many states have their own wage floor set at a higher level; moreover, some metropolitan areas have enforced minimum wage ordinances that compel companies commissioned by local authorities to pay wages higher than the legal minimum, as described in some of the articles included in the meta-analyses presented in Chapter 6. In Spain, the minimum wage has increased between 2000 and 2005, from US$4.12 to US$4.27 at 2005 market exchange rates and constant prices, which represents a slight increase from 34 to 35 per cent of gross average wages (Immervoll, 2007). In 2009, the *salario mínimo interprofesional* amounts to €624 per month (OECD website, labour statistics).

The impact of minimum wages defined in collective agreements is expected to be different. Indeed, this process leads to different wage levels according to the industry, the occupation type and the region, which allows greater flexibility in order to reduce the trade-off between employment and redistribution. Its effect also depends on the share of the workforce covered by collective agreements containing a wage convention. Whereas legal minimum wages cover the vast majority of workers, this is not necessarily the case for collective agreements.

In two of the countries analysed in Chapters 5 and 7, minimum wages are set through collective bargaining. In Sweden, minimum wages are industry-specific and nationwide (Skedinger, 2006), and about 90 per cent of the employees in Sweden are protected by collective agreements. In Germany, the coverage is not as high as in Sweden. Around two-thirds of workers are covered, but wage levels are high in international comparison, as the German bargaining model has led to a 'high skill equilibrium': workers are paid good wages, and in return, the level of conflictuality is very low, staff turnover is relatively stable and productivity is high (Eichhorst and Marx, 2009).

4.1.1 Expected Employment Effects

The neoclassical argument against the minimum wage is well-known: if the minimum wage is set above the productivity level of workers, firms will reduce their labour demand and will substitute unskilled workers for automated production processes or for higher skilled workers, while others may simply reduce their output. However, other reactions are possible: firms could simply accept that their profit margins are squeezed, or they could invest in order to increase productivity, by investing in employees' vocational training or innovative technologies, or try to develop better products that can be sold at a higher price. Moreover, the fact that low-skilled workers earn more thanks to the minimum wage can stimulate consumption and reduce labour turnover.

It is noteworthy that, at the macro level, the relationship between the level of the statutory minimum wage and unemployment is far from obvious. For instance, Spain has one of the highest unemployment rates in Europe; yet, Spain has a low minimum wage in international comparison.

Bazen mentions the 'lack of convincing evidence that minimum wages are responsible for the high unemployment rates in Europe' (Bazen, 2000: 120). However, most analyses assess the minimum wage impact on employment, rather than on unemployment, as will be shown below.

Card and Krueger (1995) have caused a massive upheaval in the world of labour economics. Based on a 'natural experiment approach', they showed that a 19 per cent increase in the minimum wage introduced in April 1992 in the state of New Jersey did not have the consequences that neoclassical theory predicts. Card and Krueger used New Jersey's fast-food industry (because it has a high share of unskilled and young workers) as the experimental group, and used the same industry in the neighbouring state of Pennsylvania as the control group, as Pennsylvania has a socio-economic structure that is very similar but did not increase its minimum wage in 1992. This method seemed more appropriate to the authors, because a regression model would certainly cause more problems as it is very difficult to control for all possible factors affecting the level of employment (demographic, economic and educational factors). Card and Krueger's results were remarkable: employment fell by 9 per cent in fast-food restaurants in Pennsylvania and rose by 2.8 per cent in restaurants in New Jersey.

However, Card and Krueger's (1995) findings have been subject to harsh criticism: it has been argued that the survey was carried out only eight months after the increase in the minimum wage level and that this time span is insufficient to evaluate the impact of an increase of the minimum wage. Other researchers think that employers had started firing employees before April 1992 because they knew the level of the minimum wage would be raised (Neumark and Wascher, 2007).

Other explanations of these results are conceivable, among which the fact that price increases did not deter consumers. The monopsony model, based on the idea that employers have a certain power in the labour market, has been used to explain this finding. Before the introduction of the new minimum wage, employers manage to keep wages as low as possible, sometimes below the market value (which can happen when the former minimum wage was not adjusted for many years and declined in real terms). When employers' scope in wage-setting is reduced, they can choose to expand their output and hire more workers to compensate the fact that their profit margins have been squeezed. In summary, different economic models lead to different predictions regarding the impact of minimum wages (Esping-Andersen, 2000).

Regarding the impact wages set by collective agreements have, the corporatist approach states that either fragmented, decentralized and uncoordinated bargaining or highly centralized and coordinated bargaining systems can lead to satisfying economic performances (Calmfors and Drifill, 1988). There is a 'hump-shaped' relationship between the type of bargaining system (coverage, centralization, coordination) and the economic performance (mainly inflation and unemployment): limited union power, as in the US, or highly coordinated and centralized bargaining, as in Sweden, can reduce unemployment (Esping-Andersen, 2000). Some authors, however, have expressed their scepticism towards Calmfors and Drifill's (1988) hump-shaped relationship model (Merrien, 2002).

In a review of 15 studies, the OECD concludes that the evidence is mixed as to the link between bargaining centralization, coordination and economic performance. The only statistically significant result is that centralized and coordinated countries have lower unemployment rates (OECD, 1997). According to Esping-Andersen (2000), the worst off countries are those where unions only represent the core workforce, but are strong enough to have an impact on the government's decisions; this situation can generate an insider–outsider divide.

In summary, 'the purportedly negative impact of the minimum wage is highly disputed' (Esping-Andersen, 1999: 126). There is a broad agreement that minimum wages set at too high a level would harm employment and that youths are most likely to be affected (OECD, 1998a) and that, 'A minimum that does not really bite cannot do much damage' (Bazen, 2000: 129); however, what 'too high' or 'a minimum wage that bites' means remains open to argument.

4.1.2 Expected Antipoverty Effects

Minimum wages have a significant impact on the wage distribution: they reduce earnings inequality in general and the gender pay gap in particular, because they 'mechanically' create a spike at the minimum wage level (Bazen, 2000). In order to understand the impact that changes in the earnings distribution may have on working poverty, I think that a conceptual and causal clarification is absolutely necessary, because, 'working poor' and 'low-wage workers' are sometimes used as synonyms; however, the reality is much more complex.

Low-wage workers are not necessarily poor and the working poor do not necessarily have very low earnings, as poverty is measured at the household level, in contrast to low pay, which is an individual characteristic (Nolan, 1998; Nolan and Marx, 2000). Many low-wage workers are not the main contributors to the household income (Nolan, 1998). Levitan and Shapiro (1988) likewise note that workers escape poverty because they live in small households or thanks to the earnings of other household members or welfare benefits.

Strengmann-Kuhn (2003) has conceptualized this essential difference as shown in Figure 4.1.

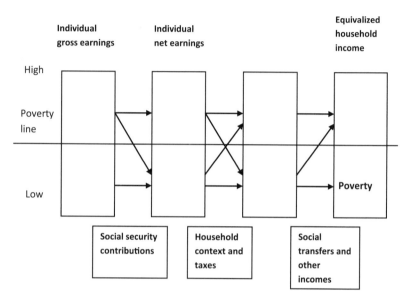

Source: Strengmann-Kuhn (2003), translated and modified for this book.

Figure 4.1 From individual earnings to household disposable income

Indeed, a minority of low-paid workers are poor, and, in many cases, a minority of the working poor have very low earnings. Of course, conclusions depend on the indicators used. Strengmann-Kuhn (2003) uses 50 per cent of the average wage as a low-wage threshold and 50 per cent of the average household income as a poverty line. About one in five workers (18 per cent) with a low pay (low remuneration rate) are poor in 14 EU countries and low-wage workers represent one-fourth of the working poor (Strengmann-Kuhn, 2003). The European Foundation for the Improvement of Living and Working Conditions defines being poor as living on an income lower than 60 per cent of the median income and setting a low-wage threshold at two-thirds of the median wage; in the EU, one in five low-wage employees are poor and 37 per cent of the working poor have a low pay (Peña-Casas and Latta, 2004). Hence, 'Generally speaking, there does not appear to be a very strong link between low pay and poverty' (Marx and Verbist, 1998: 76).

However, Nolan and Marx (2000) use two-thirds of median wage as a low-pay threshold, and 50 per cent of median income as a poverty line; that is, they define a relatively 'generous' low-wage threshold, while they use a quite restrictive poverty line. In addition, they focus on full-time full-year workers, hence excluding a large share of the female labour force. They find, too, that a limited share of low-wage workers are poor, and that about 60 per cent of the low paid are in the top 60 per cent of the household income distribution. However, in the 13 countries considered, a majority of the working poor are low paid, ranging from 54 per cent in France to 92.5 per cent in the UK (Nolan and Marx, 2000). This result is attributable to the fact that a large share of the 'secondary earners' are not taken into account.

The calculations presented in Chapter 7 also yield a relatively high share of low-wage workers among the working poor. I use hypothetical earnings based on what respondents would earn should they work full-time all year around; that is, the number of weeks spent in the labour market is also included in the calculation. Moreover, the analysis focuses on heads of households and their spouse. Still, the link between low wages and poverty is loose, and in most countries low-wage employees do not represent more than half the working poor; however, a comparison of poor and non-poor workers demonstrates that having low earnings is a significant working poverty factor.

It is noteworthy that the connection between low pay and working poverty is stronger for men and for prime-aged workers than for women and young people, due to the household context, especially the combined labour market positions of household members (Marx and Verbist, 1998). Most women in low-wage employment have a partner/husband who works too, which is less frequently the case for low-paid men (Levitan and Shapiro, 1988; Marx and Verbist, 1998; Nolan and Marx, 2000). Indeed, numerous working households can make ends meet thanks to 'supplementing earnings'. This is particularly true for working-class households. This is a very important fact, as the incidence of low-wage employment is much higher among women.

As far as youths are concerned, wages tend to increase with age and experience, in line with the human capital theory. However, for some low-wage jobs, the age-wage profile is rather flat, and can even be declining, in line with the dual labour market theory, according to which some low-wage occupations can become 'low-wage traps', such as hotel and service work, cleaning work and shop assistants (Arai et al., 1998).

Historically speaking, the link between low pay and working poverty has weakened, as female workforce participation has increased, as well as welfare state benefits. Danziger and Gottschalk (1996) provide us with a very revealing historical outlook on the situation in the US: men's earnings accounted for 82.7 per cent of family income in 1949, about 75 per cent in 1969 and 1973, and 63.4 per cent in 1991; women's earnings made up 8.5 per cent of household income in 1959 and 21.5 per cent in 1991.

The UK's case is also revealing. When Rowntree (1901 [1980]) carried out his first study of poverty in the city of York, he identified the main causes of poverty, of which a low wage was the primary cause in the majority of families. Almost a century later, this was the case in three out of ten poor households (see Table 4.1).

Table 4.1 Causes of poverty 1899 and 2001/2002

	1899 (primary poverty)	2001/2002 (60 per cent of median income)
Death of chief wage earner	15.6	5.8
Illness or old age of chief wage earner	5.1	25.7
Chief wage earner out of work/unemployed	2.3	8.6
Largeness of family	22.2	2.1
Irregularity of work	2.8	} 31.0
In regular work but at low wage	52.0	
Other	–	26.8
Total	100	100

Source: Glennerster et al. (2004), Table 2, p. 49.

Hence, in today's post-industrial economies, it does not seem absurd to conclude that 'A solution to the problem of the "working poor" will clearly require much broader measures than those relating specifically to low pay' (Gallie, 2002: 104).

4.2 SOCIAL TRANSFERS

The second approach to the fight against poverty is based on cash benefits. Social transfers can be broken down into two functional categories. Some transfers are substitution incomes: if someone loses his or her job, gets sick or disabled, benefits are a substitute for lost earnings until this person re-enters the labour market (if possible); hence, they do not affect workers directly, but they may help the non-working members of disadvantaged households. Other transfers provide a supplementing income: they increase working households' disposable income. Employment-conditional tax credits are the best-known example, as well as child allowances for workers. It is noteworthy that means-tested social assistance benefits belong to both categories, as they can supplement the income of low-wage workers or constitute the main – or even the sole – income source of a non-working person.

Substitution income transfers correspond to the traditional role of the welfare state as a 'passive' institution (Esping-Andersen et al., 2002). Most of the 'old social risks', that is, lost earnings due to illness, disability, old age, unemployment and the death of the chief wage earner, are combated mainly with cash transfers; the old welfare state was transfer-heavy (Bonoli, 2007; Huber and Stephens, 2006). On the contrary, most of the 'new social risks' – that is, risks that are typical of post-industrial societies – require an active intervention and an investment on the part of the welfare state in order to enable people to be active members of society (Armingeon and Bonoli, 2006; Esping-Andersen et al., 2002); the post-industrial welfare state is service-heavy.

It is noteworthy that, in recent years, many employment-conditional social transfers have been implemented or greatly expanded, such as tax credits for workers (US, UK, France, Canada, Sweden and so on) or child benefits for working mothers (Spain). These transfers correspond to a more recent conception of welfare state cash benefits, as they provide both an increase in disposable income and an incentive to work. Obviously, they are of no help if a person is not able to find a job.

4.2.1 Expected Employment Effects

After the oil shocks and the recession that occurred in OECD countries in the 1980s, welfare states found themselves under pressure. The influence of neoliberal theories grew, especially those stemming from the University of Chicago in the field of economic sciences (Merrien et al., 2005). Means-tested cash benefits were subject to harsh criticism for their alleged work disincentive effects (Murray, 2000). Some Conservative critics also blamed them for allegedly generating 'irresponsible' and 'morally dubious' behaviours, such as out-of-wedlock births, teenage pregnancies and so on. Even though neoliberal administrations in the US and the UK (the Reagan and Thatcher administrations) were not able to implement a large-scale, across-the-board retrenchment (Pierson, 1994), the idea that means-tested benefits could do more harm than good has remained and has been adopted by many scholars who do not share the Chicago school's ideology (Merrien et al., 2005).

In fact, no sound empirical evidence shows that the welfare state systematically has an adverse effect on employment; more specifically, neoclassical criticisms fail to explain the wide differences observed across European countries. Scandinavian countries, for instance, have generous social transfers and high employment levels. Moreover, countries with generous unemployment benefits often have lower long-term unemployment (Esping-Andersen and Regini, 2000).

This does not, by far, mean that welfare provisions have no impact at all on employment. A fundamental question concerns the marginal effective tax rates (METR) that people face when they decide to re-enter the labour market, especially welfare recipients and women getting back into the labour market after a childrearing period. These METR are due to the interaction of direct taxes with the withdrawal of benefits; however, at the macro level, the correlation between METR and unemployment levels is not very high (Whiteford and Adema, 2007).

In fact, conclusions appear to vary across countries. In the US, virtually all studies have found negative employment effects attributable to transfer payments; they are, however, rather small (Darity and Myers, 1987; Esping-Andersen, 2000). Comparative studies, on the contrary, conclude that the impact of social protection on unemployment is very limited (Esping-Andersen, 2000), especially in Europe (McFate, 1995b). In Anglo-Saxon countries more generous support to poor households is correlated to family joblessness ($r = 0.92$); on the contrary, in the Nordic countries, the correlation is negative (-0.93) (Whiteford and Adema, 2007), which reflects the fact that generous transfers are combined with an employment-maximizing strategy, as is analysed at great length in Chapter 5.

It is of paramount importance to distinguish benefits financed through payroll taxes from those financed by general taxation. Social insurance benefits financed by payroll taxes have the disadvantage of increasing non-wage costs for employers, which in turn can create hurdles for workers with a low human capital. In fact, according to Hemerijck (2002), low employment rates in Continental Europe have more to do with the heavy reliance on social security contributions than with the overall level of taxation. The impact of payroll taxes is discussed at greater length in Chapter 5.

4.2.2 Expected Antipoverty Effects

It seems that redistributive policies have a theoretically ambiguous effect on income inequality. Redistributive policies directly reduce inequality in terms of disposable income, in a static way. However, if dynamic aspects are taken into account, the same policies and institutions can reduce labour force participation, thereby increasing pre-transfer poverty (Burniaux et al., 2006).

Descriptive studies clearly demonstrate that social transfers reduce the poverty rate: the lowest poverty rates are found in countries that have 'generous' welfare states (Esping-Andersen, 1999; Eurostat, 2002; Kenworthy, 1999; McFate et al., 1995). Whiteford and Adema (2007) have evaluated the impact of a benefit strategy (mainly cash transfers and tax breaks) on child poverty rates, but behavioural responses are not accounted for. At the OECD level, the poverty rate of working single parents is reduced by 49.7 per cent, by 39.3 per cent for double-earner households and by 43.0 per cent for single-earner households (Whiteford and Adema, 2007).

Interestingly, targeting cash benefits to the poorest segments of the population is not necessarily the most efficient approach, as poverty rates are significantly lower in Scandinavian countries – where it is mainly universal benefits and services that contribute to the fight against poverty – than in Anglo-Saxon countries, where welfare state benefits are targeted at the poorest of the poor.

The indirect, long-term effects of social transfers also seem to be positive. A few researchers have developed regression models that account for the potential negative effects of social transfers on employment and economic growth, in order to go further than the usual descriptive comparison of pre-tax/pre-transfer and post-tax/post-transfers poverty levels, with regression models that explain levels of 'absolute' poverty or pre-tax/pre-transfer poverty (Brady, 2004; Kenworthy, 1999; Moller et al., 2003). These models control for a large array of economic, demographic and policy factors and show that the welfare state has a positive antipoverty effect, even when the possibility that social benefits reduce economic growth and employment is accounted for. Moreover, it seems that social spending and welfare-state benefits have a bigger antipoverty impact than economic performance in post-industrial countries.

However, these rather favourable conclusions do not rule out that 'too generous' benefits can have a detrimental impact on labour market participation, by generating high reservation wages and high marginal effective tax rates, which in turn can increase pre-transfer poverty.

Another noteworthy aspect regarding child poverty and the cost of combating it is that child poverty can be reduced through cash transfers or by increasing the labour force participation of parents and by reducing childcare costs (Whiteford and Adema, 2007). The second strategy is more costly than the first; however, if mothers work more, they will also pay more taxes, which reduces the net costs of childcare services (Esping-Andersen, 2002b). This 'servicing strategy' is analysed in the section devoted to childcare.

Apart from 'traditional' social transfers, employment-conditional benefits are often brought to the forefront in the working poverty literature; these complex policy tools require a more elaborate treatment and are the subject of the following sections.

4.2.3   Tax Credits for Working Families/Workers

Tax credits for working families have received a large amount of attention in recent years and belong to the group of 'make work pay' (MWP) policies (Immervoll and Pearson, 2009; Pearson and Scarpetta, 2000). Their main aim is to enhance the labour market participation of disadvantaged workers and to increase their disposable income. It should be emphasized that minimum wage legislations are often included in MWP policy mixes.

The main categories of MWP instruments are the following (OECD, 2003; Pearson and Scarpetta, 2000):

- tax credits for workers;
- childcare tax credits for working parents;
- tax allowances for work-related expenses;
- employment-conditional child benefits.

Other MWP policies exist; they mainly aim at increasing the labour market participation of specific groups of workers, such as decreases in employers' payroll taxes. These MWP policies, however, do not generally support poor workers; they rather help non-working persons to enter the labour market or to get back into it. These antipoverty strategies are not evaluated in the present work, as they do not directly aim at reducing poverty among those already in work.

I focus here on tax credits for workers that have existed for some time and for which a certain number of evaluations are available. The first of these

programmes is the Earned Income Tax Credit (EITC), which was introduced in the US in 1975. This is by far the most discussed employment-
conditional benefit. In the UK, a tax credit for working families has also
become an important antipoverty tool. In 1971, the Family Income Supplement (FIS) was introduced, replaced in 1988 by the Family Credit, then by
the Working Family Tax Credit in October 1999 (Dilnot and McCrae,
2000), and eventually by the Working Tax Credit (WTC) in 2003.

During the 2000s, similar programmes have been introduced in many
OECD countries (Immervoll and Pearson, 2009), such as: the 'Employment Premium' (*Prime pour l'emploi*) in France in 2001; the Family Income
Supplement and three other credits in Ireland; the Family Tax Credit and
the In-Work Tax Credit in New Zealand; the Working Income Tax Benefit
in Canada and additional programmes at the provincial level (some of
which existed before the 2000s); an Earned Income Allowance in Finland;
and earned income tax credits at the local level in Sweden. Belgium used to
have such a programme, but it got replaced by a rebate on employee's social
security contributions in 2004. Other countries such as the Netherlands and
Australia have employment-conditional benefits that are not completely
comparable to earned income tax credits but have similar objectives.

4.2.3.1   The Earned Income Tax Credit (EITC) in the US

The EITC was enacted in 1975 and was only supposed to offset payroll
taxes paid by low-income families with children (Howard, 1994). Since
then, it has become 'the centerpiece of antipoverty efforts in the US'
(Husby, 2000: 24). In the 1980s, the EITC survived welfare retrenchment
during the Reagan era: while the Omnibus Budget and Reconciliation Act
of 1981 slashed welfare expenditures by US$4 billion, increasing the
poverty rate by 2 percentage points, the Tax Reform Act of 1986 indexed
the EITC to inflation (Ventry, 2001). From 1984 to 1996, EITC expenditures grew by 1191 per cent (Ventry, 2001), far out-distancing expenditures
on Temporary Assistance for Needy Families (TANF) and the Food Stamp
Program (MaCurdy and McIntyre, 2004).

The EITC is an employment-conditional benefit based on Federal
income tax returns and does not depend on the number of hours worked
(MaCurdy and McIntyre, 2004). A first range, called the phase-in range,
corresponds to a large earnings subsidy (MaCurdy and McIntyre, 2004;
Meyer and Holtz-Eakin, 2001; Nagle and Johnson, 2006). As of 2007, the
phase-in rate for families with two or more children amounts to 40¢ for
each additional dollar up to the maximum credit, which is allowed over a
range of income called the 'plateau', which represents the flat range of the
credit. The end of the plateau corresponds to the beginning of the phase-
out range. It is important to note that the poverty line is about where the

EITC starts phasing out (MaCurdy and McIntyre, 2004). The phase-out range is meant to prevent so-called threshold effects, that is, the sudden withdrawal of benefits due to a one-dollar increase in earnings. The phase-out rate of the credit is 21¢ on the dollar, and the breakeven point, that is the point above which households receive no EITC, is clearly above the poverty threshold (Burkhauser et al., 1995; Greenstein, 2005; Nagle and Johnson, 2006; Scholz, 1994). A very important feature of the EITC is the fact that it is refundable: if the amount of the credit exceeds what the taxpayer owes to the IRS, he or she will receive a payment from the US Treasury (Nagle and Johnson, 2006; Scholz, 1994).

Originally, the EITC was designed to support working families with children. However, there is also a modest EITC for childless workers enacted in 1994 (Nagle and Johnson, 2006; Scholz, 1994). In 2006, only 2 per cent of the EITC goes to childless workers (Furman, 2006). Around two-thirds of EITC dollars went to single mothers in the early 2000s and more than two-thirds of payments went to families with two or more children (Meyer and Holtz-Eakin, 2001). The parameters of the EITC are adjusted for inflation every year by the Internal Revenue Service (IRS) (Levitis and Johnson, 2006; Okwuje and Johnson, 2006). However, the situation is less favourable in the phase-in range, because the matching rate used to calculate the credit has been set at 40¢ per dollar earned for many years now, and the minimum wage is not adjusted for inflation. Indeed, for many households that have to live on a minimum wage, the EITC is not generous enough to lift a two-parent family with two children above the federal poverty line (Nagle and Johnson, 2006). Given that the EITC is administered by the IRS, the take-up rate is very high (80 to 86 per cent according to Scholz, 1994). By contrast, fewer than half of eligible working families participate in the Food Stamps Program (Fishman and Beebout, 2001).

The EITC has enjoyed broad bipartisan support throughout the 1980s and the 1990s. In recent years, however, some Conservative politicians have been deeply disturbed by the fact that a majority of EITC recipients are non-poor according to the official definition (Husby, 2000; Ventry, 2001). Moreover, high error rates were found by the IRS; this has led some critics to name the programme a 'tax credit for crooks' (Ventry, 2001). In 1994, the IRS examined the returns of 2046 randomly selected EITC claims, and concluded that there was an overclaim rate of 25.8 per cent (the percentage of total dollars paid out in error). It is difficult, however, to identify cases where the misreporting is voluntary and cases of unintentional mistakes, due to the complexity of certain rules (McCubbin, 2001). The IRS has increased the number of returns that are controlled and can levy penalties against individuals who abuse the EITC (Greenstein, 2005; Ventry, 2001).

In addition to the federal programme, a growing number of states have introduced their own EITC, set at a flat percentage of the federal credit: they 'piggyback' directly on the federal credit. As of 2006, 21 states had enacted an EITC, at a given flat percentage ranging from 5–6 per cent in the states of Illinois, Indiana, Maine, Oklahoma and Oregon, to 30 per cent and more in the states of New York and Vermont, and the District of Columbia. Delaware, Iowa, Maine and Virginia have enacted a non-refundable tax credit. All states but Maryland, New Jersey and Wisconsin, allow childless workers to claim a state EITC (Levitis and Johnson, 2006; Okwuje and Johnson, 2006).

Regarding the *expected employment effects* of the EITC, the credit in the phase-in range has an ambiguous effect in terms of work incentives due to the offsetting impact of income and substitution effects (Hoynes, 2007). In the plateau, the theoretical effect is unambiguously negative (Burkhauser et al., 1995; Hoynes, 2007), especially for women in married households with children (Furman, 2006; Scholz, 1994). In the phase-out range, the impact should be unambiguously negative, due to both negative income and substitution effects (Ventry, 2001). However, contrary to what microeconomic theory predicts, given that a majority of recipients are either in the plateau or the phase-out range (Meyer and Holtz-Eakin, 2001), the overall employment effect of the EITC appears to be positive, as will be shown in the meta-analysis of the EITC in Chapter 6.

As far as its *expected antipoverty effect* is concerned, according to Census data, in 2003, 4.4 million people living in the US were lifted out of poverty, including 2.4 million children (Greenstein, 2005); for 1999, Meyer and Hotz-Eakin (2001) estimate that 3.7 million people escaped poverty; these estimates, however, do not account for employment effects. It is noteworthy that the EITC combined with food stamps allows a family of four to escape poverty if there is one full-time minimum-wage worker in the household (Greenstein, 2005).

It is fundamental to underline that the expansions of the EITC took place in a very specific social and economic context: during the 1990s, the US enjoyed the longest period of economic expansion in its history (Sawhill and Thomas, 2001). Moreover a major welfare reform took place in 1996, with the introduction of a lifetime limit of five years of benefits receipt, leading to a strong decrease in welfare caseloads (Blank, 2000; Sawhill and Thomas, 2001). By 1999, TANF caseloads had dropped by nearly half, and nearly two-thirds of mothers who left TANF had a job (Loprest, 2001). Hence, most evaluation results are based on a rather exceptional period of time. As Sawhill and Thomas (2001: 49) put it, 'the employment effects … will remain relevant only so long as there are jobs to be had … the assumption that there is a strong demand for labour among employers ... will almost certainly prove problematic in a time of economic downturn'.

4.2.3.2   The Working Family Tax Credit (WFTC) in the UK

Britain also has a long history of tax credits for workers. The Family Income Supplement (FIS) was introduced in 1971, a means-tested benefit for families with an adult working at least 24 hours per week. In 1988 the FIS was renamed Family Credit and its generosity increased. The WFTC was introduced in October 1999 and replaced the former Family Credit (FC). Within the WFTC, there was a Childcare Tax Credit that amounted to up to £150 per week (Blundell, 2006). The WFTC itself was replaced by an integrated children and employment tax credit in 2003, but the approach was not fundamentally altered; indeed, the new WTC is an extension of the WFTC (Marx and Verbist, 2008).

As of 2009, there has been a new Child Tax Credit for all parents, whether they work or not, and a Work Tax Credit for working households that includes a childcare element if approved or registered childcare services are used; the Child Tax Credit is paid on top of the Work Tax Credit, the latter being also paid to workers who do not have children. Childless workers need to work at least 30 hours per week to be entitled, with some exceptions, whereas working parents of children under 16 or of full-time students have a lower work requirement threshold, namely 16 hours per week. The childcare element is worth up to 80p in tax credit for every £1 per week spent on approved childcare, with maximum amounts between £140 per week for one child and £240 per week for two or more children. Workers in dual-earner couples can choose who gets the WTC, while the childcare element and the Child Tax Credit are paid to the main carer of all children in the family (UK HM Revenue & Customs' website).

In what follows, the WFTC is the only programme described, even though it does not exist under this label anymore and has been slightly modified, because virtually all available evaluations pertain to this programme. The 'third way' in welfare reform began when Tony Blair and the Labour Party won the general election of May 1997 (Hills and Waldfogel, 2004) and the WFTC was a 'flagship policy' for New Labour (McLaughlin et al., 2001). The introduction of UK's first national minimum wage was also a major reform in the New Labour's agenda in 1998. Three goals were pursued: first, the very low level of labour force participation of specific demographic groups, both in the UK and the US, in the early 1990s, was a strong motivation (Blundell, 2006). In the UK the employment rate of single mothers was very low (Blundell, 2006), and there was an increase in the percentage of workless couples. The second objective was to reduce child poverty through significant real increases in the universal child allowance and other means-tested benefits as well as increasing the tax credit for working parents. The third part of New Labour's strategy was to reduce welfare dependency with programmes that provided childcare or other services to pre-school-aged children, in order to break the intergenerational cycle of disadvantages. In addition, programmes helping teenagers to stay in school were implemented, with allowances paid to those who chose to do so (Hills and Waldfogel, 2004).

The WFTC was notably more 'generous' than its predecessor, the Family Credit: the maximum credit was higher and the rate at which the WFTC was withdrawn was less steep, namely 55p to the pound instead of 70p. The amount paid was dependent on the number and age of children, the earned and unearned income of parents and whether the parents had incurred approved substitute childcare expenses (McLaughlin et al., 2001).

Like its American counterpart, the WFTC is not administered by traditional welfare authorities, but by the UK's Inland Revenue. Contrary to the EITC, the WFTC has a minimum work-week requirement, namely at least 16 hours per week; moreover the credit is boosted if the head of the household works at least 30 hours per week (Blundell, 2006; Brewer, 2001; Sawhill and Thomas, 2001). Another major difference between the WFTC and the EITC is that the WFTC does not have a phase-in range: at 16 hours per week, the recipient gets the maximum credit he or she is eligible to; in addition, the UK system displays a much steeper withdrawal.

Regarding expected employment and antipoverty effects, it is very important to note that the introduction of the WFTC occurred at the same time as other policy reforms, which is crucial in understanding the impact of the WFTC (Blundell, 2006). Indeed, this feature of welfare reform in the UK allows the explanation of a pronounced puzzle: while the WFTC had a maximum credit that was twice as high in real terms than its American counterpart, the impact of the WFTC was about half of what it was in the US (Blundell, 2006). While the welfare reform in the US was based on a decrease in real terms of welfare benefits and the introduction of a lifetime five-year limit, the level of means tested benefits in the UK were increased, because reducing child poverty also was a strong priority in the UK (Blundell, 2006).

4.2.3.3 The 'Employment Premium' in France (*Prime pour l'emploi PPE*)

The Employment Premium was introduced in May 2001. Its main stated goals were to provide incentives to get back to work or to stay in employment through a decrease of the marginal effective tax rates (Cahuc, 2002), notably for recipients of the minimum income scheme. The first programme's eligibility criteria were linked to earnings, namely earnings between 0.3 and 1.4 times the full-time minimum wage (SMIC being its acronym), with an upper limit of 2.1 SMIC for workers in jointly filing households who have an inactive partner or whose earnings do not exceed 0.3 SMIC in full-time equivalent. Taxable household income is also taken into account.

This approach is completely different from those presented above, as the group of eligible workers is very large, namely one in four compared to one in 20 for the WFTC (Cahuc, 2002), and the credit is much smaller than its more generous but also more targeted Anglo-Saxon counterparts (Cahuc, 2002). In 2001, the average credit amounted to €144 per year and the maximum credit amounted to slightly less than €400 per year, namely for a worker earning the SMIC in a single-earner household. The context in which the PPE was implemented was also different. First, the unemployment rate was high, especially for low-skilled and young workers (Legendre et al., 2004). Moreover, the minimum wage (SMIC) is one of the highest among OECD countries, when expressed in per cent of average earnings, as already mentioned.

First evaluations showed that these tax credits could not have any effect on employment in a country with a compressed wage distribution and generous welfare benefits (Cahuc, 2002). Hence, the main effect and advantage of the PPE was redistributive. Moreover, the PPE mainly accrued to full-time SMIC workers, which is not the most disadvantaged group in the French workforce. Another drawback is that the benefit calculation is very complex, as it depends on both individual earnings and household income, making it very difficult to understand for recipients (Legendre et al., 2004).

Given all these drawbacks, the programme was reformed as early as 2003. It increased the amount paid to part-time workers, with a 45 per cent supplement for workers with less than a half-time job (Legendre et al., 2004). As of 2003, the maximum credit amounted to €444 per year for a minimum-wage worker on full-time year-round employment (1820 hours in France); as indicated above, a yearly workload of less than 910 hours meant that the credit was multiplied by 1.45 (Legendre et al., 2004).

The calculation remains, indeed, very complex. It depends on the earnings and hours worked indicated in the tax return, but also on the average wage rate. It also depends on the characteristics of the fiscal unit: married couples, single parents, and single-earner couples get different amounts that, in addition, depend on the number of children. Even after the increase of 2003, the PPE level remained low: €27 per month for a SMIC-worker working half-time and €37 for a SMIC-worker on full-time employment. Thanks to the increase for part-time workers, the PPE is better targeted; however, 12 per cent of the global amount accrued to workers in the fifth income decile (Legendre et al., 2004).

Given the small amounts at stake, and the specificities of the French labour market, notably high unemployment rates and a compressed wage distribution, the *employment and antipoverty effects* of the PPE are expected to be small.

In June 2009, a new benefit was introduced, namely the RSA (*Revenu de solidarité active*); its main aim is to replace the existing minimum income schemes (the minimum income guarantee RMI and a benefit for lone parents); in practice, workers entitled to both RSA and PPE must declare the amount of money received through the RSA, and fiscal authorities calculate PPE benefits including the RSA in household taxable income.

The next section deals with social transfers that are not conditioned on employment (with the exception of Greece); they can be universal or means-tested.

4.2.4   Family Cash Benefits, Child Allowances/Benefits

According to the OECD family database, as of 2007, approximately half the OECD countries provide family cash benefits that are not means-tested (they are, hence, universal). This is the case in Austria, Belgium, Cyprus, Denmark, Estonia, Finland, France, Germany, Greece, Hungary, Ireland, Latvia, Lithuania, Luxembourg, the Netherlands, Norway, Slovakia, Sweden, Switzerland and the UK.

The level of these benefits varies widely across countries, from less than 1 per cent of the average wage in Greece to 10 per cent in New Zealand. In some countries these cash benefits are an important component of low-income families' material well-being; for instance, they represent around 10 per cent of disposable income in Germany for families in the bottom decile of the income distribution (Whiteford and Adema, 2007). Eligibility in terms of the child's maximum age also varies widely, from 12 years in Japan and Lithuania up to 19 in Austria. In the large majority of OECD countries, the age limit is higher for students. There are employment conditions in Greece, and a reduction of benefits in proportion to days not worked in Italy; in other countries, eligibility is not linked to parental employment.

In some countries, family cash benefits take the form of a tax credit (they should not be confused, however, with childcare tax credits nor with earned income tax credits), namely in Australia, Austria, Canada, Germany, New Zealand and the UK.

Regarding the *expected employment effects*, most of the findings pertaining to social transfers in general (except for employment-conditional cash benefits) should apply to family cash benefits. It should be noted that universal benefits have the great advantage of preventing threshold effects, but their cost is notably higher, as most children do not grow up in disadvantaged families.

The antipoverty effect of these benefits is not easy to assess: in a static sense, obviously, they reduce child poverty, and figures based on a pre-transfer/post-transfer approach are provided in many studies, one of the best-known being Whiteford and Adema's report (2007). It is important, however, to account for behavioural responses, as these benefits could have a negative employment effect, especially in countries in which childcare services are in limited supply and/or expensive, as low-skilled mothers might be financially better off staying at home with their children, or reducing their labour force participation, if family benefits are high.

Among the numerous analyses that do not include behavioural responses, Fagnani and Math's (2008) study is very interesting. They use the 'model family method' to analyse the distribution of family cash benefits in an 11-country comparison:[1] for each model family – varying according to the number of children and earners – the family package is calculated as the difference between the net income after transfers and taxes for a household with children and the net income of a childless couple, with both families living on identical earnings. The components included in the calculation of the disposable income are: earnings, income tax, social insurance contributions, local taxes, family cash benefits, housing benefits, social assistance and guaranteed child support. Finally, the overall family package is measured in € in Purchasing Power Parities (PPP).

Austria and the UK stand out as the most generous countries when it comes to cash provisions for families, be it for couples with children or for lone-parent families. Regarding couples with children, France, Belgium and Germany follow the leaders Austria and the UK, while Scandinavian countries are at the bottom of the ranking. The situation is fundamentally different for lone-parent families: here, the Scandinavian countries follow the leaders, and France, Germany and Belgium are the lowest-ranked countries. Overall, it can be said that the UK is the most generous state toward low-income families; the UK and Ireland favour the working poor in their family policy. France and Belgium tend to encourage larger families and Scandinavian countries provide more support to single parents than to couples.

But being the most generous country in terms of average cash benefits per supported family does not mean being the most efficient in the war on poverty; in terms of child poverty, the UK is the worst performer among these 11 countries. Moreover, it probably takes more than cash benefits to reduce social inequalities. Nordic countries put much more emphasis on benefits in kind and on family services than on cash benefits (Fagnani and Math, 2008). Indeed, the fact that a country puts more emphasis on cash benefits or on family services matters a great deal. In the latter case, the approach is not mainly based on social transfers, but on the maximization of employment; this strategy is analysed in section 4.3 below.

Another important category of social transfers, namely social assistance benefits (or welfare benefits), must be discussed, as their main aim is to prevent poverty.

4.2.5 Social Assistance Benefits

In fact, most of the elements presented above regarding social transfers in general (except for employment-conditional benefits) apply to social assistance benefits in particular, be it work disincentive effects as well as antipoverty effects. As indicated above, social assistance benefits can act both as substitution income for unemployed and inactive persons and supplementing incomes for the working poor. In most countries, however, the unemployed are the largest proportionate category of recipients (Eardley et al., 1996).

The specificity of welfare benefits is that they are associated with stigma (Leu et al., 1997; Van Oorschot, 1991), as opposed to social insurance benefits, as the entitlement to the latter is derived from social security contributions paid by the recipient and is, hence, perceived as a due right. Even in countries in which the general public's attitude towards the welfare state is clearly positive, such as Sweden, the perception of social assistance benefits is rather negative (Bergmark, 2000).

The antipoverty and employment effects of social assistance will not be systematically assessed in Chapter 6. An abundant literature already exists, and these impacts constitute a research topic of their own. Moreover, these evaluations usually do not concern workers in the first place; most of them are either devoted to disincentive effects for those not in the labour force or measure antipoverty effects without accounting for dynamic aspects. However, some of the evaluations meta-analysed in Chapter 6 contain the level of welfare benefits as a control variable; these findings will be reviewed.

Let us now direct our attention to the third approach to the fight against working poverty: the employment maximization strategy.

4.3 MAXIMIZATION OF LABOUR FORCE ATTACHMENT

This third approach can also have an impact on working poverty, because a low degree of labour force attachment is one of the three working poverty mechanisms I have been able to identify. Policies that allow increasing female employment (especially maternal employment) and employment among low-skilled workers of both sexes can, hence, efficiently contribute to the fight against working poverty.

In the US everything is done to maximize labour market participation, which translates into a strong emphasis on employment-conditional benefits, especially the EITC, and the existence of a five-year lifetime limit for welfare benefits; in Scandinavia, this maximization strategy translates into generous parental-leave schemes and an access to largely available and affordable childcare. In addition, Nordic countries have a long tradition of active labour market policies (Esping-Andersen, 2002b). It should be noted, however, that in neither country the fight against working poverty was the main aim of the employment-maximizing approach. In the US, the main goal was to reduce welfare dependency, especially among single mothers (Meyer and Holtz-Eakin, 2001); whereas in Scandinavia it was a response to labour shortages in the 1960s and a way to take feminist claims into account (Bonoli, 2007).

Labour market participation has not been the number-one priority in many Continental European countries, in which early retirement, disability pensions, low female labour force participation and labour shedding have often been perceived as appropriate ways to regulate labour supply in periods of high unemployment (Esping-Andersen, 1999; Hemerijck, 2002). In the recent past, however, there has been a departure from the 'welfare without work' strategy and Continental welfare states are 'in the midst of a general paradigmatic shift ... towards ... employment-friendly welfare systems' (Hemerijck and Eichhorst, 2009: 23).

This third approach can also be divided into two subcategories. The first one consists of incentives and productivity-enhancing measures in the form of state-provided childcare services, parental leaves and active labour market policies. The other one is rather based on 'coercion', for example welfare-to-work programmes or employment-conditional benefits: people are compelled to hold a job in order to receive financial support. Interestingly, some researchers consider that employment-conditional benefits encourage rather than force people to work (see for example Meyer and Holtz-Eakin, 2001). Indeed, in the US, welfare-to-work policies and other measures aiming at forcing people back into employment are qualitatively different from work-conditional benefits, notably tax credits for workers.

The employment-maximization approach based on incentives implies a conception of the welfare state seen as an enabling institution, that is, a social investment state pursuing prevention rather than protection (Bonoli and Bertozzi, 2008; Esping-Andersen et al., 2002; Van der Veen, 2009). Labour protection is replaced by the promotion of work. In Scandinavian countries, the social investment approach, with an accent on activation and human capital, has been promoted for decades (Esping-Andersen, 2002a).

The *potential employment effects* of the employment-maximization strategy are self-evident. As far as the *potential antipoverty effects* are concerned, female unemployment and employment rates are significantly correlated to relative poverty (with the threshold set at 50 per cent of median income) over the period 1993–2000, while it is not the case for men, confirming the central role of women's earnings in reducing poverty risks (Burniaux et al., 2006). Indeed, female employment is one of the most effective means of combating poverty (Bonoli, 2007; Esping-Andersen, 2002c). Moreover, as will be shown in Chapter 7, countries with high maternal employment rates have a smaller share of working lone mothers who are poor. More generally, virtually all studies I am aware of show that unemployment and inactivity are important poverty factors, while double earnership reduces the poverty risk.

Finally, it is noteworthy that combating working poverty per se can also be seen as a social investment approach, as many poor workers have children. There is growing evidence that poverty has a detrimental effect on the mental health and cognitive development of children. Two models explain this impact. The first is the Family Stress Model: as families experience economic hardship, parents and other caregivers are subject to emotional distress and sometimes behavioural problems, which in turn leads to interparental conflict and inconsistent parenting practices (Conger and Jewsbury Conger, 2007). Another model, the Investment Model (IM), is primarily concerned with the advantages for the developing child of family financial prosperity: learning materials available in the home, stimulation of learning, specialized tutoring or training and so on (Conger and Jewsbury Conger, 2007). For instance, in the mid-1990s, the state of Wisconsin launched an experiment called New Hope, which provided adults with earnings below 150 per cent of the federal poverty line who worked at least 30 hours per week with wage supplements, subsidized health insurance and childcare subsidies. Not only did the programme decrease poverty, but it also improved children's academic achievement (Gupta et al., 2007).

4.3.1 Active Labour Market Policies (ALMP)

ALMP could be considered as a useful tool in the fight against working poverty, by contributing to the maximization of workforce attachment. Indeed, ALMP may increase the likelihood that unemployed or inactive members of working households find a job and retain it. However, whereas an abundant literature exists regarding the effectiveness of ALMP in the fight against unemployment, these policies are rarely considered as potential anti-working poverty tools outside the US (Hamilton et al., 2001; Kluve, 2006; Martin and Grubb, 2001). Moreover, the impact of ALMP on employment goes far beyond the scope of the present work, and, as indicated in the introduction, is not analysed here.

4.3.2 Childcare Services

Subsidizing childcare is another strategy that can be pushed in order to boost the labour market participation of poor workers and of inactive members of poor households.

Regarding family policies in general, an important fact is that the level of spending varies considerably across countries. Within the EU, the Nordic countries spend the most on family policy, broadly speaking (Fagnani and Math, 2008). More importantly, the structure of the spending varies widely: the majority of public spending on family policy in Nordic countries is devoted to the provision of services and tax breaks are virtually non-existent. In absolute terms, spending on services exceeds 1 per cent of GDP in Denmark, Finland, Iceland, Norway and Sweden; France is also notable. In France and Germany, the distribution between services, cash benefits and tax breaks is quite balanced, with tax breaks playing a more important role in Germany than France. In the US, the bulk of public spending on family benefits consists of tax breaks. In Europe, Mediterranean countries display the lowest levels of spending overall (Whiteford and Adema, 2007).

In summary, in many countries, family policy mainly belongs to the realm of social transfers, while in others it mainly aims at maximizing employment, especially maternal employment. The availability and the cost of childcare services are the two main approaches to the employment maximization strategy analysed here; however, although tax credits for workers are classified as employment-conditional transfers, they also belong to the category of instruments designed to increase employment rates, especially among single mothers.

4.3.2.1 Expected employment effects

Policies that improve the work–family life balance and, hence, the labour force participation of mothers are the following: increasing the availability of formal childcare, lowering childcare fees, making childcare expenses deductible from taxable income or from the calculation of means-tested benefits, childcare-related cash benefits, as well as tax credits for working mothers/parents (Immervoll and Barber, 2005). In the chapter devoted to meta-analyses of existing programmes, I focus on tax credits for working parents, and on childcare availability and costs/fees.

In their analysis of 21 countries, Immervoll and Barber (2005) show that, at both extremes of the distribution of two important variables, namely the share of children in formal childcare and the maternal employment rate (mothers of children under the age of three), the situation is clear: in Greece, Italy, Spain and Germany, a maternal employment rate of 45 to 56 per cent corresponds to a low share of children in formal childcare (less than 10 per cent). At the other end of the two distributions, Sweden and Denmark display both a high rate of labour market participation for mothers (more than 65 per cent) and a high share of children under three in formal childcare (65 and 64 per cent respectively). Regarding 'in-between' countries, the evidence is less clear. A first group of countries displays employment rates for mothers of children under three between 55 and 65 per cent, whereas the share of children in formal childcare lies between 10 and 30 per cent (Canada, the US and Switzerland). A second group of countries, namely France, Belgium, Austria, the Netherlands and Portugal have maternal employment rates of 65 to a high 74 per cent and a share of children in formal childcare below 30 per cent (it equals 30 per cent in France and Belgium).

All in all, these figures tend to show that mothers' labour force participation partly depends on the share of children in formal childcare, which in turn depends on the availability of childcare slots. However, a simple regression model in which maternal employment is regressed on the share of children in formal childcare yields a coefficient of determination that is rather modest, namely $R^2 = 0.16$; that is, 16 per cent of the variation in maternal employment is explained by the share of children in formal childcare (Immervoll and Barber, 2005).

Childcare fees doubtlessly play an important role, too. The average fees charged by childcare centres, for a two-year-old in 2001 in full-time care amounted, on average, to 16 per cent of gross earnings of an average production worker, ranging from 6 per cent in Sweden, the Slovak Republic, Hungary and Spain, to 37 per cent in Switzerland (Immervoll and Barber, 2005).

Immervoll and Barber (2005) show that childcare costs can be a heavy burden for working parents in OECD countries, but massive variations exist across countries. The situation of various family types is assessed in their report. For a dual-earner family with both parents earning 100 per cent of the average production worker (APW) wage, the cost of childcare for two children in full-time care, including tax and benefits concessions, expressed in per cent of family net income, ranges from 6 per cent in Germany, Sweden and Greece to 29 per cent in Ireland and Switzerland. For dual-earner households with earnings amounting to 133 per cent of the wage of an APW, these costs range from 5–6 per cent in Germany, Denmark and Finland, up to 32 per cent of family net income in New Zealand and 40 per cent in Ireland. For lone parents who earn an APW wage, differences are even larger, from 4–5 per cent in Germany and Norway, to 38 per cent of net income in the US, 42 per cent in New Zealand and a stunning 53 per cent in Ireland. For low-wage lone parents, the ranking is notably different, reflecting the fact that the US has targeted the bulk of its social policy effort on this population group: for a lone parent earning two-thirds of the APW wage, childcare costs range from 2 per cent of net income in the US (and Finland), to 42 per cent in Canada and 58 per cent in Ireland.

In summary, in some countries, childcare costs constitute a large obstacle to maternal employment, even for families living on average earnings, whereas in other countries, family policy efforts make childcare services affordable, most notably in Scandinavian countries.

The relative impact of childcare costs on the incentives to take up employment is summarized in Tables 4.2 and 4.3; some policy mixes can have a different impact on parents who hold low-wage jobs (–) than on those who hold higher wage jobs (+). Interestingly, results are different for married parents (Table 4.2) and for lone parents (Table 4.3).

Table 4.2 Work incentives and childcare costs for married couples

Impact of childcare cost on income gain	Financial incentives to take up employment (net income gain)		
	Low incentives	Average	High
Low	Denmark Hungary Slovak Republic	Finland (–) Iceland	Sweden
Average	Finland (+)	Belgium Norway	Greece Korea
High	Australia (+) Ireland New Zealand (–) Portugal (–) Switzerland (Zurich) UK	Australia (–) Austria (Vienna) Canada (Ontario) France (+) Japan (–) Netherlands Portugal (+) US (Michigan)	France (–) Japan (+) New Zealand (+)

Notes: (–) low-wage jobs; (+) higher wage jobs.

Source: Immervoll and Barber (2005).

Table 4.3 Work incentives and childcare costs for lone parents

Impact of child-care cost on income gain	Financial incentives to take up employment (net income gain)		
	Low incentives	Average	High
Low	Austria (Vienna) (–)	Finland (–)	Greece
	Denmark	Belgium	Norway
	France (–)	Iceland	Sweden
	Slovak Republic	Germany	UK (–)
		Japan (–)	US (Michigan) (–)
		Netherlands (–)	
		Portugal (–)	
Average	Austria (Vienna) (+)		Australia (–)
	France (+)		Hungary
	Netherlands (+)		
High	Canada (Ontario)	Portugal (+)	Korea (+)
	Ireland	Australia (+)	US (Michigan) (+)
	Japan (+)		
	Korea (–)		
	Australia (+)		
	New Zealand		
	Switzerland (Zurich)		
	UK (+)		

Notes: (–) low-wage jobs; (+) higher wage jobs.

Source: Immervoll and Barber (2005).

Childcare costs appear to play an important role in terms of work incentives. However, low financial incentives do not only depend on childcare costs. The tax and benefits system also plays a fundamental role. The cost of childcare acts as a major barrier to work in Canada, Ireland, New Zealand and Switzerland, but 'inactivity traps' can also exist in countries where childcare is much more affordable for low-wage lone parents, such as Austria, Denmark, France and the Slovak Republic (Immervoll and Barber, 2005).

Moreover, it is noteworthy that Swedish mothers entered the labour market long before the childcare policy was strongly developed. In 1970, half of the mothers with pre-school children were employed, while only 9 per cent of the pre-school children were in public childcare (Nyberg, 2006). The case of Greece is also interesting in this regard; mothers' labour market attachment is weak whereas the financial incentives to work are high.

In addition, it is also important to know whether women work full-time or part-time. Esping-Andersen (2002c) shows that in most countries, except for Scandinavian countries (and surprisingly also Italy), the presence of infant children has a very strong negative effect on full-time work, for instance in France, Germany and Southern Europe. In Scandinavia, part-time employment is increasingly not necessary for working mothers; they no longer need to work part-time to reconcile work and family life, thanks to a generous childcare policy (Hemerijck, 2002).

It is noteworthy that the phenomenon of 'statistical' discrimination may also depend on childcare policies. In countries in which employers expect that women will experience a productivity decline due to births, they will be more reluctant to hire them in the first place, to invest in their human capital and to pay them equal wages (Esping-Andersen, 2002c).

In summary, the cost of childcare appears to be a major determinant of maternal employment; however, other factors also play an important role, such as the tax/benefits system and the overall employment performance. Another key factor is the availability of childcare slots. If the number of childcare slots is low, then the price is quite unlikely to have much of an influence (Del Boca and Vuri, 2007; Kalb, 2009). In fact, there are different ways to achieve a high degree of childcare coverage. The first approach is typical of Scandinavia, a region in which childcare centres are heavily subsidized by the state; another approach is found in the US, a country in which childcare services are bought on the market. In the US, however, it is possible to find affordable childcare services, due to a wide earnings dispersion: childcare workers are low-paid. Indeed, Bonoli and Reber (2010) demonstrate that both public spending on family services and earnings dispersion have a statistically significant and positive impact on the percentage of children aged 0–3 in formal childcare.

Another important factor pertains to 'cultural values', or perhaps more precisely to social norms, as it appears that opinions about what 'a good mother' should and should not do have an impact on childcare use and employment. Comparative studies based on regression models that include employment and sociodemographic variables, public policy factors, as well as opinion questions concerning maternal employment show that the latter have a significant impact on the availability of childcare, all other things being equal (Berninger, 2009).

It is important to note that the impact of childcare services goes beyond its immediate effect on maternal employment. In fact, the more women stay in the labour market, the more jobs are created in the personal services sector. According to Esping-Andersen (1999), this 'multiplier' could amount to 10 per cent, that is, approximately one extra job in personal services for ten mothers who stay in the labour market.

4.3.2.2   Expected antipoverty effect

Interestingly, as will be shown in Chapter 6, the number of studies evaluating the antipoverty effects of childcare policies is limited. Most available evidence pertains to the employment effects and the impact on fertility of these policies. Here, I present some descriptive evidence found in the literature, whereas evaluations based on regression models and simulations are presented in Chapter 6.

The potential impact of childcare costs on poverty is easy to grasp. For instance, in 2001 in the US, 43 per cent of all working parents with children pay, on average, around US$5044 per year for childcare (the amount ranges from US$1958 to US$6587 per year). On average, childcare payments eat up one-fifth of the incomes of poor and lower middle-income working families who have to buy childcare services (Sawhill and Thomas, 2001).

Childcare policies can increase multi-earnership as well as the work volume of single parents. Indeed, single earnership has become a significant poverty factor in countries in which double earnership has become the norm. Moreover, there is also a long-term effect: a full-time worker who interrupts her career for five years will forego 1.5–2 percentage points per annum in potential lifetime earnings (Esping-Andersen, 2002c). This is due to skills erosion and lost seniority. In short, childcare policies can contribute to the reduction of working poverty by increasing earned income both in the short and in the long term.

Maximizing parents' labour force participation may not be sufficient, though. The OECD published a report (Whiteford and Adema, 2007) that aimed at evaluating the respective impact of a benefit strategy (mainly cash transfers and tax breaks) and of a work strategy on child poverty. Whiteford and Adema's conclusions are fundamental: 'while encouraging employment of the jobless and increasing the share of two earner families is likely to be an essential part of any effective policy to reduce child poverty, complementary strategies are required' (Whiteford and Adema, 2007: 31). This is due to the fact that the employment-maximization approach can play a fundamental role, but may not combat all types of working poverty.

NOTE

1. Belgium, UK, France, Austria, Netherlands, Germany, Ireland, Norway, Finland, Sweden and Denmark.

5. The real world of social policies: the welfare regime approach

In the real world of social policy, the instruments I present and meta-analyse separately, for the sake of analytical clarity, interact with each other. Moreover, not all possible combinations of these tools are found in post-industrial economies. Hence, a systemic approach is requested and I briefly analyse which of the existing welfare regime typologies found in the literature seems to be appropriate for the analysis of poverty among workers. There is disagreement among sociologists and political scientists (Bonoli, 1997): Esping-Andersen's typology (1990) has been criticized, either from a feminist perspective or because other indicators were suggested to draw a typology; moreover, additional regimes have been proposed (Bonoli, 1997). Eventually, I have chosen a four-category typology: 'liberal', conservative corporatist, social-democratic and Mediterranean welfare regimes.

The US, Germany, Sweden and Spain have been chosen to illustrate the welfare regimes used in this book. For each country, I first analyse the main dimensions that underpin the fight against working poverty and, second, highlight other features of its welfare state that appear to have an impact on working poverty. Third, all welfare regimes were hit by strong exogenous shocks, namely globalization, deindustrialization and technological changes in developed economies. There were objective evolutions, capital becoming much more mobile thanks to the development of transportation and communication (Wood, 1994) and the removal of many barriers to international trade, but also cognitive changes, due to the crisis of the Keynesian model in the 1970s and 1980s, which allowed neoclassical 'outsiders', the 'Chicago boys' in particular, to make their way to the top and impose their viewpoint: the welfare state undermines economic competitiveness, generates disincentives to work and irresponsible behaviours and is, hence, the cause of poverty rather than an efficient solution to it (Merrien et al., 2005; Murray, 2000). Globalization should, according to this approach, mechanically lead to a strong reduction in welfare expenses; however, differences between welfare regimes remain striking (Merrien et al., 2005; Stiglitz, 2002). In what follows, I show that each country has had different reactions to these massive shocks. The fourth stage includes indicators of poverty, income redistribution and employment performance gathered from official statistics and some academic publications.

5.1 WHICH TYPOLOGY OF WELFARE REGIMES IS APPROPRIATE FOR WORKING POVERTY ANALYSES?

This section does not aim at analysing at great length the various welfare regime typologies that have been proposed and the theoretical and empirical elements they are based on; this is a research topic of its own. My goal is to identify, among existing typologies, one that appears to be well suited for the analysis of poverty among workers in post-industrial economies.

Esping-Andersen's (1990) famous typology of welfare regimes (liberal, social-democratic, conservative corporatist) is based on three criteria: the first is the degree to which people's well-being is independent from the market (decommodification); the second is the impact of the welfare regime on the class composition; and the third is the respective role the public and the private sphere play.

There is no agreement among scholars as to the best welfare regime typology to use. The choice depends on the point of departure; for instance, social assistance types differ from employment-based typologies or from family policy typologies. Moreover, some authors have suggested adding new clusters, for instance the Antipodes or Mediterranean countries, because they thought that some of Esping-Andersen's categories were too heterogeneous. Other authors have suggested the use of further indicators to define welfare regimes (Bonoli, 1997), which is the approach I follow here.

Moreover, feminist critics blame Esping-Andersen for not having taken gender-specific elements into account (Berninger, 2009; Merrien, 2002) and distinguish regimes in which the male-breadwinner model is encouraged, even in a modified form, from regimes that promote dual-earner families. It could be said that Esping-Andersen (1990) probably underestimated the role families played in various welfare regimes and, as a consequence, gender-specific issues.

What typology shall I use, then? As shown in Chapter 4, there are mainly three approaches to the fight against working poverty and each of these approaches can be broken down into two subcategories (see Table 5.1).

Table 5.1 The approaches to the fight against working poverty that underpin the typology of welfare regimes

Minimum wages	
Legal minimum wages	Collectively bargained wages
Social transfers	
Substitution income	Supplementing income
Maximization of labour force participation	
Incentives	Coercion

In my view, it is possible to define welfare regimes on the basis of the two (out of six) approaches that have the largest impact on working poverty. Obviously, sharp distinctions can only be made within the framework of an ideal-typical approach, ideal types being simplified representations of reality which allow classifying countries by the type they resemble the most. Many countries combine all approaches: substitution and supplementing benefits coexist, as well as coercive and productivity-enhancing measures; in many OECD countries there is a legally enforced minimum wage and collective bargaining. However, some combinations are not really possible in the real world of welfare regimes. For instance, a highly regulated labour market may impair a country's ability to pursue labour force maximization as a strategy.

The role of the family, female employment patterns and family policies are also important dimensions of the fight against working poverty. This means that a useful typology should put enough emphasis on the design of family policies and their impact; hence, a brief review of some recent evidence regarding the impact of welfare regimes on the work–family life balance is important.

The European Foundation for the Improvement of Living and Working Conditions (hereafter Eurofound) has established a typology of welfare states according to the type of work–family life balance they tend to shape, in a life-course perspective (Eurofound, 2007). First, Eurofound notes that it is well established that female employment rates are higher in countries which support the employment of mothers through the provision of publicly financed childcare (Eurofound, 2007). The typology developed by Eurofound (2007) is the following:

- Nordic regimes (Denmark, Finland and Sweden);
- Liberal regimes (Ireland and UK);
- Continental regimes (Austria, Belgium, France, Germany and the Netherlands);
- Mediterranean regimes (Greece, Italy, Portugal and Spain).

In addition, a cluster of new member States of the EU is defined (Czech Republic, Cyprus, Estonia, Hungary, Latvia, Lithuania, Malta, Poland, Slovakia and Slovenia). Two acceding countries (Bulgaria and Romania, situation in 2004) and a candidate country (Turkey) are also included.

Eurofound (2007) identifies three models of female/maternal employment:

- *A continuous model* found in Denmark, Sweden, Slovenia, Latvia and Portugal. In these countries, the participation rate of women in employment is high and continuous over the life course, even during the childrearing phase. In France and Belgium, the situation is quite similar in terms of continuity, but the labour market participation level is lower. The high and continuous level observed in most of these countries is mainly due to extensive childcare facilities. In Portugal and Latvia, on the contrary, mothers rather work out of financial necessity. Interestingly, the continuous model is also predominant in North America (Esping-Andersen, 2002c).
- *A traditional model* is found in former 'West Germany', Ireland and the Netherlands, as women significantly decrease their labour force participation once they have children and do not necessarily increase their participation when their children start going to school. In Spain, Greece, Italy and Poland, mothers have low employment rates; however employed mothers tend to work full-time. A common pattern among all of these countries is a lack of childcare facilities.
- *A transitional model* in which women significantly reduce their working hours when they have pre-school age children, but then significantly increase their labour force participation when their children start going to school. In this cluster we find most post-socialist countries, especially Estonia, the Czech Republic, Lithuania, Bulgaria, Slovakia, Hungary and Romania; Austria, the UK and former 'East Germany' also belong to this group of countries with a transitional model.

The overlap between the three to four clusters of welfare states and the three clusters of female paid employment in a life-course perspective is only partial; nonetheless some regularities can be stressed (see Table 5.2).

Table 5.2 Welfare regimes and their impact on the female employment pattern

Employ-ment pattern	Welfare regime				
	Social-democratic	Mediterranean	Contin-ental	Liberal	Other countries
Continu-ous	Denmark Sweden (2/3)	Portugal (1/4)	France Belgium (2/6)		Slovenia Latvia (2/11)
Traditional		Italy Spain Greece (3/4)	Germany (West) Nether-lands (2/6)	Ireland (1/2)	Poland Turkey (2/11)
Transi-tional	Finland		Austria Germany (East) (2/6)	UK (1/2)	Estonia Czech Republic Lithuania Bulgaria Slovakia Hungary Romania (7/11)

Source: Eurofound (2007), table created for the purpose of this research.

Clearly, the social-democratic welfare regime, with its extensive childcare system, leads to a continuous model. A large majority of post-socialist countries exhibit a transitional model. The countries that belong to the conservative regime are spread across the three types of female working time models, which shows that it is probably too heterogeneous a cluster. Southern European countries are associated with the traditional model, with the notable exception of Portugal, where many mothers of young children work out of financial necessity.

It should be noted that Esping-Andersen (1999), though highlighting some specificities in Mediterranean countries, does not think it is necessary to create a separate cluster for Southern Europe. However, in addition to the traditional model, other specific patterns are noticeable: mothers tend either to be inactive or to work full-time, whereas in the rest of Continental Europe most mothers work part-time. In addition, the level of expenses on family policies is much lower in Southern Europe. Moreover, these countries rely much more on labour market regulation by law and far less on collective bargaining than most other Continental European countries, with the notable exception of France. These aspects are further discussed below.

Eventually, I will use the following typology in Chapters 6 and 7, as it appears to be the most appropriate for working poverty analyses:

- *Social-democratic*, exemplified by Sweden. Working poverty levels and the composition of the affected population are mainly explained by an employment-maximization strategy based on incentives and collective bargaining (even if social transfers are high, they are mainly aimed at non-working persons).
- *Liberal*, exemplified by the US, a country in which the fight against working poverty is mainly based on an employment-maximizing strategy based on both forcing people to work and on financial incentives, as well as complementing income in the form of tax credits.
- *Conservative corporatist*, exemplified by Germany. The size and composition of the working poor population are mainly explained by collective bargaining and by social transfers in the form of substitution income and family cash benefits.
- *Southern European countries*, exemplified by Spain, experience a type of working poverty that is mainly due to the fact that labour markets are strongly regulated and by the use of social transfers in the form of substitution income.

The following sections are devoted to the four countries that epitomize these four types of welfare regimes. It is fundamental to note that the crisis that has hit all advanced economies since 2008 is not analysed at great length here. Obviously, it has had a negative impact on poverty and employment. The harmonized unemployment rate amounts to 6.8 per cent in Germany and 8.3 per cent in Sweden in the third quarter of 2010 (OECD website, labour statistics). The 'at-risk-of-poverty rate' increased by 24 per cent in Germany and by 27 per cent in Sweden between 2007 and 2009. However it remained below the average of the old member states of the EU (Eurostat website, income, social inclusion and living conditions). In the US, the increase in unemployment has been massive: between 2007 and the third quarter of 2010, unemployment rose from 4.6 to 9.6 per cent (OECD website, labour statistics). Moreover, in the US in 2009 poverty reached its highest level since the 1960s (US Census Bureau, 2010). Spain is very hard hit. The harmonized unemployment rate reached 20.5 per cent in the third quarter of 2010, while it amounted to 8.3 per cent in 2007 (OECD website, labour statistics). As is the US, one of the main culprits was the bursting of the construction bubble (FEDEA, 2009; Garrido and Gutiérrez, 2009). However the 'at-risk-of-poverty rate' remained stable between 2007 and 2009 (Eurostat website, income, social inclusion and living conditions), which is partly attributable to the very specific situation of young workers; they are much harder hit by unemployment than the rest of the Spanish workforce, but most of them live with their parents until their thirties, as explained below, which reduces the impact of unemployment on their income.

It is too early, however, to know what the long-term consequences of this crisis will be. Will employment and poverty get back to their pre-crisis levels and will the working poverty mechanisms be modified? These are questions that will need to be answered once this crisis is over.

5.1.1 Sweden

5.1.1.1 Main approaches to the alleviation of working poverty

In Sweden, waged work is perceived as being the primary route out of poverty (Jones et al., 2006). Public childcare, which is available at low cost, provides poor families with incentives to work and with a real opportunity to increase their living standard (Lindbom and Rothstein, 2004). Particularly noteworthy is the very high female labour market participation, almost 73 per cent in 2003 (Jones et al., 2006). In Sweden, as in other Nordic countries, the main goal is to maximize citizens' employability and productivity (Esping-Andersen, 2002a). Scandinavian welfare states in general, and the Swedish one in particular, have promoted the right to work for everyone and have focused their policy on the maximization of labour force participation, rather than income transfer strategies like in Continental European countries. Sweden is a 'universalist work-centred society' (Leibfried, 2000). This approach is pursued through a generous, state-financed social service provision (Clayton and Pontusson, 2000), notably in the field of childcare and active labour market policies, financed by general taxation, while social insurance is mainly financed by employers' payroll taxes (European Commission's website, employment, social affairs and equal opportunities, MISSOC tables).

As far as labour market policy is concerned, Sweden is, among the four countries analysed here, the biggest spending country with 1.24 per cent of its GDP spent on public employment services and administration, training, employment incentives, integration of the disabled, direct job creation and start-up incentives; whereas this share amounts to 1.15 per cent in Germany, 0.72 per cent in Spain and 0.16 per cent in the US (OECD, 2006).

Sweden has been a frontrunner in the development of publicly provided childcare, which is partly attributable to a shortage of labour in the 1960s

(Lundin et al., 2008) and the fact that Sweden did not rely on immigration to fill the gaps. During the 1970s, mothers' employment grew from 30 to 70 per cent. As early as 1976, the Government and the Swedish municipalities agreed to build 100,000 childcare slots within the next five years (Lundin et al., 2008). Since 1995, the legislation obliges local governments to supply childcare to working parents (or full-time studying parents) within four months of the parents' request. The price is largely subsidized and in 2002 a major reform of childcare fees was implemented, with the introduction of a maximum fee, which substantially reduced expenses for most parents of pre-school children (Brink et al., 2007). After the reform, the average family paid only 4 per cent of its after-tax income on childcare (Lundin et al., 2008).

Sweden is also characterized by a very strong emphasis on collective bargaining, which is highly centralized and coordinated; there is no legally enforced minimum wage and agreements apply to all firms in the industry, whether the workers are unionized or not; the bargained minimum wages are industry-specific and nationwide (Skedinger, 2006). About 90 per cent of the employees in Sweden are protected by collective agreements. An important aspect that deserves our attention is the very high unionization rates found in Sweden. This can be explained by the 'Ghent system' of unemployment compensation: access to unemployment benefits requires union membership (Bonoli, 2006). This implies that women, white-collar employees, part-time workers and workers with 'atypical' contracts are well represented in the labour movement. By contrast, most unions in Continental European countries tend to mainly protect older male blue-collar workers who are in the core workforce and public service employees (Ebbinghaus, 2006).

5.1.1.2 Further aspects of the welfare regime that have an impact on working poverty

Sweden displays a high degree of employment protection. It was higher than in other Nordic countries in 1990; however it has decreased ever since and is now comparable to the Finnish and the Norwegian level (OECD website, overall EPL strictness), which is still above the OECD average.

Social transfers, though generous in international comparison, are not the main tools in the fight against working poverty; however they indirectly support many low-income workers by supporting a non-working partner or a child. As will be clearly demonstrated below, social transfers in Sweden also contribute to the fight against working poverty. Social transfers in Sweden reflect a strongly egalitarian ethos and universalist style (Goodin et al., 2000). Another very important intention is to emancipate individuals from dependency on the family (Jones et al., 2006), in complete opposition to the Spanish welfare regime, as will be demonstrated below. In Sweden, redistribution plays a very important role by strongly reducing income inequality (Kenworthy, 2004). It should be noted that income replacement benefits in Continental Europe are equally as generous as in Scandinavia, but they require longer periods of labour market participation (Bonoli, 2007).

The very large size of the public sector is also of paramount importance. Empirical evidence gathered by Armingeon (2006) demonstrates that, in the fight against new social risks, a crucial variable is the size of the public sector, because public-sector employees tend to favour the expansion of the welfare state. Moreover, many well-paid low-skilled jobs are provided by the state (Iversen and Wren, 1998) and contribute to the shaping of the social stratification in Sweden (Esping-Andersen, 1993).

In short, the combination of a compressed wage distribution, a high employment rate and a work-related welfare system, with high replacement rates for unemployment, sickness and disability compensation (Kenworthy, 2004), leads to the fact that Swedes who are in the lower income decile are better-off than their counterparts in many other European countries and much better-off in purchasing parity terms than Americans in the lower decile (Freeman, 1995).

Interestingly, many institutions and services provided prevent the emergence of a large low-income segment within the Swedish labour force; yet, none of them were specifically designed to combat working poverty, except for collective bargaining which aims at reducing the incidence of low-wage employment, an important poverty factor in the industrial era (Bonoli, 2007).

It is fundamental to understand why Scandinavian countries have been frontrunners in combating new social risks; interestingly, the main reasons are not connected with exogenous macroeconomic shocks. Before World War II, Sweden's birth rate was one of the lowest in Europe, which was a source of concern. Moreover, the timing of various sociodemographic and macroeconomic changes often included in the label 'post-industrial changes' varies greatly across nations. Based on an index combining the share of service employment in total employment, the female employment rate and the divorce rate, Bonoli (2007) demonstrates that Sweden entered the post-industrial era in 1970, the US in 1975, Germany in 1989 and most Southern European countries in the 1990s. It is noteworthy that:

> In countries that have entered the postindustrial age relatively early, new demands generated by the ongoing social transformations found comparatively little competition ... In contrast, in countries that have developed into post-industrial societies more recently, demands for protection against new social

risks are in strong competition with demands for the preservation, in spite of population ageing, of the current level of protection provided (Bonoli, 2007: 511).

In Sweden, the economic boom of the 1960s was accompanied by the emergence of second wave feminism and a strong representation of women in the labour movement and in the Social Democratic party, and this resulted in a series of measures, such as the implementation of individual taxation for married couples, pre-school services for young children and the right to work for six hours per day without loss of status for parents with pre-school children. A parental leave insurance was introduced in 1974 (Daguerre, 2006). This explains why Sweden's bulk of social spending on family policies is devoted to the provision of services and to generous parental leave schemes, while cash benefits are less important, quantitatively and qualitatively speaking. This is in sharp contrast with Continental Europe.

5.1.1.3 Shocks to the system: globalization, deindustrialization and recent changes in the welfare regime

Comparative welfare state research systematically emphasizes that Sweden spends nearly twice as much on its social policies, in per cent of the GDP, as the US. What is far less well documented is the fact that this enormous difference is a recent phenomenon, in spite of exogenous pressure toward convergence, as some Anglo-Saxon countries which already had the leanest welfare states carried out a significant retrenchment, both in terms of expenditure and social rights, while in Sweden, the universalist nature of benefits and services created their own political support and made long-term retrenchment difficult (Lindbom and Rothstein, 2004). Most of the main social security programmes are related to work performance. But the political effect of work-related programmes is largely similar to that of universal programmes, namely a broad support among the population, as most citizens both contribute to the financing and can benefit from these programmes. This also explains why support for social assistance schemes became increasingly negative in the 1990s in a country in which pro-welfare state attitudes are very widespread (Bergmark, 2000).

The 1990s were years of change, as Sweden experienced the most severe macroeconomic crisis since the 1930s. Unemployment rose from 1.7 per cent to 8.3 per cent between 1990 and 1993; moreover, at a time when unemployment soared, Sweden received the largest waves of immigrants in modern history (Palme et al., 2002). Swedish governments instituted some important cutbacks in welfare programmes in the 1990s: eligibility rules were tightened, while replacement rates and benefits levels were reduced in almost all earnings-related schemes (Palme et al., 2002). The number of social assistance recipients increased; in 1998, 43 per cent of social assistance recipients were in fact unemployed but not eligible for the unemployment benefit, a quite widespread feature among young adults and recent immigrants (Lindbom and Rothstein, 2004). Another cause was the fact that the proportion of children aged 0 to 17 years living in households with annual incomes under the level of eligibility for social assistance increased from 6 to 16 per cent over the period 1991–97 (Bergmark, 2000). Higher childcare fees were introduced, whereas there was an expansion in the number of children enrolled with 82 per cent of 3−6-year-olds in childcare at the end of the decade (from 64 per cent at the beginning of the 1990s).

As far as collective bargaining is concerned, the wage solidarity policy through a centralized negotiation between the Swedish Labour Confederation (LO) and the Swedish Employers' Confederation (SAF) was undermined as early 1983; collective bargaining has been decentralized, which partly explains the increase in the wage dispersion that took place in the recent past (Halleröd and Larsson, 2008).

But after the economic crisis was over in the late 1990s/early 2000s, replacement rates were raised (Lindbom and Rothstein, 2004) and resources increased (Bergmark, 2000), and 'the commitment to a high-equality, high-employment society remains largely intact in Sweden, and as of the writing the effort can be judged rather successful' (Kenworthy, 2004: 136). For instance, despite reduced benefits, the level of social assistance in Sweden is at approximately two-thirds of an average wage (Jones et al., 2006). In addition, the crisis did not lead to women leaving the labour market and there is no evidence that older workers were pushed out of working life (Palme et al., 2002).

However, even if the Swedish economy and welfare system seem to be back on track, some negative elements remain: earnings inequality grew and temporary forms of employment have become more common (Bergmark, 2000; Palme et al., 2002). Short-term employment was the lot of 17.5 per cent of Swedish employees in 2007, a 3 percentage point increase in ten years (OECD website, labour statistics). Moreover, the 9th-to-1st earnings decile ratio increased from 2.01 in 1990 to 2.31 in the mid-2000s (OECD website, labour statistics). However the incidence of low pay remains very low in international comparison; indeed, the increasing degree of earnings inequality mainly took place in the upper segment of the distribution and real median wages increased by 22 per cent over the 1990s, because there was a strong relative decline for public sector employees, which contrasted with a strong increase in the managerial wage in the private and public sector (Palme et al., 2002).

More importantly, working poverty in Sweden is a quantitatively small, but growing problem (Halleröd and Larsson, 2008), a phenomenon that particularly affects young and single workers; the working poor rate is now slightly higher than in Germany (own calculations based on EU-SILC 2006 data presented on the next page). Finally, at the end of the 1990s, the overall costs and number of recipients of social assistance declined, but long-term receipt was at considerably higher levels than before the crisis (Bergmark and Backman, 2004) and the yearly exit rates into work were low (Bergmark and Backman, 2004). Even if the size of this group of welfare recipients is rather modest, this represents a growing number of persons durably excluded from the labour market.

In summary, even though the generosity of the Swedish welfare regime is clearly above average and poverty levels are low, the expansionary phase of the Swedish welfare state has probably come to an end (Lindbom and Rothstein, 2004).

5.1.1.4 Poverty, income redistribution and employment performance

Interesting figures are provided by Notten and De Neubourg (2007), based on the US official poverty line adjusted with purchasing power parities (PPP). When measured with this absolute threshold, poverty is lowest in Germany and Sweden; it is noticeably higher in the US and extremely high in Spain (see Table 5.3).

Table 5.3 Poverty incidence, measured with the US official poverty line in PPP, in per cent

	1995	2000
Germany	7.5	5.1
Spain	29.1	19.1
Sweden	n/a	5.7
US	10.6	8.7

Source: Notten and De Neubourg (2007).

In relative terms, too, Sweden appears as a country with a limited poverty problem (see Table 5.4).

Table 5.4 Poverty rates based on thresholds set at 50 and 40 per cent of median disposable income (most recent wave, around mid-1990s, around mid-1980s and mid-1970s)

Year	Poverty rate (50 per cent threshold)	Poverty rate (40 per cent threshold)	Child poverty in two-parent families (50 per cent)	Child poverty in single-parent families (50 per cent)
Sweden, 2005	5.6	2.6	3.3	10.4
Sweden, 1995	6.6	4.7	1.5	6.6
Sweden, 1987	7.5	4.4	3.2	5.5*
Sweden, 1975	6.5	2.8	2.3	3.4

Note: * = estimates based on 15 to 30 observations only. Figures as of 28 September 2008.

Source: Luxembourg Income Study (LIS) Key Figures.

Child poverty is very low and does not exceed a proportion of one in ten among children living in single-parent households, an extremely low percentage in international comparison, because parents are able to reconcile work and family life (Bonoli, 2006). In Sweden, lone mothers have a very high labour force participation rate. This specificity of Scandinavian countries is mainly due to childcare services and public employment. A low child poverty rate is a logical consequence of having low poverty rates among the working-age population in general and among single mothers in particular.

Regarding 'in-work poverty', the share of workers who have spent at least six months in the labour market in the previous year and have an income lower than 60 per cent of median disposable income is similar, although slightly higher, to the percentage measured in Continental European countries: 7 per cent in Sweden (vs 6 per cent in France and 5 per cent in Germany in 2006) (Eurostat website, in-work at-risk-of-poverty rate). Even measured with a poverty line set at 50 per cent of median income and a definition including all workers, the working poor rate is slightly higher in Sweden than in Germany (5.3 and 4.4 respectively, own calculations with EU-SILC data 2006).

The effect of redistribution on child poverty due to taxation and the benefit systems is one of the largest across OECD countries (poverty measured as having a household income lower than 50 per cent of median disposable income, Whiteford and Adema, 2007). Focusing on the situation of working families, we get a good proxy of the impact of the Swedish redistributive system on working poverty. Child poverty among working lone-parent households is reduced by 83.3 per cent (OECD average: 49.7 per cent), among dual-earner families by 68.8 per cent (OECD average: 39.3 per cent) and among single-earner couples with children by 75.4 per cent (OECD: average 43.0 per cent) (Whiteford and Adema, 2007). It is noteworthy that, 'If tax and benefit systems could be made as effective as … [in] Sweden, it is estimated that child poverty in OECD countries would be more than halved' (Whiteford and Adema, 2007: 28).

In terms of labour market performance, despite the deep recession of the 1990s, in 2000 Sweden displayed the highest level of labour market participation and an unemployment level that was slightly higher than in the US but significantly lower than in Germany and Spain (OECD website, labour statistics). The harmonized unemployment rate amounted to 5.6 per cent, with an overall employment rate of 77.4 per cent (civilian labour force divided by the population aged 15–64) and a female participation rate of 71 per cent. Seven years later, before the worldwide recession began, the unemployment rate had slightly increased and amounted to 6.1 per cent; however total and female employment rates had also increased, with 80.5 and 77.8 respectively. Moreover, the maternal employment rate (for mothers of children under 16 years of age) was much higher than in the other countries with 82.5 per cent of mothers in employment. Of the four countries analysed in this chapter, Sweden is the best performer in terms of participation rates and second best in terms of unemployment levels.

Hence, Sweden seems well equipped to face the challenges caused by post-industrial mutations: 'Sweden has the most well established [new social risk] policies and has developed labour market activation through training [and] has supported access to employment' (Kananen et al., 2006: 85). In fact, only in the social-democratic welfare regime did the poverty rates of the overall working-age population, of children and of single mothers decrease since 1980 (Huber and Stephens, 2006).

5.1.2 The US

5.1.2.1 Main approaches to the alleviation of working poverty

The US is characterized by an employment-centred approach, that is, by strict work requirements for welfare recipients and the provision of supplementing income to those who are compelled to work but do not earn enough to make ends meet. This welfare-to-work approach, the fact that there is a lifetime limit for benefit receipt of five years, as well as the fact that the Earned Income Tax Credit (EITC), a work-conditional tax credit, has become the main antipoverty policy since the 1990s (Husby, 2000;

Meyer and Holtz-Eakin, 2001; Nagle and Johnson, 2006) with a much higher level of expenditure than the means-tested Temporary Assistance for Needy Families (TANF) (MaCurdy and McIntyre, 2004), are the most distinct dimensions of this 'work-first' approach. The welfare state is conceived as a work-enforcing mechanism (Leibfried, 2000).

In the US, as in Scandinavia, the maximization of labour market participation is a priority; however the services families need in order to increase their volume of work must be bought in the market: 'What Scandinavians are compelled to pay in taxes, their US equivalents are compelled to pay out of their own pockets' (Esping-Andersen, 2002a: 14). These services are affordable to many households due to very low wages in the low-end service sector. However, low-wage workers may find it difficult to buy childcare services in the market and pay for other work-related expenses and, hence, face disincentives to work. Childcare for a four-year-old in a childcare centre averages US$4000 to US$6000 per year in cities and states around the country, and families with younger children face even greater costs (Schulman, 2000). This problem is partly solved by the existence of the EITC as well as childcare-related tax credits, which aim at making work pay for lone mothers and low-wage workers. However, despite these tax credits, unaffordable childcare can be a serious poverty trap for low-wage workers (Esping-Andersen, 2002b).

In fact, the difference between an enabling approach of the maximization of labour force participation and a more 'coercive' approach is not clear-cut. In Scandinavia too, there are constraints imposed on unemployed persons to follow training, and this trend has increased in recent years, while in the US the welfare reform of 1996, namely The Personal Responsibility and Work Opportunity Reconciliation Act (PRWORA), also emphasized the provision of childcare services and training for welfare recipients in order to improve their employability and life chances (Bryner and Martin, 2007; Pierson, 1994).

The PRWORA replaced the main means-tested programme named Aid for Families with Dependent Children (AFDC), created by the Social Security Act of 1935, with a programme named Temporary Assistance for Needy Families (TANF). The name of the 1996 PRWORA is revealing: the emphasis is put on both responsibility and opportunities. Among American politicians there are different interpretations of workfare: 'Large gaps remained between the liberal vision of "rehabilitative" workfare and conservative perceptions of "deterrent" workfare' (Pierson, 1994: 122). Likewise, states differ in the way they have implemented their reforms. Some states sought to promote basic education, job training and other skills. Others aimed at moving recipients as quickly as possible into the workforce (Bryner and Martin, 2007).

The bottom line is, however, that the US relies more on a 'work-first' approach than Nordic countries, by putting more emphasis on 'incentives' to work and obligations than on providing protection against new social risks (Bonoli, 2007).

With regards to income transfers, the US antipoverty approach for working-age persons and their children relies mainly on means-tested benefits. This is, of course, the case for welfare recipients; for the working poor, the main antipoverty tool is a means-tested work-conditional benefit that provides a supplementing income, namely the EITC. However, the breakeven point of the credit is set at a much higher level than the official poverty line.

In summary, the main approach in the US consists in getting as many disadvantaged persons as possible back into the labour market and in providing those on low-wage employment with supplementing income sources in the form of a refundable tax credit. In addition, if the combination of earnings and tax credits does not suffice, workers are entitled to further means-tested cash or in-kind benefits, such as food stamps. The main post-industrial challenges have been regulated essentially by market mechanisms (Bonoli, 2006) with notable interventions of the Federal government and states in order to compensate market imperfections.

5.1.2.2 Further aspects of the welfare regimes that have an impact on working poverty

The US has the least regulated labour market of all OECD countries (according to the OECD's EPL index) and a decentralized and uncoordinated type of collective bargaining. As mentioned above, there is a low federal minimum wage; however a growing number of states have implemented their own minimum wage, set at a higher level. Moreover, some metropolitan areas have implemented living wage ordinances: private companies commissioned by local authorities must pay wages above the legal minimum.

In addition, it should be noted that having a systemic approach seems of paramount importance here, because the composition of the US labour force is different from most European countries. There are more single-parent households, but also more multi-earner households. And perhaps more importantly, the US has an earnings distribution that is totally different from European countries (Marx, 2008). As will be shown in Chapter 6, employment-conditional benefits appear to have a very limited impact in Continental European countries, partly because the composition of the workforce and the distribution of earnings are very different from that in the US.

Overall employment performance has been strong from the late 1980s until 2008 and the employment rate is high in international comparison; however unemployment levels have shot up during the economic crisis of the late 2000s. Contrary to what is commonly believed, the US economy did not create mainly low-skilled, low-wage service sector jobs; the jobs created in the 1980s and the 1990s were disproportionately in high-paying occupations and sectors. In fact, 'in the 1990s the distribution of new employment was U-shaped, with a relative shortage of job growth in mid-paying occupations' (Kenworthy, 2004: 143).

Regarding female labour force participation, there is a strong emphasis on gender equality issues among workers. Thanks to strictly enforced antidiscrimination laws, gender equality in the US has progressed faster than in other countries (Bonoli, 2006). Interestingly, the results regarding the reconciliation of work and family life in the US are quite similar to those achieved in Scandinavia, but the distributional consequences are fundamentally different across educational levels and income brackets.

Regarding the tax and benefit system, contrary to Sweden, reducing income inequality is not a priority; its goal is to improve the living standards of the worst off in society with targeted benefits (Goodin et al., 2000), a fact reflected, inter alia, in the low level at which the official poverty line is set. However successive EITC expansions have led to the fact that households with an income clearly above the poverty line also get a small benefit.

5.1.2.3   Shocks to the system: globalization, deindustrialization and recent changes in the welfare regime

In the 1980s, when unemployment rates skyrocketed and reached two-digit levels, due to very heavy losses in industrial employment, the Reagan administration tried to redesign welfare towards 'workfare', as concerns about the disincentive effects of benefits and welfare 'dependency' had surfaced among liberals as well as conservatives (Pierson, 1994). At the same time, the EITC was expanded considerably in the Tax Reform Act of 1986 and 'stands out as the great political success of the retrenchment era' (Pierson, 1994: 125). The next steps were the in-depth welfare reform of 1996 mentioned above, when the TANF replaced the AFDC. The word 'temporary' reflects a fundamental change in the programme, as no one should receive welfare benefits more than five years during their lifetime (Lindbom and Rothstein, 2004; Meyer and Holtz-Eakin, 2001). The AFDC programme had been subject to criticism for a long time and it turned out to be the most vulnerable means-tested programme in the 1980s (Pierson, 1994).

In fact, the increase in the number of working poor since the mid-1970s made it increasingly unfair, for a majority of citizens, for the government to provide welfare recipients with benefits and services that the working poor did not receive. In addition, a large share of the population did not expect the state to provide for these goods and services, as they had already bought them on the private market (Lindbom and Rothstein, 2004); means-tested welfare benefits became increasingly unpopular.

States were given much more room for manoeuvre; some emphasized sanctions and shorter time limits while others put emphasis on incentives. A major shift in the structure of social expenditures took place, from 77 per cent of total spending on welfare programmes in 1997 to 44 per cent in 2002, while the proportion of spending on childcare, training and education rose from 23 to 56 per cent (Bryner and Martin, 2007).

In recent years, a controversial problem has been tackled, namely the lack of universal healthcare coverage. In 1997, the Federal government created the State Children's Health Insurance Program (SCHIP), providing funds to states so that they can expand healthcare coverage through Medicaid or a separate programme. By 2000, 37 states provided coverage to children in all households with an income up to 200 per cent of the poverty line (Kenworthy, 2004). At the time of writing, a nearly universal healthcare programme is being proposed by the Obama administration.

In sum, in a social investment perspective, the US has undergone remarkable changes in the recent past, with an increased generosity of the EITC and childcare subsidies, as well as the implementation of the SCHIP. However, as shown in the next section, levels of child poverty remain high in international comparison.

5.1.2.4 Poverty, income redistribution and employment performance

A closer look at the absolute poverty rates provided by Notten and De Neubourg (2007) leads to the conclusion that the US has a non-negligible share of its population suffering harsh financial poverty. The US poverty rate, measured with an absolute threshold set at the low official level, is 71 per cent higher than in Germany and 53 per cent higher than in Sweden, but notably lower than in Spain.

The difference between the US, on the one hand, and Germany and Sweden on the other hand, appears larger when it is measured with relative poverty lines. Indeed, based on relative indicators, the US appears to have the biggest poverty problem among the four countries analysed in this chapter (see Table 5.5).

Table 5.5 Poverty rates based on thresholds set at 50 and 40 per cent of median disposable income (most recent wave, around mid-1990s, around mid-1980s and mid-1970s)

Year	Poverty rate (50 per cent threshold)	Poverty rate (40 per cent threshold)	Child poverty in two-parent families (50 per cent)	Child poverty in single-parent families (50 per cent)
US, 2004	17.3	11.4	13.5	48.5
US, 1994	17.8	11.8	14.8	57.1
US, 1986	17.8	12.4	16.1	62.8
US, 1974	15.9	10.7	11.6	60.1

Note: figures as of 28 September 2008.

Source: Luxembourg Income Study (LIS) Key Figures.

Child poverty is notably higher in the US than in Sweden, Germany and Spain, whereas in the case of Spain the difference is less marked (see corresponding tables in the sections devoted to these countries). The incidence is staggeringly high for children living in lone-parent households: half of them are affected by relative poverty. Some factors explain the incidence of poverty among single mothers: as of 2003, around 30 per cent of single mothers did not work; this rate amounted to nearly 40 per cent for never-married mothers (Sherman et al., 2004). Many of these non-working single mothers got TANF benefits. In fact, two-thirds of TANF families had only one adult recipient in 2000 (US Department of Health and Human Services, undated). In addition, the level of TANF benefits is set at a low level – in most states they amount to 20 to 40 per cent of the Federal Poverty Level (Bryner and Martin, 2007). The situation of working mothers is more enviable, thanks to the EITC, as will be evaluated in Chapter 6.

As far as in-work poverty is concerned, in the US case, obviously, I cannot use Eurostat's figures, nor my own calculations based on EU-SILC; however the US Bureau of Labor Statistics (2003) provides figures on working poverty in the US. The official poverty line is, as already indicated, set at a very low level in international comparison (around 40 per cent of median income in the early 2000s); nonetheless around 5 per cent of workers were poor in 2003 (US Bureau of Labor Statistics, 2003), which means that if Eurostat's in-work at-risk-of-poverty rate was calculated, it would be very high. In fact, working poverty has been a source of concern since the early 1980s, as the working poor rate grew markedly in that decade (Levitan and Shapiro, 1988) and, since the 1980s, large numbers of workers have remained poor, even in periods of prosperity (Gupta et al., 2007).

Regarding the impact of the tax and benefits system in the US, I consider the reduction in child poverty among working families as a proxy for the reduction in the working poor rate. For all working-family types, the poverty reduction effect is below average: –21.2 per cent for single-parent households (OECD: –49.7), –23.6 per cent for dual-earner families (OECD: –39.3) and –16.7 per cent for single-earner couples with children (OECD: –43.0 per cent). It should be kept in mind that these calculations encompass the impact of the taxation system and, hence, take into account the effect of the EITC (Whiteford and Adema, 2007). However, it is fundamental to note that the poverty threshold used here is 50 per cent of median disposable equivalence income, as in virtually all OECD studies. Let us remember that the official poverty line in the US amounted to around 42 per cent of median disposable income in 2002 (Smeeding, 2005). Hence, when US researchers and policymakers make claims about lifting people out of poverty, it usually means lifting them above the 'Orshansky threshold', whereas most of them are still poor according to usual poverty lines used in comparative research. This partly explains the quite low impact of the tax system and cash benefits described in this section.

All in all, of the four countries analysed in this book, the US is the worst performer in terms of relative poverty, but the judgement is less negative when an absolute poverty line is used, as median income is high in the US.

In terms of employment and unemployment, the US performs well according to the OECD labour statistics. In 2000, the harmonized unemployment rate amounted to 4 per cent only and 4.6 per cent in 2007, which makes it the best performer among the countries analysed in this chapter. Regarding the employment rate, the US ranked second just behind Sweden with 76.3 per cent of the 15–64-year-olds in civilian employment in 2000 (1.1 percentage point less than Sweden). However, during President Bush's two terms, employment stagnated and amounted to 75.6 per cent in 2007, leading to a larger gap between Sweden and the US (4.9 points), as Sweden increased its participation rate over the 2000s. The same trend applies for female employment. As far as mothers are concerned, however, the differences are more marked: according to the OECD, as indicated above, more than eight in ten mothers of children under 16 held a job in Sweden in 2007, whereas this share amounted to around two-thirds in the US, a level similar to that of Germany (OECD website, family database).

In short, among the countries analysed in this chapter, the US ranked first in terms of unemployment and second in terms of employment until recently, before unemployment went through the roof and the employment rate declined due to the recession.

5.1.3 Germany

5.1.3.1 Main approaches to the alleviation of working poverty

Germany epitomizes non-Mediterranean Continental Europe; one of the main characteristics of this group of countries is that social insurance financed through social security contributions gives good protection to those with stable employment; for this reason, these countries have a high degree of employment protection (Esping-Andersen, 2002a). The basic functioning of the 'corporatist' welfare regime, founded in Germany in the 1880s, is that 'you get what you pay for and pay for what you get' (Goodin et al., 2000: 172).

This model relies on passive income maintenance for those who are not able to earn a living, be it because of a job loss, sickness, injuries or disability, and provides strong job guarantees for those in work. This model tends to favour those who have a stable and continuous employment pattern. Hence, Germany is a typical strong breadwinner regime (Daguerre, 2006) and has relied on a strategy of paying generous social transfers and subsidizing exit from the labour market, or even inactivity, to regulate labour supply (Goodin et al., 2000), which has led to a 'welfare without work' approach (Hemerijck and Eichhorst, 2009). The level of social transfers is generous, in some instances even more generous than in Scandinavia, especially pension benefits (Armingeon, 2006). Germany devotes a large share of its GDP to family policies, especially family cash benefits, with significant increases in tax credits for parents in the recent past, as will be further analysed below.

Fixed labour costs are high due to payroll-based social insurance financing: they amount to more than 40 per cent of gross wages (Kenworthy, 2004). Indeed, high payroll taxes have regularly been seen as the main culprit for Germany's modest employment performance (Andress and Seeck, 2007). Recently, however, Germany, as many other Continental European countries (such as France, Belgium, the Netherlands, Spain and Portugal) has introduced a reduction in social security contributions for low-skilled workers.

At the end of the 1990s, nine in ten workers with a pre-transfer income below the poverty line (defined as 50 per cent of average income) received social transfers, namely a child allowance (*Kindergeld*, 63.8 per cent), unemployment benefits (22.2 per cent) and pensions (27.8 per cent) and housing subsidy (*Wohngeld*, 11.5 per cent) (Strengmann-Kuhn, 2003).

Obviously, in the case of unemployment and old-age benefits, the support to workers is provided indirectly by supporting non-working household members. However, less than one in ten working poor (9.7 per cent) received social assistance, due to a low take-up rate caused by phenomena such as feelings of shame and lacking knowledge on the side of potential beneficiaries, as well as errors on the side of social workers and practical aspects such as the opening hours of welfare services (Boos-Nünning, 2000; Leu et al., 1997; Strengmann-Kuhn, 2003).

In Germany, industrial relations are fully autonomous from state intervention and are based on collective bargaining (Bonoli, 2006; Hemerijck, 2002). Social partners play a very important role in the administration of the social insurance system. The coverage of collective bargaining was very high in former West Germany (Bonoli, 2003a) and is still rather high in reunified Germany with approximately two-thirds of the labour force covered, which is, however, lower than in Spain and Sweden (International Labour Organization, 2008). Trade unions tend to represent blue-collar, core-workforce male breadwinners as well as civil servants, contrary to their Nordic counterparts (Ebbinghaus, 2006).

Minimum wages are defined in collective agreements, usually at the industry level. Extension laws exist, but they are used with much more parsimony than in France or Spain (Bonoli, 2003a). For many years, collective bargaining between trade unions and employers in Germany was highly centralized and led to a high-wage economy with a low level of income inequality (Andress and Seeck, 2007) and a very low degree of labour conflictuality with few strike days (ILO website, database of labour statistics LABORSTA). German wages are high in international comparison, but high productivity levels have kept German firms competitive (Kenworthy, 2004). This strategy has led to a 'high-skill equilibrium' which explains the very weak development of the private service sector, notably personal services (Eichhorst and Marx, 2009).

Contrary to Sweden and the US, the goal is not to maximize labour force participation: the employment rate drops sharply after age 55 and women under 35 years of age tend to display relatively low employment rates (OECD website, OECD family database). The main goal of this welfare regime is to prevent poverty wages and maintain a certain income level in the event of earnings loss, so that Conservative countries mainly promote income stability, while Scandinavian countries aim at reducing income inequality (Goodin et al., 2000).

5.1.3.2 Further aspects of the welfare regimes that have an impact on working poverty

The situation of mothers in Germany stands in striking contrast to that of Swedish mothers. In Sweden, a very important goal has been to help wage earners combine work and family life; in Germany, on the contrary, social policy still rests upon the idea that children should be looked after by their mothers. For decades, former West Germany epitomized the male-breadwinner model and there were generous transfers for mothers of young children to stay at home (Anderson and Meyer, 2006). Germany has a male-breadwinner biased social security rights and taxation system. Social policy in general and family policy in particular still entails aspects of the traditional family model. The organization of 'half-day schools' (*Halbtagschule*) and of most childcare centres is revealing of the persistence of the male-breadwinner–housewife model[1] (Fischer, 2000), even if the housewife is, more often than not, a part-time worker. The proportion of part-time workers in Germany is high in international comparison. The existence of a very long maternity leave (three years), that was reformed only recently, as well as that of the aforementioned child-raising allowance are further proofs of a conception of motherhood seen as a period spent out of the labour market (Butterwegge, 2000). However, in 2006, the Grand Coalition (Christian Democrats/Social Democrats) enacted a major reform of the parental leave.

As already mentioned above, Germany spends much more on cash benefits for families and much less on childcare services and parental leaves than Sweden; this can prove problematic because the provision of services in kind rather than benefits may be key to European antipoverty strategy (Esping-Andersen et al., 2002). Indeed, public childcare for children under three is practically non-existent (Giesselmann and Lohmann, 2008). In 2005, the maternal employment rate was lower than in most EU-15 member states and only slightly higher than in Spain (OECD website, family database). Employment has been on the increase among women, as well as has part-time employment between 1982 and 2000 (Anderson and Meyer, 2006).

Cash benefits for families with children are generous, especially *Kindergeld* (Strengmann-Kuhn, 2003), a tax credit that does not phase out as earnings increase (Bäcker, 2000; OECD website, family database). Other cash transfers also help, especially the income-tested child-raising allowance (*Erziehungsgeld*) which is designed for parents who work less than 19 hours per week (Strengmann-Kuhn, 2003) as well as the supplementary child allowance (*Kinderzuschlag*) which is paid to parents to prevent them from having to apply for unemployment benefit II/social welfare benefits only because of the maintenance of their children (OECD website, family database). Overall, the level of spending on family policy amounts to around 3 per cent of GDP and is nearly as high as in Sweden, and much higher than in the US and Spain (OECD website, family database). This generosity, amongst other factors, explains why child poverty is low in Germany.

In summary, the German model is based on a husband working full-time and his wife part-time (Andress and Seeck, 2007), that is, on a modified male-breadwinner model, and 'the idea that mothers are primarily responsible for childcare has prevailed in Western Germany to this day' (Giesselmann and Lohmann, 2008: 110). In the Eastern part of the country, however, women tend to work more than in the West; during the Communist rule, women would usually hold a full-time position, and the dual-earner model was dominant in the German Democratic Republic (Andress and Seeck, 2007; Giesselmann and Lohmann, 2008).

5.1.3.3 Shocks to the system: globalization, deindustrialization and recent changes in the welfare regime

After the strong increase in unemployment in the 1980s and the 1990s, the adjustment of the welfare state to new social risks has often been prevented by the fact that an overly transfer-biased policy is not well suited to combat mass unemployment and social exclusion. The social insurance model is not well suited to face economic stagnation and unemployment, and it may reinforce the insiders/outsiders divide (Bonoli, 2006; Esping-Andersen, 2002b). In addition, post-industrial mutations emerged later than in the US and Scandinavia, at a time when the welfare state was already under strong financial pressure.

Legislative changes pertaining to employment regulation mainly affected those at the margins of the labour market, while the position of core workers was actually improved, and this trend has been reversed only recently (Clasen and Clegg, 2006). However employment regulation is not the only aspect that matters in this regard; Germany's main problem may indeed be its high level of payroll taxes that average 42 per cent of gross wages (evenly split between employees and employers), compared to 15 per cent in the US, which may prevent job creation in the service sector (Kenworthy, 2004). Moreover, the corporatist model is difficult to modify, due to the capacity of entrenched social actors to prevent change (Kananen et al., 2006).

However, Germany, which was seen as the 'sick man of Europe' throughout the 1990s (Eichhorst and Marx, 2009), has experienced many far-reaching changes in the recent past. Atypical work contracts have become more widespread through the deregulation of a so far rather 'rigid' labour market, with a significant decline in the OECD's employment protection legislation index between 1990 and 1998. However, the degree of protection remains fairly high in international comparison (OECD website, EPL strictness). Moreover, a series of far-reaching reforms, dubbed the Hartz reforms (named after the President of the commission that proposed them), have changed the philosophy that underpins the German welfare state. In 2003, the government introduced an employee subsidy in the form of a reduction in payroll contributions: workers in jobs paying less than €400 per month (called the 'mini-jobs') were fully exempted from payroll contributions and employers only pay 5 to 15 per cent of this wage for the employee's pension (website of the German Minijob-Zentrale), while those on jobs paying between €400–800 per month (the 'midi-jobs') were partially exempted with low and linearly growing payroll taxes (Andress and Seeck, 2007; Eichhorst and Marx, 2009; Jacobi and Kluve, 2007; Kenworthy, 2004). The number of 'mini-jobs' increased markedly after the reform (Jacobi and Kluve, 2007). Moreover, labour market insiders' employment has also become more flexible; this flexibilization did not take place through an easing of dismissal protection, but rather through a liberalization of collective bargaining in the form of agreements with opening clauses (Eichhorst and Marx, 2009). Interestingly, the share of low-wage workers increased in the Western part of the country, while it decreased in the Eastern part (the former GDR). The share of fixed-term contracts, however, remained relatively constant.

Another major change concerned unemployment benefits and social assistance that have been redesigned to reduce the disincentives to work they supposedly generated (Andress and Seeck, 2007); this was the fourth part of the Hartz reforms (dubbed Hartz IV). Compulsory unemployment insurance has existed in Germany since 1927 and was organized as follows at the time the reform was implemented: after a first period of receipt of unemployment benefits (six to 32 months) with a replacement rate of 67 per cent, an unemployed person would get unemployment assistance with a 57 per cent rate, without time limit. These relatively generous benefits were combined with high benefit reduction rates that taxed away most of the additional earned income of a benefit recipient; hence, incentives to take up a job were low (Jacobi and Kluve, 2007).

After the implementation of Hartz IV, an unemployed person receives a so-called 'type I benefit' for six to 12 months and thereafter a lump sum means-tested benefit, the 'type II benefit' (Jacobi and Kluve, 2007). In fact, the former unemployment assistance and social assistance for those able to work have been merged into the type II benefit (ALGII), while social assistance (*Sozialgeld*) remains for persons unable to work (Christoph, 2008; Eichhorst and Marx, 2009; Jacobi and Kluve, 2007). In addition, sanction elements have been introduced, and the functioning of public employment services modified in order to operate more efficiently, and public job creation has been redesigned for merely targeting those who are very hard to place; for this latter group, wage subsidies paid to employers were also introduced (Jacobi and Kluve, 2007).

In a review of existing evaluations *before* the introduction of the Hartz IV reforms, Jacobi and Kluve (2007) conclude that the impact on placement services was positive, as well as the impact of new training measures, wage subsidies to employers and temporary work deregulation. The evidence is more mixed for the midi-jobs and the mini-jobs, even though a large number of mini-jobs were created. Indeed, there are strong disincentives to work more due to a marked increase in taxes and social insurance contributions above €400 (Eichhorst and Marx, 2009). Jacobi and Kluve's (2007) conclusion is rather positive, though: 'On balance, we ... find that the Hartz reforms in their entirety seem to have contributed to a better functioning of the German labour market and the effectiveness of specific active labour market policies' (Jacobi and Kluve, 2007: 61).

Germany's unemployment rate has decreased in the recent past: as of April 2009, and despite the worldwide recession, Germany's unemployment level was below the EU-25 average and very similar to Sweden's (Eurostat website). In summary, Germany does not have a passive welfare state anymore and has put much more emphasis on activation (Hemerijck and Eichhorst, 2009).

Regarding the impact of Hartz IV, namely the restructuring and recalibration of unemployment benefits and social assistance, fears have been expressed that poverty might increase. Indeed, according to Eurostat, the poverty risk (income below 60 per cent of median income) has been on the increase in Germany since 2005, from 12 to 15 per cent (Eurostat's website, living conditions and welfare indicators), with a strong increase in the Eastern part of the country; earnings inequalities have increased too (Müller and Steiner, 2008).

Family policy, however, has become more 'generous'. Between 1991 and 2004, many tax allowances were increased, as was the tax credit for families (*Kindergeld*). As of 2000, child allowances represented 11.8 per cent of the income of a family with two children relying on the earnings of a full-time industrial worker, while this share amounted to 4.7 per cent in 1995 (Andress and Seeck, 2007). Around the year 2000, family cash benefits represented 10.3 per cent of disposable income in the lowest income decile (Whiteford and Adema, 2007).

An important element needs to be highlighted here: in the former GDR, a high number of companies went bankrupt and a large number of jobs were destroyed after the Reunification process (Offermann, 2000). Unemployment in the Eastern part of Germany has been high ever since; in 2007, while the unemployment rate in Baden-Württemberg (in the Western part of Germany) amounted to less than 5 per cent, it exceeded 16 per cent in former GDR regions such as Mecklenburg-Vorpommern and Sachsen-Anhalt (Statistisches Bundesamt Deutschland's website).

After the electoral loss of the Red−Green coalition in 2005, a Grand Coalition formed by the Christian Democrats and the Social Democrats came to power. The new government took a more moderated stance on labour market reforms, reflecting growing concerns about widening inequalities (Eichhorst and Marx, 2009; Müller and Steiner, 2008). In addition, as already indicated, the Grand Coalition implemented a significant reform of the parental leave and benefit in 2006.

5.1.3.4   Poverty, income redistribution and employment performance

Notten and De Neubourg's (2007) figures show that Germany had the lowest level of 'absolute' poverty in 2000. Regarding relative poverty, the Luxembourg Income Study provides the following figures (see Table 5.6).

Table 5.6 Poverty rates based on thresholds set at 50 and 40 per cent of median disposable income (most recent wave, around mid-1990s, around mid-1980s and mid-1970s)

Year	Poverty rate (50 per cent threshold)	Poverty rate (40 per cent threshold)	Child poverty in two-parent families (50 per cent)	Child poverty in single-parent families (50 per cent)
Germany, 2000	8.4	4.6	4.7	38.1
Germany, 1994	8.2	4.5	5.6	41.0
Germany, 1984	7.9	3.4	4.8	49.3
Germany, 1973	6.7	3.6	3.3	28.8

Note: figures as of 28 September 2008.
Source: Luxembourg Income Study (LIS) Key Figures.

Relative poverty rates are low in Germany: they were slightly higher than in Sweden in 2000, but significantly lower than in Spain and in the US. More recently, poverty levels in Sweden and Germany have been very similar. The child poverty rate among two-parent families is very low; by contrast, around four in ten children living in single-parent households are poor, which is clearly the biggest difference between Germany and Sweden in terms of poverty outcomes. I get back to this point below. It should be noted that child poverty and working poverty are only loosely correlated in Germany, because more than half of poor families with children are jobless (Whiteford and Adema, 2007).

Regarding in-work poverty, official figures show that Germany displayed the lowest level among the four countries analysed in this chapter in 2006 (Eurostat website, in-work at-risk-of-poverty rate). Even at the 50 per cent level and including all workers (contrary to official figures that only include those who have spent at least six months in the labour market in the previous year), the working poor rate was lowest in Germany (4.4 per cent, own calculations with EU-SILC data 2006). It is noteworthy that full-time employment is an almost watertight protection against poverty: as of 2004, only 3.3 per cent of full-time workers holding an open-ended contract lived in a household with an income below 60 per cent of median disposable income (Andress and Seeck, 2007).

Regarding income redistribution among working families, the tax and benefit system displays a far above average efficiency for dual-earner families (poverty was reduced by 94.3 per cent vs 39.3 at the OECD level), but a below-average performance for single-parent households (–39.6 per cent vs 49.7 at OECD level) and an average impact for single-earner two-parent families (–46.7 per cent vs 43.0) (Whiteford and Adema, 2007).

In summary, among the four countries analysed here, Germany is probably the best performer in terms of working poverty, whereas the difference with Sweden is only slight; moreover, Sweden performs better as far as single-parent families are concerned.

Regarding employment performance, in 2000, the harmonized unemployment rate amounted to 7.5 per cent and increased to 8.4 per cent in 2007. In the recent past, however, despite the worldwide recession, Germany's employment performance has improved. The employment rate is lower than in Scandinavian and Anglo-Saxon countries, but higher than in Spain: in 2000, it reached 70.9 per cent among the 15–64-year-olds and increased to 75.9 per cent in 2007, a level slightly higher than in the US. One of the key differences between Germany and Sweden is the maternal employment rate, which is much lower in Germany (in 2007, the difference amounted to 14.4 percentage points), and not far above Spain's level (6.2 percentage points), the country with the lowest level among the countries under review (OECD website, family database, 2007). Another key feature, as in many other Continental countries, is the low participation rate of workers older than 55, which lies below the 50 per cent mark (48.4 per cent in 2006, Statistisches

Bundesamt Deutschland's website). In terms of employment, then, Germany's performance is neither very good nor disastrous.

5.1.4 Spain

5.1.4.1 Main approaches to the alleviation of working poverty
Southern European countries share many features with other Continental European countries, notably the fact that they mainly rely on a passive approach based on substitutive income transfers, especially unemployment benefits and means-tested transfers, and on employment protection.

In Spain, workers who have an open-ended contract are highly protected (Bonoli, 2003a). On the OECD's overall strictness of employment protection legislation index (version 2), Spain displays the fourth highest score behind Turkey, Portugal and Mexico (OECD website, overall EPL strictness); in addition, there is a statutory minimum wage (*Salario Mínimo Interprofesional*) set at 45 per cent of median wage in 2008 (OECD website, labour statistics). Workers dismissed for objective reasons can get up to 12 months' wages; in the event of an unfair dismissal, the maximum amount can reach 42 months' wages (OECD website, indicators of employment protection). Moreover, though the unionization rate is lower than 20 per cent, the degree of coverage of collective bargaining exceeds 70 per cent (International Labour Organization, 2008), thanks to extensions laws, imposing agreements to employers and workers who did not sign them (Bonoli, 2003a).

The other major pillar of the fight against working poverty in Spain is the use of social transfers, which mainly benefit non-working household members, especially unemployed adult children and/or partners. Spain displays a relatively high aggregated level of social expenditure, namely 21.2 per cent of its GDP in 2005 (which is comparable to Norway or the UK), half of which is spent on old age and unemployment benefits, while expenditures on family benefits and active labour market policies amount to less than 2 per cent of GDP (OECD website, social expenditure database). Spain has experienced one of the largest growths in social spending among EU countries, in purchasing power parities (PPP), between 1980 and 1993 (Guillén and Alvarez, 2002). Social transfers are financed by social security contributions that are rather high, namely 36.95 per cent of gross earnings for the average paid workers in 2004, whereas this level is lower than in Germany with 41.1 per cent. However, contrary to Germany's equirepartition principle, Spanish employers pay 82.81 per cent of total social security contributions (Zubiri, 2007).

Among social transfers, two benefits mainly contribute to lowering poverty among working families: unemployment benefits (and further

subsidies) and minimum income schemes (*rentas mínimas*), both supporting unemployed or inactive members of working households. The unemployment insurance offers generous benefits with high replacement rates
(Zubiri, 2007), namely 70 per cent of reference earnings for a maximum
period of six months (and there is no waiting period), then 60 per cent of
reference earnings for the remaining period of the benefits (which can last
24 months).

Minimum income schemes were introduced at the level of the autonomous communities (*Comunidades Autónomas*) between 1988 and 1995. The
minimum income level is set at the regional level and ranges from 40.2 to
64.3 per cent of the minimum wage, except for the Basque country (76 per
cent) (Arriba González de Durana and Pérez Eransus, 2007); that is, their
level is low. Indeed, even if minimum income schemes alleviate the difficulties of many poor families, they do not lift them above the poverty line
(Pérez Eransus et al., 2009). Many reforms of the minimum income
schemes have taken place, with a growing emphasis on social inclusion and
activation; however, the coverage and the expense levels have remained
nearly unchanged (Pérez Eransus et al., 2009).

5.1.4.2 Further aspects of the welfare regimes that have an impact on working poverty

There is an important difference with the conservative welfare regime: in
Spain, the level of spending on family policies is rather low with less than
1.5 per cent of GDP in 2005, a feature shared with other Mediterranean
countries (Greece, Italy and Malta). In the same year, for instance, France
and Germany spent more than 3 per cent of their GDP on family policies
(OECD family database). More generally, a familialist approach characterizes Spanish social policies (Esping-Andersen, 1999; Esping-Andersen et
al., 2002). In fact, the role played by the family is one of the most
characteristic traits of the Mediterranean regime (Moreno, 2002). Hence, I
share the conclusion that Southern European countries constitute a welfare
regime of their own; this cluster contains Spain, Portugal, Greece and to
some extent (Southern) Italy (Leibfried, 2000), though there are notable
differences among these countries.

Other components of the Spanish welfare state are, contrary to family
policy, very generous: since 1986, a healthcare system financed by general
taxes is provided 'for free' to the entire population. Moreover, as already
indicated, unemployment benefits are also characterized by high replacement rates. However, some elderly persons were not able to contribute the
minimum years of service and only get assistance pensions, while many
long-term unemployed have exhausted their unemployment benefits and
receive minimal assistance.

Another very important feature of the Spanish labour market that must be brought to the forefront, is, at least in part, a consequence of the very high degree of protection workers on open-ended contracts enjoy: Spain has the highest share of workers on short-term employment among OECD countries, namely 31.9 per cent in 2007, a much higher share than in Continental countries such as France (13.7 per cent) and Germany (14.1 per cent) (OECD website, labour statistics), a figure that skyrocketed after the modification of the Workers Status Act in 1984 (Ruesga, 2007). Many analysts consider Spain as an extreme case of dualization. However, while a majority of workers under the age of 30 hold a fixed-term contract, the incidence decreases markedly after that age (Garrido and Gutiérrez, 2009). The Spanish labour market can be seen as a long waiting queue, which leads us to the fundamental role played by the Spanish family and the correlated implicit intergenerational pact: children have a long and hectic pattern of integration into the labour market, but they live with their parents who hold well-protected jobs (Garrido and Gutiérrez, 2009). Most people leave the parental home in their thirties (García Espejo and Ibáñez Pascual, 2007). As a consequence, compared to EU average values, Spain displays a higher average household size (Gutiérrez Palacios et al., 2009).

Spain's unionization rate is low (18.1 per cent in 2001), and more than twice as high among employees with open-ended contracts than among those on fixed-term employment contracts (Simón, 2003). Moreover, and maybe as a consequence of these features, conflictuality is rather high in the Spanish labour market, with a high number of strike days over the last two decades (ILO website, LABORSTA). However this number has been decreasing in the recent past.

The role of the family is, as already mentioned, very important. Traditionally, Spanish institutions have favoured married male workers with families, which largely explains the very high degree of employment protection. The role of the family has undergone profound changes in recent years; however it remains very important (Garrido and Gutiérrez, 2009; Moreno, 2002). Cultural values and social norms play a role, and so do the institutional framework and the economic situation, and it is difficult to disentangle the influence of these factors. For instance, a low level of spending on family policy partly explains the type of conciliation of work and family life observed; simultaneously, however, it is important to note that state intervention in family matters brings back memories of Franco's authoritarian policies (Moreno, 2002). Likewise, the drop in the fertility rate, which is now one of the lowest in the EU, can be partially explained by the fact that young workers struggle to find a job with an open-ended contract and live with their parents for a long period of time, which postpones family formation; however the fertility decline is also attribut-able to changes in people's values and lifestyles and a relaxing of religious codes (Moreno, 2002). Moreover, part-time employment is rather marginal in Spain and many mothers have to combine full-time employment and domestic activities. Women with higher educational levels who have an access to better jobs sometimes choose not to have a second child (Moreno, 2002).

5.1.4.3 Shocks to the system: globalization, deindustrialization and recent changes in the welfare regime

A fundamental aspect is often neglected, namely that Spain is a young democracy (as are Portugal and Greece) that emerged, at the end of the 1970s, from four decades of dictatorship. As clearly demonstrated by Sen (1999), the absence of freedom is an obstacle to economic development and arguably one of the main poverty factors. The emergence of a social dialogue in Spain can be dated back to 1978, when the political transition occurred (Ruesga, 2007); at that time, a large share of the labour force was still in the agricultural sector and industrialization was recent.

Put differently, Spain simultaneously faced the challenges of the transi-tion to democracy, on the one hand, and deindustrialization and globaliza-tion, on the other hand (Garrido and Gutiérrez, 2009). Unemployment skyrocketed from 4.5 per cent in 1975 to 21 per cent ten years later, because the labour market was totally inflexible, a high proportion of the labour force worked in agriculture, many companies were inefficient but were protected by tariffs and export subsidies, and the average educational level was low (Zubiri, 2007).

Given this point of departure, some achievements are quite impressive: an immense increase in the employment rate (+14.4 points between 1996 and 2007) (Garrido and Gutiérrez, 2009), especially among women who represented 41.2 per cent of the workforce in 2007, whereas they only made up 27.5 per cent of the labour force when Franco died in 1975 (OECD website, labour statistics), a large increase in the number of persons with tertiary educational level (+150 per cent between 1996 and 2007) combined with the retirement of a large share of persons without post-compulsory education – this combination has sometimes been dubbed the 'educational overturn' – and the partly correlated massive influx of immigrants, a more than 900 per cent increase over the same period, to fill the gaps in low-skilled occupations (Garrido and Gutiérrez, 2009). However, this influx does not seem to have had a major impact on the employment of native workers (Carrasco et al., 2004; Felgueroso and Vázquez, 2009).

In summary, Spain experienced far-reaching transformations within a short time span and entered the post-industrial era in the 1990s (Bonoli,

2007). As Zubiri (2007: 382) put it, 'In the last thirty years, Spain has undergone a radical ... change. Dictatorship has been transformed into democracy, a closed overprotected and underproductive economy has given rise to a modern ... economy, and a country with low social expenditure has been turned into a very generous welfare state'.

Between 1996 and 2007, employment increased by a stunning 7.5 million persons, a phenomenon some called the 'Spanish miracle', which appeared to have been partially due to unsustainable factors (Arellano and Bentolila, 2009; Felgueroso and Jiménez, 2009). However, though many low-skilled and precarious jobs were created, an analysis of the occupational composition of the labour force between 2000 and 2008 shows no trend toward a deterioration, with the strongest increases in senior corporate and public sector managers and other higher-level occupations (Garrido and Gutiérrez, 2009). The share of short-term contracts remained fairly constant, while gross earnings inequality and the share of low-wage workers decreased (OECD website, labour statistics). In the Spanish case, it is impossible to identify a general relationship between labour market performance and trends in earnings inequality, in line with analyses at the OECD level (Esping-Andersen and Regini, 2000; Gutiérrez Palacios et al., 2009; Kenworthy, 2004).

However, an increase in relative poverty took place between the mid-1990s and the mid-2000s (Luxembourg Income Study (LIS) key figures; OECD, 2008). This is probably due to the strong increase in real median income (Luxembourg Income Study (LIS) key figures; Instituto Nacional de Estadística's consumer price index).

The main factors that have contributed to the massive decrease in unemployment and increase in employment until 2007 are an above-average economic growth, wage moderation, a reduction in dismissal costs (which remain, nonetheless, very high in international comparison) and a more efficient economy (Zubiri, 2007). Overall, Mediterranean countries have achieved some of the biggest employment gains since the mid-1990s and female employment is rapidly catching up to Northern European averages (Hemerijck and Eichhorst, 2009). However, the crisis of the late 2000s gave a massive blow to these positive developments; in Spain, unemployment has been extremely high since 2009 and at the time of writing, signs of recovery are nowhere in sight.

5.1.4.4 Poverty, income redistribution and employment performance

In absolute terms, the poverty rate in 2000 was more than twice as high as in the US and more than three times as high than in Germany and Sweden (Notten and De Neubourg, 2007). It is noteworthy, however, that a very significant decrease took place over a short period of time, namely a 34 per cent decrease between 1995 and 2000 (see Table 5.3); this trend probably continued until the beginning of the recession of the late 2000s, given the strong economic growth that characterized these years. In relative terms, differences between Spain and the other three countries are less pronounced (see Table 5.7).

Table 5.7 Poverty rates based on thresholds set at 50 and 40 per cent of median disposable income (most recent wave, around mid-1990s and 1980)

Year	Poverty rate (50 per cent threshold)	Poverty rate (40 per cent threshold)	Child poverty in two-parent families (50 per cent)	Child poverty in single-parent families (50 per cent)
Spain, 2000	14.2	7.6	N/A	N/A
Spain, 1995	13.7	8.4	16.6	34.0
Spain, 1980	12.1	6.7	12.3	21.5

Note: figures as of 28 September 2008.

Source: Luxembourg Income Study (LIS) Key Figures.

It is noteworthy that relative poverty is less widespread in Spain than in the US, while the poverty rate is notably higher than in Germany and Sweden. Child poverty among single-parent families is slightly lower than in Germany, whereas it is much higher among two-parent families. This, in part, is due to relatively low female labour force participation rates and to a redistributive system that appears to be less efficient than in Continental European countries, as analysed below.

The fact that the difference between Spain and the other three countries analysed here is more marked in absolute than in relative terms is due to important differences in income levels. In 2000, the real median income in Spain amounted to €12,718.46 (approximately US$12,188 as of mid-June 2000), less than half the amount in the US of US$27,168.50 (OECD website, social and welfare statistics); even accounting for PPP, this difference is very large (OECD website, purchasing power parities for private consumption).

Regarding the 'in-work at-risk-of-poverty rate', Eurostat's figures for 2006 show that the incidence of in-work poverty is noticeably higher in Spain (10 per cent) than in Germany (5 per cent) and Sweden (7 per cent) (Eurostat website). I reach similar conclusions with my own calculations based on SILC 2006 data, with the poverty line set at 50 per cent of median disposable income and an encompassing definition of 'working': they show that the working poor rate is notably higher in Spain (6.9 per cent) than in Sweden and Germany (5.3 and 4.4 per cent respectively).

As far as income redistribution is concerned, unfortunately, Whiteford and Adema's (2007) report does not contain data on poverty reduction among working families in Spain. As an imperfect proxy, I compare Eurostat's pre-tax/pre-transfer at-risk-of-poverty rates with the corresponding post-tax/post-transfer rates and obtain the following results shown in Table 5.8.

Table 5.8 A comparison of pre-tax/pre-transfer and post-tax/post-transfer poverty rates in 2006

	Pre-tax/ pre-transfer %	Post-tax/ post-transfer %	Poverty reduction %
Germany	26	13	−50.0
Sweden	29	12	−58.6
Spain	24	20	−16.7

Source: Eurostat website.

Obviously, these results include non-working households, and, thus, only allow a crude comparison with Whiteford and Adema's (2007) findings presented above for the US, Germany and Sweden. Nevertheless, I get an interesting picture: poverty reduction is highest in Sweden, followed by Germany and much lower in Spain. Interestingly, then, Spain has a strict employment protection legislation but a low degree of redistribution (Bonoli, 2003a). This leads to the conclusion that the Spanish welfare regime relies heavily on labour market regulation in the fight against working poverty (and on families in the event of a difficult integration into the labour market).

In terms of employment and unemployment, Spain is the worst performer among the four countries analysed here. Employment rates are lower, especially female labour market participation. The participation rate of mothers of children under the age of 18 remained low by international comparison in 2008 (nearly four in ten mothers did not work) (OECD website, labour statistics). Regarding unemployment, among the four countries analysed here, Spain displayed, by far, the highest level at the turn of the millennium, but the gap was closed with Germany in 2007 (8.3 and 8.4 per cent respectively). However, the unemployment rate has massively increased in Spain since 2007 – it has more than doubled – while the German level has remained surprisingly stable.

Having now identified promising tools in the fight against working poverty and analysed the four countries that epitomize the four clusters of the welfare regime typology I have decided to use, I can now proceed to the empirical work. Chapter 6 is based on meta-analyses of evaluations of specific policy tools, while Chapter 7 deals with the impact of welfare regimes on the composition of the working poor population and on the three mechanisms that lead to working poverty.

NOTE

1. The male-breadwinner model strictly speaking is a model in which the husband works and his wife does not. Hence, today's Germany is sometimes described as a 'modified' male-breadwinner model.

6. What works where and for whom? A meta-analytical approach

In Chapter 4, I have presented the main tools that can be used to combat working poverty and presented their potential employment and antipoverty effects. These effects must now be evaluated empirically. Since there is, for most effects assessed here, a large body of evidence available, the empirical contribution of this chapter consists in meta-analyses of systematically identified and retrieved studies published between 2000 and 2010 that provide empirical estimates of the antipoverty and employment effects of these policies. This meta-analytical approach consists of a weighted vote-counting procedure, coupled with a significance test.

Moreover, as I am also interested in the way these policies operate in the 'real world' of social policy, findings are also broken down by welfare regime; in addition, a more qualitative and detailed examination of results is also provided. This paves the way for the next chapter, which assesses the overall impact of welfare regimes on the three working poverty mechanisms and, hence, on the size and composition of the population of low-income workers.

The main policies that have been identified as potentially efficient anti-working poverty tools are the following:

- minimum wages, legally enforced or through collective bargaining;
- tax credits for workers;
- cash transfers towards families;
- the provision and cost of childcare services.

Before meta-analysing each policy, it is necessary to precisely define how the evaluation of each policy will be carried out.

6.1 RESEARCH SYNTHESIS

Attempts to synthesize empirical findings are not new. In the early 1900s, the British statistician Karl Pearson was asked to review the evidence on a vaccine against typhoid (Cooper, 1998; Rosenthal and DiMatteo, 2001).

However, it was not until the 1970s that researchers began to develop systematic methods for reviewing evidence in order to replace traditional, qualitative literature reviews, and until recently social scientists placed little attention on how to integrate past research (Cooper, 1998). The massive development of social sciences over the past decades has generated an immense corpus of books, articles, conference proceedings, position papers, working papers and so on (Rosenthal and DiMatteo, 2001); hence, research synthesis has become more important than ever. Moreover, the recent development of efficient search engines, scanning the content of thousands of journals within a few seconds, has facilitated the development of research synthesis.

Many terms are used to describe the type of analysis carried out in this chapter: literature reviews, research synthesis and meta-analysis. *Literature review* is a very broad term and can encompass both theoretical reviews and syntheses that focus on empirical studies. The term *research synthesis* is more specific and more accurately fits the empirical work described in this chapter. *Meta-analysis* is even more specific, whereas it is often used as a synonym of research synthesis, although it implies the use of quantitative procedures in order to combine study results (Cooper, 1998; Cooper and Hedges, 1994; Lipsey and Wilson, 2001). Meta-analysis can be seen as a statistical approach similar to that used in usual primary research, the statistical unit being research findings (significance tests, directions of relationships, size effects) rather than individuals, households and other units that primary research usually examines.

The question I want to answer is the same for each policy: does policy X efficiently combat poverty without having a negative impact on employment? Moreover, there is a corollary question in the event of a positive answer: where does it work and for whom?

6.1.1 Conceptual Issues and Operationalization

A difficulty research synthesists face is that it is often complicated to aggregate evidence because social scientists use different scales to express their findings. However, this variety of operations can also be perceived as having the potential of stronger inferences (Cooper, 1998) by giving various perspectives on the same topic, which is doubtlessly one of the pros of meta-analysis. The only general recommendation that can be made is to begin the literature search with the broadest conceptual definition in mind, leaving the possibility of restricting the sample at a later stage of the meta-analysis (Cooper, 1998).

An obvious example in the present research pertains to the definition of poverty: some studies measure the impact of social policies on the head-count ratio (with various poverty lines), while others use poverty measures that also account for the depth of poverty and even for the severity of poverty (for instance the Foster–Greer–Thorbecke (FGT) index described above). Moreover, some studies conclude that a given policy significantly increases disposable income. This can lead to the conclusion that it reduces the poverty gap; however, it is not possible to determine whether it reduces the incidence of poverty. In some evaluations, it is the probability of escaping poverty in the following year that is assessed.

Similar variations exist in estimations of the potential employment effects, measured with employment rates and employment-to-population ratios, with conditional probabilities to hold a job in the following year, or in terms of hours per week or weeks per year.

6.1.2   Systematic Collection of Relevant Studies and Choice of Relevant Findings

An important aspect of data collection is, obviously, the use of scientific search engines; they have revolutionized meta-analysis by allowing very far-reaching searches. In addition, they allow reducing the impact of subjective factors that may lead a researcher to subconsciously omit some publications. In what follows, a predefined procedure has been established, providing a non-subjective approach. The use of various keywords is also advised (Lipsey and Wilson, 2001), an approach that has been applied in this book.

The approach presented here contains one important source of bias, because it mainly focuses on articles written in English, an approach that is common, especially in comparative research (Lipsey and Wilson, 2001). It is possible that significant results obtained in non-English speaking countries are not reviewed (Delgado-Rodriguez, 2001). An attempt has been made to partly reduce the impact of this bias in the third phase of the article search described below, based on the other languages that I can read, namely French, German and Spanish. This allowed the identification of some interesting articles. But obviously, a further step might be taken by using scientific search engines that allow identifying articles written in German, French and Spanish in a more systematic fashion.

Another practical aspect pertains to problems in library retrieval (Cooper, 1998). I have an access to two universities' online journals retrieval systems (University of Lausanne and University of Neuchâtel, Switzerland), and the number of relevant articles I could not retrieve was quite marginal. To the extent that the number was very small (never more than three articles for a given policy) and that the journals that were not available did not seem to have anything in common, which suggests that there is no systematic bias, I do not account for missing articles. However, to be absolutely accurate I should have attempted to obtain these few articles by other means, for instance, through a direct contact with primary research-ers, but the extra effort requested was not deemed justified given the small amount of articles at stake.

A fundamental step is, obviously, to assess whether all the identified articles are reliable and relevant (Cooper, 1998). Basically, there are two main dimensions to assess: the first dimension pertains to the quality of the methodology (research design, statistical method, data quality and so on), whereas the second concerns the degree to which the study's findings can be generalized (sample size and representativity, standard errors, confidence intervals and so on). However, it is important to highlight that the judge-ment on the relevance and validity of a study's results is coloured by the evaluator's predispositions. Cooper (1998) mentions seven studies of evalu-ator agreement about research quality and concludes that agreement on judgements of methodological quality is less than one would think, due to personal biases. Indeed, 'methodological quality is something that seems to exist largely in the eye of the beholder' (Lipsey and Wilson, 2001: 22).

In this chapter, I take into account Cooper's advice not to exclude studies a priori, an approach that is probably too subjective (Cooper, 1998). Some researchers have criticized this conception of no a priori exclusion of studies based on a poor methodology on the grounds that it does not allow a better understanding of the phenomenon studied, because of the 'gar-bage in-garbage out' principle (Cooper 1998; Rosenthal and DiMatteo, 2001). Indeed, some researchers blame proponents of meta-analysis for refusing to exclude bad studies, which may completely bias the true out-come (Eysenck, 1994). I did not exclude studies a priori, but rather evaluated the pertinence of articles *ex post* and excluded studies that were either purely descriptive (that is, that did not contain regression-based or microsimulation results) or based on small samples (less than 1000 observa-tions for individual level data). Moreover, the decision not to include a study in the meta-analysis is mentioned in the summary tables, as well as a justification of the decision. Detailed summaries of the retrieved studies are provided (see Appendix), allowing the reader to draw his or her own conclusions about the evidence, my main concern being transparency and intellectual honesty. Based on the studies deemed reliable, data-sets that contained empirical estimates were produced and submitted to a statistical analysis (see Appendix).

Regarding the choice of the estimates included in the meta-analysis, I made the decision to only include results from the main specifications and their main variations, whereas results from models that were only specified to assess the findings' robustness are not reported in the vote-counting tables, but if, and only if, this intention is explicitly stated by the author(s). Moreover, when an article provides econometric models with and without macroeconomic controls (GDP growth, GDP per capita, unemployment rate and so on), only the models including economic controls have been kept, as it has been shown above that the economic situation, business cycles in particular, can have a decisive impact on poverty. Finally, some US articles contain regional estimates that were reported in the summary tables; in the vote-counting procedure, however, as US studies are largely represented, these regional findings were dropped.

6.1.3   At the Heart of Meta-analyses: The Statistical Treatment of Findings

Until recently, research synthesists did not systematically apply standard statistical techniques to their data. However, due to growth in the amount of research and the development of computerized retrieval systems, the introduction of statistical procedures into research synthesis has become a necessity. Recent meta-analysis has become more and more interested in quantifying the effects identified in the literature, rather than identifying whether or not the relationship between variables exists. This means that meta-analysis, in a restrictive sense, only applies to empirical research studies that produce quantitative findings, and aims at integrating information about the effect sizes (Lipsey and Wilson, 2001).

There are two main sources of variation across studies, namely sampling error, on the one hand, and methodological differences and/or different sample compositions, on the other hand. Meta-analysts have access either to information that can be used to calculate size effects, and/or information about whether a test found significant relationships, and/or information about the direction of the effects. Vote-counting procedures are useful for the second and the third types of data (Bushman, 1994). More sophisticated techniques are necessary for synthesizing size effects.

6.1.3.1   Vote-counting methods
The simplest methods for integrating findings are vote-counting methods, which take into account the statistical significance and/or focus on the sign of the estimates (Bushman, 1994). Basically, the synthesist classifies findings into three categories: statistically significant findings that have the expected direction, usually named positive findings; statistically significant findings in the unexpected direction (negative findings); and non-significant findings (Bushman, 1994; Cooper, 1998). The conventional vote-counting procedure counts the number of times the three above

mentioned categories appear, and the modal category is declared the winner (Bushman, 1994); this approach has been used quite often (Cooper, 1998).

It appears, however, that this strategy is conservative and often leads the synthesist to conclude that the relationship does not exist, especially when counting the number of non-significant findings. An alternative vote-counting method consists in comparing the frequency of significant positive and significant negative findings, with a statistical test based on the assumption that the number of positive and negative findings is equal, but as it ignores non-significant findings it may have a low statistical power. A third vote-count approach consists in counting negative and positive effects regardless of the significance, which has the advantage of using all the findings.

A sign test can be performed (Bushman, 1994; Cooper, 1998) and the test statistic can be defined as follows (Cooper, 1998):

$$Z = \frac{N_p - \dfrac{N}{2}}{\dfrac{\sqrt{N}}{2}}$$

Z follows a standard normal distribution, with N_p the number of positive findings (that is, findings that have the expected direction). With a confidence level of 5 per cent (error type I), the critical value is 1.96; for 1 per cent it is 2.58.

In what follows, the expressions 'negative effects' and 'positive effects' have different meanings that relate to the effects various policies have on employment and on poverty. If a study examines the antipoverty effects of a policy, the result is deemed positive if this policy reduces the poverty rate or the poverty gap; a study examining the employment effects of a policy is deemed to have positive effects if employment increases or unemployment decreases.

Vote-counting procedures have been criticized for not taking account of sample size; however, as sample size increases, the probability of obtaining a significant result increases. In addition, this method does not allow us to determine whether a treatment 'wins by a nose or in a walkaway' (Bushman, 1994: 194); that is, this procedure does not provide estimates of the effect size. Furthermore, when effect sizes are medium to small, the conventional vote-counting procedure usually fails to detect any effect. These drawbacks have led to the development of more refined meta-analytical techniques.

6.1.3.2   More sophisticated meta-analysis techniques

A vote-counting procedure does not attempt to evaluate the magnitude of the effect, which prevents the synthesist from answering the 'how much?' question. Still, vote-counting methods appear as an 'informative complement to other meta-analytic procedures and can even be used to generate an estimate of the strength of a relationship' (Cooper, 1998: 119).

The most advanced statistical procedures used for meta-analysis weight the findings according to their sample size, for instance, by using the inverse of the standard error, so that studies that have more accurate estimates – that is, smaller standard errors – are given more weight. In addition, if several findings come from the same study, the meta-analyst may want to weight them less than a finding that is the only contribution of another study (this weighting is applied in the vote-counting procedure presented below).

Detailed meta-analysis requires information on the number of findings, the directional outcome of each finding and sample size. The key concept in this kind of approach is the effect size, which necessitates defining a common metric for all studies based on a standardization of findings: the effect size statistic must be the same across studies (Lipsey and Wilson, 2001).

Some research designs, such as those found in experimental studies, are easy to quantify, by calculating the difference between the experimental and the control group, often adjusted with standard deviations. Odds ratios are also often used in the context of experimental research. If the findings have a quantitative nature, correlation coefficients can be calculated.

In more complex research designs, such as those found in most evaluations reviewed in the present work, other metrics have to be used. For *ex post* evaluations based on regression models, the findings can be expressed in terms of elasticities (Doucouliagos and Stanley, 2009). Sometimes, however, it is difficult to calculate them, for instance, if the outcome is not the employment rate, but the probability of being in employment in year $t + 1$ conditional on being in the labour force in year t in a logit or probit specification.

In fact, multivariate analysis results in general, be it multiple regression, discriminant analysis, factor analysis, structural equation modelling and so on, are difficult to transform into a size effect statistic. Indeed, research synthesists have not yet developed an adequate statistic (Eysenck, 1994; Lipsey and Wilson, 2001). Other findings reviewed below are derived from simulations for which it seems difficult to estimate an elasticity (it might be possible if a large number of scenarios were tested, which is usually not the case). Hence, the most recent meta-analytical techniques are not easily used for the kind of evaluations reviewed in the present work.

Another complex step consists of analysing the variance in effect sizes across findings, that is, the meta-analyst must pay attention to violations of the assumption of homogeneity of variances, which require, usually, a weighted least square regression.

Finally, some meta-analysts go even further in order to adjust findings to their needs. For instance, findings that are deemed too extreme (outliers) can be winsorized (Lipsey and Wilson, 2001), or biases due to a small sample or to measurement errors can be corrected.

6.1.4   Difficulties Facing Meta-analysts

A fundamental problem in meta-analysis is the 'apples and oranges' problem. Ideally, samples/populations and 'treatments' should be comparable, but they vary markedly across studies (Eysenck, 1994). Indeed, meta-analyses often summarize results from studies that vary notably in their operationalization of variables and are based on very different types of samples of various population groups. However, 'It can be argued ... that it is a good thing to mix apples and oranges, particularly if one wants to generalize about fruit, and that studies that are exactly the same in all respects are actually limited in generalizability' (Rosenthal and DiMatteo, 2001: 68). A related problem is the above mentioned 'garbage in-garbage out' phenomenon, due to the fact that studies do not have similar quality standards. Some meta-analysts advocate some kind of quality weighting (Rosenthal and DiMatteo, 2001); weighting findings according to their standard error being one of these methods.

Another important aspect of meta-analysis is the independence of estimates (Lipsey and Wilson, 2001). A single study may contain multiple tests of the same relationship, either because there are various measures of the same phenomenon, for instance in an article using the FGT indicator with various values of α, say 0, 1 and 2, or because different subsamples might be used in the same study, for instance, a first estimate is based on all families, another on single-parent families only, a third on couples with children and a fourth on childless couples.

Statistical units can be the studies themselves, samples or estimates. If the statistical unit is the study, the meta-analyst will have to average estimates for each study. This is not the option chosen in the present work. If samples, usually population groups, are the analysed units, the meta-analyst should weight their impact by the sample size; moreover, in some studies, some results pertain to the entire sample and others to certain subsamples, for instance, single mothers in general and single mothers without a high school diploma in particular. In such cases, units are not independent. A third option is to take the estimates of a relationship as the statistical unit; likewise, if several estimates stem from the same study and the same population, the assumption that estimates are independent will be violated, which can be a problem for meta-regression techniques (as it requires more sophisticated regression models that correct for these violations of technical assumptions).

Other important aspects are common to all quantitative studies, be they primary studies or meta-analyses, namely the problem of missing data and outliers. In such cases, I clearly mention the problem in the tables (see Appendix).

Other potential problems need to be highlighted here. Some authors mention the existence of a publication bias: in the case of the minimum wage literature, studies showing that minimum wages have a significant negative impact on employment may be more likely to be published (Card and Krueger, 1995; Doucouliagos and Stanley, 2009), as they are in line with neoclassical, mainstream economics. One way to detect this bias is to draw a funnel plot, that is, a scatterplot of precision versus estimated effect, for instance of the inverse of the standard error versus the elasticity. If the scatterplot is asymmetric, this is taken as evidence of a publication bias (Doucouliagos and Stanley, 2009). Another noteworthy difficulty is the 'file drawer problem': it seems that studies that produce significant effects are more likely to be written-up and published (Lipsey and Wilson, 2001).

The bottom line is that the most persistent criticism of meta-analysis concerns the diversity of the studies reviewed, and the fact of applying statistical techniques to studies that are not easily comparable – the above mentioned apples and oranges problem – leading to an aggregate statistical measure that can be a relatively fuzzy grand mean effect size (Lipsey and Wilson, 2001), however sophisticated its calculation might be.

6.1.5   Why is Meta-analysis Better than Traditional Literature Reviews?

Given the difficulties enumerated above, one may wonder why it is important to carry out a meta-analysis, that is, to perform a statistical analysis of the estimates contained in the articles retrieved.

To start with, it should be noted that traditional reviews are also confronted with the problem of comparing apples and oranges, due to the use of evaluations that vary greatly in terms of countries, population groups, sample size, estimation techniques, operationalization of both the policy variable and the effect variable and so on. Hence, this problem is at the heart of any research synthesis. However, in my view, the use of statistical techniques helps reduce the uncertainty associated with this scientific endeavour.

Probably one of the main advantages of meta-analysis is to provide *objective decision criteria*. A problem associated with any research synthesis is that most articles do not provide crystal-clear results; the impact of a given policy may be positive for one group of workers and negative for another group. This is not completely surprising in many cases, as some groups of workers are expected to react to the incentives provided by the policy, while others are not supposed to. Moreover, some specifications yield significant results, while others do not; in addition, some specifications can produce positive coefficients, while others produce negative coefficients. For instance, adding a time trend, an interaction term or a quadratic term, and adding further control variables to the model can markedly affect results, and these differences are not always easy to interpret.

In addition, the variable of interest can be measured in various ways; for instance, in the case of the minimum wage, relevant indicators include the Kaitz index, the share of the workforce affected by a rise in the minimum wage or the level of the minimum wage; conclusions may vary depending on the definition of the policy variable. Likewise, different operationalizations of the dependent variable are conceivable; for instance, the antipoverty impact can be measured in many ways, as already indicated, and results may depend on the operationalization of the dependent variable. Moreover, some studies contain a large number of estimates, because many models are calculated, while other studies are based on more complex regression or microsimulation models and contain fewer estimates.

These difficulties are particularly problematic for traditional literature reviews. Hence, statistical techniques contribute to the clarification of certain problems. For instance, using a weighting procedure that takes into account the number of estimates contained in each evaluation can reduce a first bias: a qualitative review may lead to biased interpretations if one study contains a large number of estimates that confirms one of the researcher's hypotheses, while a sophisticated simulation that contains only one result contradicts it. The researcher may be tempted, subconsciously, to infer that there is more evidence that confirms his or her hypothesis than that which infirms it. However, this high number of similar findings may be the result of slight modifications of the same regression model, based on the same data-set. Hence, I think it is very important to weight results according to the number of estimates per article. In addition, many researchers advocate to weight results according to the accuracy of the estimates – typically by using standard errors.

Moreover, as overall results are usually fuzzy and difficult to synthesize (Kluve, 2006), using a significance test allows the researcher who employs a vote count procedure to draw conclusions that are not subjective: the test is either significant or not. Hence, the test is a clear indication concerning the interpretation of the results (most articles are positive, most articles are significant and so on): do they really say something about the impact of a policy or should this majority be interpreted with caution? Hence, in the present work, I have systematically used conditional formulations when results were not significant.

Finally, it should be noted that a meta-regression is better than the type of vote-counting procedures I have used here, but its purpose is different. It is better in the sense that it partly solves the 'apples and oranges problem', because the regression model allows controlling for the population group studied, for other institutional variables that may also have an impact on poverty or employment and for macroeconomic performance as well as for specific sociodemographic factors. In the present work, as indicated below, I have partly solved the comparability problem by carrying out overall meta-analyses and, whenever possible, meta-analyses for each welfare regime. In addition, these statistical procedures are accompanied by a qualitative review of the evidence that highlights differences between categories of workers.

It is fundamental to note, in addition, that meta-regression techniques require having a number of estimates that is large enough (which, in fact, is the case for any regression model) and focusing on a small number of policies. Most of the time meta-regression analyses focus on a single policy.

In summary, meta-analysis is superior to traditional literature reviews because it limits the impact of researchers' subconscious preconceptions, which is, in my view, a great advantage. Meta-regression techniques better contribute to the resolution of the apples and oranges problem than the meta-analyses I have carried out.

6.1.6 My Approach to Meta-analysis

The research synthesis presented here consists of vote-counting procedures (based on significance, effect direction and a combination of both) applied to weighted data with sign tests. This approach lies, hence, somewhere between meta-regression techniques and traditional vote-counting proce-dures. The goal of this chapter is not so much to precisely quantify the impact a specific social policy may have on poverty and employment in a given context. It is an attempt to evaluate which policies work in which institutional and economic context, and for whom, as my meta-analysis includes a broad spectrum of policies ranging from family policy to labour laws, and provides results that are broken down by welfare regimes. What then follows is the global assessment of the impact of welfare regimes on the three working poverty mechanisms and the composition of the working poor population is provided in Chapter 7.

My analysis is based on a systematic strategy for the identification of articles. More specifically, I used the search engine provided by Thomson Reuters, namely ISI Web of Knowledge, one of the most widely used engines, with a focus on twenty-first century articles (2000–2009/2010) written in English. The specific keywords used and the number of hits they yielded are described in the sections devoted to each policy (minimum wages, tax credits, family policy). Other search engines have been used, which proved useful when some countries where overwhelmingly represented in the sample of articles (especially the US) or when the amount of articles was low (especially for antipoverty effects). The goal of this second stage of the search for articles was to fill the gaps left by the first research based on the ISI Web of Knowledge. The search engine of the IZA, the Institute for the Study of Labour (a private non-profit research institute that works in close cooperation with the University of Bonn in Germany) and the IFAU, the Institute for Labour Market Policy Evaluation in Sweden, were used. A third stage was carried out with Google Scholar, with specific targets, such as articles dealing with a specific country or the search of further articles on the poverty effects of some policies in a given welfare regime. This last step also included French, German and Spanish keywords.

Three types of vote count are provided: the first one counts whether significant or non-significant findings are predominant, the second focuses on significant findings and assesses whether positive or negative findings are dominant, and the third establishes whether positive or negative findings are dominant, regardless of their significance.

In most cases, all studies published between 2000 and 2010 were reviewed; however, the number of articles identified that fulfilled the quality criteria I present below was relatively low, ranging from four for the antipoverty effects of childcare policy to 18 for the antipoverty effects of minimum wages. There are two exceptions, however. First, the impact of minimum wages on employment has been the subject of a large number of evaluations published in the recent past, mainly in the Anglo-Saxon world, which is partly attributable to the publication of Card and Krueger's book (1995). The second topic that generated many evaluations, especially in Europe, is the effect of childcare policies on maternal employment. In both cases, the number of articles analysed amounts to 20, on pragmatic grounds: first, the systematic search for other policies and their effects, as indicated above, never yielded more than 18 articles usable for meta-analysis purposes. Setting the limit at 20 provides a comparable number of articles for most policies. Second, I have been able to identify, for both topics, encompassing literature reviews published in the 2000s that, of course, include some of the studies I have identified and included in my meta-analysis, but cover a longer time period. Hence, for these two topics, I present the most recent estimates stemming from my meta-analysis and comment on the findings contained in these literature reviews.

The statistical units are empirical estimates (rather than articles or population groups), and a simple weighting procedure has been defined, so that estimates from studies containing a large number of findings are given less weight, namely the inverse of the number of estimates in the article, adjusted to keep the size of the sample of estimates constant. For instance, a literature search for a given topic yielded 20 articles containing 150 estimates in total; if one of these articles contains ten estimates, each one gets a weight of 0.1 multiplied by 150/20 (the average number of findings per article), that is, 0.75.

However, each estimate has not been weighted according to the sample size[1] of the study it stems from, because the evaluations analysed here rely on large data-sets of many thousands of observations, sometimes tens of thousands. The bias due to the fact that sample size is not included in the calculation of weights is limited, as I have decided to exclude studies with 'small' samples (that is, based on less than 1000 cases).

Empirically unreliable studies were not removed from the summary tables (see Appendix), only from the vote-counting procedure, and the reason for their exclusion is written in bold in the tables. I have removed studies from the vote-counting procedure on the basis of clear criteria (the absence of regression and simulation results, and sample size). Table 6.1 summarizes the results of the article search.

Table 6.1 Number of articles and estimates pertaining to the antipoverty and employment effects of selected policies

Effect/policy	Number of articles	Number of estimates
Employment effect, minimum wage	20	141
Antipoverty effect, minimum wage	18	87
Employment effect, tax credits for workers	17	162
Antipoverty effect, tax credits for workers	10	51
Employment effect, family cash benefits	11	66
Antipoverty effect, family cash benefits	7	29

Effect/policy	Number of articles	Number of estimates
Employment effect, childcare services	20	171
Antipoverty effect, childcare services	4	12

Overall, I have read and summarized 93 studies and reviews, most of which have been included in the vote-counting procedure, for a total of 719 estimates.[2]

An important element of the meta-analysis carried out here must be discussed at this point, as one of the three vote counts is based on significance. In the case of microsimulation results, there is no indication of significance (with a few exceptions, when the simulation is based on structural equations parameters, that is, regression coefficients associated with significance tests). I made the decision to classify a simulated effect as significantly different from zero if it exceeded ± 5 per cent, because in most studies based on regression models a 5 per cent increase or decrease is usually associated with a significant impact. Hence, simulation results expressed in absolute numbers (for example 30,000 persons escape poverty) or in percentage points had to be transformed into per cent, so that a decision could be made.

For most policies, the choice of this pragmatic 'significance threshold'[3] is very unlikely to have an impact on the conclusions drawn: there is no single simulation result for the employment effects of minimum wages and only nine out of 87 for their antipoverty effects, four of which are above 5 per cent. Likewise, six out of 66 estimates of the employment effects of family cash benefits are derived from simulations (four of which are larger than 5 per cent), six out of 29 estimates of the antipoverty effects of family cash benefits (two are greater than 5 per cent and one is less than 1 per cent), 19 out of 171 for the employment effects of childcare services (three are greater than 5 per cent and eight are less than 1 per cent). As far as the antipoverty effect of childcare services is concerned, the number of estimates is very limited and, hence, they will not be submitted to a statistical treatment.

On the contrary, many estimates of the employment and antipoverty effects of employment-conditional tax credits are based on simulations, namely 55 out of 162 estimates of employment effects and 19 out of 51 estimated antipoverty effects. The large majority of these simulation results were calculated for Continental European countries in which no such tax credits exist. The goal was to assess what would happen if the WFTC (or, in a few cases, the EITC) were implemented. Hence, the robustness of findings for the Continental European welfare regime will be assessed with alternative 'significance levels', namely 2 and 3 per cent.

Now that methodological aspects have been clarified, the meta-analyses of four social policy and labour market policy instruments, namely minimum wages, tax credits for workers, family cash benefits and childcare policies, are presented in the following sections. First, existing literature reviews are summarized; they were either identified through the article search or often mentioned in the retrieved articles. Second, an overall statistical analysis, for all risk groups and all welfare regimes is provided, followed by break downs by welfare regime. Third, a qualitative review of some results allows me to further ascertain aspects that remain unclear after the quantitative procedure.

6.2 MINIMUM WAGES

6.2.1 Existing Literature Reviews

A study published by Neumark and Wascher in 2007 appears to be a reference publication for many scholars participating in the debate on the employment effects of minimum wages, and, hence, on the allegedly limited explanatory power of neoclassical labour supply and demand equilibrium models.

Neumark and Wascher (2007) highlight the fact that the minimum wage has always been a contentious issue in the US. Nobel Laureate Stigler suggested, as early as in 1946, that a minimum wage could raise employment in a labour market characterized by monopsony, a fact that is central in Card and Krueger's (1995) work. However, in the early 1980s there was a broad consensus that minimum wage hikes harmed the employment prospects of low-skilled workers, with labour demand elasticities ranging from –0.1 to –0.3. However, in the 1990s, many researchers challenged this view.

This is why Neumark and Wascher (2007) carried out an encompassing review of what they call the 'New Minimum Wage Research'. They note that many factors explain the broad range of findings observed. Many new studies rely on a 'natural experiment approach' or case study approach: for instance, the employment levels in a state experiencing an increase in the minimum wage are compared with those of a state with no such increase (Card and Krueger, 1995). Most of the other studies rely on panel data studies; in the US case they often rely on state-year observations, whereas some use county-level data.

Another line of contention involves the appropriate minimum wage indicator to be used in regression models: the Kaitz index,[4] the fraction of workers affected by a minimum wage hike or the level of the real minimum wage. Regarding the dependent variable, results often differ depending on whether it is the employment rate or the number of hours (or weeks) worked that are predicted. In countries in which working hours are lightly regulated, the employment rate might remain constant, but employers may reduce the number of hours worked by their employees.

Other debates pertaining to model specifications are noteworthy. For studies based on state-level panel data, the inclusion of year fixed effects (year dummies) in the regression model is subject to criticism. The difference between contemporaneous and lagged effects of minimum wage increases is also subject to controversy, as firms may adjust some non-labour inputs slowly, and it may take more than a year for a minimum wage hike to have a negative employment impact. Finally, there are also potential endogeneity problems, especially if the variations in the minimum wage are partly explained by macroeconomic factors that are used as controls in the econometric model, for instance if there is a decrease in the youth minimum wage as a reaction to a strong increase in youth unemployment or a global increase in the minimum wage allowed by a booming economy.

In addition, as already indicated, there may be a publication bias: authors who provide analyses that confirm the 'textbook model' of labour supply have a higher likelihood of being published, as well as an 'author bias', which occurs when economists run regressions until they find a specification with the desired effect.

Eventually, Neumark and Wascher (2007) review 87 studies, 42 of which analyse the US case, five Canada, one Sweden, seven the UK, four Australia, three New Zealand, three France, one the Netherlands, one Spain, two Portugal, one Greece, four Brazil, one Mexico and Colombia, one Mexico on its own, one Colombia on its own, one Chile, one Costa Rica, one Trinidad and Tobago, one Puerto Rico and four Indonesia. The authors conclude that, 'two-thirds give a relatively consistent (although by no means always statistically significant) indication of negative employment effects of minimum wages, while only eight give a relatively consistent indication of positive employment effects' (Neumark and Wascher, 2007: 121). In summary, the evidence regarding alleged disemployment effects is mixed, but tendentially indicate a slightly negative impact.

6.2.2 Overall Meta-analysis

Thanks to the search engine provided by Thomson Reuters, I searched for articles published during the period of 2000–2009. Searching for 'minimum wage*poverty' yielded 37 hits, 44 hits with 'minimum wage poverty', whereas 'minimum wage*employment' led to no less than 310 hits. In the case of articles dealing with antipoverty effects, all 44 articles and proceedings' abstracts were read; those clearly not dealing with the impact of minimum wages (either legally defined or set through collective agreements) were dropped. As for the employment effect, the literature is plethoric, which is attributable to the strong impact that Card and Krueger's publication (1995) has had in the field of labour economics. As indicated, I started with the most recent article available, until 20 articles directly dealing with this issue were reviewed.

The vast majority of poverty-related articles and around half of those dealing with employment effects analyse the situation in the US. Hence, in order to find articles on antipoverty effects in other countries, other search engines were used: notably the IZA, the Institute for the Study of Labour; the IFAU, the Institute for Labour Market Policy Evaluation in Sweden; and Google Scholar. I searched the IZA discussion papers series for articles with 'minimum wage' in the title, dropping articles dealing with employment effects or based on US data (that is, the overwhelming majority) and identified a few interesting articles. With the IFAU search engine using 'minimum wage', I could only find one article dealing with poverty issues (out of 82 hits) that had already been found through the ISI Web of Knowledge. The same search was carried out on IFAU's website, without success. Finally, I used Google Scholar with the keywords 'minimum wage poverty', 'Mindestlohn' and 'Mindestlohn Armut' (that is, minimum wage and poverty in German), 'SMI pobreza', 'salario mínimo pobreza' and 'salario mínimo interprofesional' (the latter being the official denomination of the statutory minimum wage in Spain) and 'salaire minimum pauvreté' and 'SMIC pauvreté' (minimum wage and poverty in French). The vast majority of the articles found dealt with employment effects.

All in all, some elements are noteworthy: first, a large majority of the articles devoted to minimum wages deal with employment effects, while the literature on the antipoverty impact is much scarcer (Müller and Steiner, 2008; Vedder and Galloway, 2001). Second, as already indicated, most of the evidence comes from the US: regarding employment effects, nine articles study the US labour market, two Canada, one New Zealand, one Japan, one Austria, one France, one Portugal, one Finland and one Sweden. As for antipoverty effects, 13 out of 18 articles study the US, while two study the UK and one New Zealand. Third, while most evaluations measure the impact of statutory minimum wages, some analyse countries in which minimum wages are set through collective bargaining (Sweden, Finland and Austria). Fourth, the large majority of the evaluations are empirical estimates based on econometric models. Fifth, the overwhelming majority of evaluations of employment variations are based on low-skilled groups or groups largely over-represented among low-wage workers, such as teenagers, young adults, high school drop-outs, low-skilled immigrants, middle-aged married women in Japan or low-wage industries, such as the retail trade industry and hotels and restaurants (see Appendix).

6.2.2.1 Employment effects
Overall results pertaining to the employment effects of minimum wages are presented in Table 6.2: the first row of the table indicates whether the majority of estimated effects are positive or negative, regardless of their significance. The second row shows whether or not the majority of estimates indicate a statistically significant effect of a policy. The third vote count accounts for statistically significant estimates only, and indicates whether significant findings are mainly positive or negative.

For each vote count, a Z test establishes if the majority identified (based on the sign of the effect, its significance or both) is statistically significant, or if the conclusion might just as well be the other way around, at usual significance levels, namely 1 and 5 per cent.

Finally, if a vote count shows a 'fifty-fifty' situation or approximately so (49 per cent–51 per cent is the limit), the result is deemed inconclusive, as it is not possible to determine a majority. This situation is different from the one in which a majority can be identified but is not significant.

Table 6.2 Employment effect of minimum wages, based on all estimates, weighted vote count with sign test

Type of vote count	Majority	Significance of majority
Sign (regardless of significance)	99/141 negative effects	**
Significance (regardless of sign)	71/140 inconclusive	n.s.
Sign among significant effects	55/73 negative effects	**

Notes: **significant at the 1% level; n.s. not significant at the 5% level.

Overall, then, I reach similar conclusions as I did based on Neumark and Wascher's (2007) literature review. It seems that the employment effect of minimum wages is globally negative; however, findings are mixed in terms of significance, as around half of them find a non-significant effect. Hence, it appears that the effect on low-skilled workers might be negative, but probably limited in magnitude.

6.2.2.2 Antipoverty effects

Table 6.3 Antipoverty effect of minimum wages based on all estimates, weighted vote count with sign test

Type of vote count	Majority	Significance of majority
Sign (regardless of significance)	63/86 positive effects	**
Significance (regardless of sign)	65/87 insignificant effects	**
Sign among significant effects	21/22 positive effects	**

Note: **significant at the 1% level.

As shown in Table 6.3, minimum wages appear to have a positive, yet statistically insignificant impact on working poverty. As will be shown below, it is probably safe to say that the impact on the incidence of poverty is small, due to the fact that a large majority of low-wage workers are not poor, but that minimum wages reduce the poverty gap.

In what follows, I further my first conclusions by analysing results by welfare regimes, because in the real world of social policy, the impact of a given instrument depends on a large set of institutional, economic and demographic factors that varies considerably across regimes. Given the very limited number of estimates at my disposal for Southern European countries, I made the pragmatic decision to include them in the conservative cluster; this is the case for all policies reviewed in this chapter.

6.2.3 Meta-analysis by Welfare Regime and Further Considerations

6.2.3.1 Employment effects
For the liberal, Anglo-Saxon cluster, results pertaining to the employment effects of minimum wages are shown in Table 6.4.

Table 6.4 Employment effect of minimum wages in the liberal welfare regime, weighted vote count with sign test

Type of vote count	Majority	Significance of majority
Sign (regardless of significance)	68/99 negative effects	**
Significance (regardless of sign)	51/98 insignificant effects	n.s.
Sign among significant effects	36/48 negative effects	**

Notes: ** significant at the 1% level; n.s. not significant at the 5% level.

Results are similar to the global analysis, which is not very surprising, given that a majority of estimates (78 out of 141) are based on Anglo-Saxon data. The employment impact is negative, if there is any impact at all. Indeed, results tend to show a non-significant impact of minimum wages on employment, but the slight majority of insignificant effects could be an artefact.

With regards to the Continental European welfare regime cluster, results are similar; they should, however, be interpreted with caution, as they are based on a small sample of 28 estimates (see Table 6.5).

In Continental Europe, conclusions are very similar; minimum wages are likely to have a slightly negative impact on employment. Hence, in this cluster too, the impact is probably small in magnitude, if there is any disemployment effect at all.

A closer look at estimates in the social-democratic cluster reveals that the number of observations is very small, namely 14 (weighted) estimates stemming from two articles: the majority of estimates show a negative impact on employment for Finnish workers under 25 and Swedish unskilled workers in the hotel and restaurant sector.

Table 6.5 Employment effect of minimum wages in the conservative corporatist welfare regime, weighted vote count with sign test

Type of vote count	Majority	Significance of majority
Sign (regardless of significance)	20/28 negative effects	*
Significance (regardless of sign)	16/28 significant effects	n.s.
Sign among significant effects	13/17 negative effects	*

Notes: *significant at the 5% level; n.s. not significant at the 5% level.

After this first, merely quantitative approach, which leads to the conclusion that minimum wages are likely to have a slightly negative impact on the employment of low-wage workers, a more qualitative interpretation of the findings is necessary to improve our understanding. It is notable that the impact of the minimum wage depends on other labour market institutions, for instance, hiring and firing legislations (Neumark and Wascher, 2007), payroll taxes (Kenworthy, 2004), and the composition of the workforce (share of unskilled workers, share of migrants and so on). The impact of the minimum wage may be different in the US, where the labour market is lightly regulated, firing employees is easy and the share of low-skilled labour is large, especially among a large migrant population, than in some European countries with highly regulated labour markets, high payroll taxes and a lower share of unskilled workers.

Put differently, minimum wages in Continental Europe, even if set at an equivalent level in purchasing power parities (PPP), have a bigger impact on a company's payroll, because of higher taxes. Moreover, employers in Continental Europe probably have less room for manoeuvre in terms of quantitative flexibility, as it is more complicated to hire and fire employees and the composition of their workforce is different.

Hence, a qualitative review of unweighted data based on contrasting cases appears necessary, and comparing the French and the US case can be interesting in this regard. In the US, in international comparison, the minimum wage is low, the labour market lightly regulated and payroll taxes are low. In the present work, around half of the estimates are insignificant, while the majority are negative. Significantly negative estimates pertain to very low skilled and/or disadvantaged groups, mostly teenagers, sometimes teenagers in low-wage industries, single mothers who are high school drop-outs or workers in the retail industry. Only two findings out of 67 suggest that the employment effect for all workers is significantly negative. The fact that the US minimum wage only has a negative impact on very low-skilled workers is not all too surprising, given that its level is relatively low, as well as payroll taxes.

France is in strong contrast to the US: its minimum wage, expressed as a share of the average wage (Kaitz index) is high by international comparison, and so are payroll taxes. Moreover, employment protection legislation is rather strict. The only evaluation identified in the present work provides two estimates, and both conclude to a statistically significant negative effect of the French minimum wage on employment for male and female workers. Neumark and Wascher (2007) were able to identify three studies for France published in the 1990s, but none in the 2000s. The first study compares two periods – one with a strong increase in the minimum wage and one with no increase – and concludes that unemployment rose more for groups with a greater proportion of workers paid at or below the minimum wage; the pattern for employment rates is weaker but in a consistent direction. However, the first period included a recession, while the second was characterized by a recovery, so it is difficult to draw a clear-cut conclusion. The second study analyses youth employment in 32 economic sectors that vary in their proportion of young workers: the estimates are negative and statistically significant. The third evaluation, which in fact is a set of three studies by the same authors, leads to clear conclusions: the authors consistently find considerably higher transitions to non-employment for workers newly bound by the minimum wage, with very high elasticities. Of course, six studies are not enough to draw conclusions about the impact of the minimum wage. Still, all of them seem to show that the French minimum wage has a detrimental impact on the employment prospects of low-skilled workers.

This qualitative interpretation of a subset of findings may be summarized as follows: when the minimum wage is low, as is the case in the US, that is, approximately one-third of gross average wage of full-time workers (its after tax value amounts to slightly less than 40 per cent of the average net wage) (Immervoll, 2007) and payroll taxes/social security contributions are low, namely around 15 per cent of an employee's wage, the employment impact is very minimal to non-existent. If the minimum wage is set at a high level, with an after-tax value of around 60 per cent of the net average wage of full-time workers (or around 45 per cent of gross average wage), and social security contributions are high (around 35 to 40 per cent of an employee's wage), as is the case in France (Immervoll, 2007), the minimum wage is likely to have an impact on low-skilled and young workers. It is not only the minimum wage, but a combination of institutional factors that appears to have this detrimental impact.

6.2.3.2   Antipoverty effects

As to the antipoverty effects of minimum wages, the vast majority of evaluations meta-analysed here pertain to the situation in the US; a few findings concern the UK and New Zealand and only four findings concern Continental European countries. Hence, the vote count presented in Table 6.6 is based on the Anglo-Saxon cluster.

Table 6.6 Antipoverty effect of minimum wages in the liberal welfare regime, weighted vote count with sign test

Type of vote count	Majority	Significance of majority
Sign (regardless of significance)	53/76 positive effects	**
Significance (regardless of sign)	61/77 insignificant effects	**
Sign among significant effects	16/17 positive effects	**

Note: **significant at the 5% level.

The conclusion is straightforward: the minimum wage in the liberal cluster, especially in the US, has a positive, yet statistically insignificant impact on poverty. This vote count might be too conservative, though; hence, it cannot be excluded that the minimum wage has a slightly positive impact on poverty.

For the conservative cluster, only ten weighted estimates are available, all of which are positive; half of these estimates point to significant effects. Hence, in Continental Europe, I do not rule out a significant effect on the incidence of working poverty. This would not be very surprising, given that minimum wages are higher than in the US. No estimate was found for the social-democratic cluster.

An in-depth review of the US evidence can be interesting in this regard. A large majority of estimates (54 out of 70) are not significant. This is not very surprising given the relatively low level of the minimum wage in the US. Actually, a full-time worker with two children earning the minimum wage in 2006 brings home about 89 per cent of poverty-level income

(Levitis and Johnson, 2006). Moreover, a large majority of minimum-wage workers are not poor, most of them living in middle-income households, a fact often mentioned in the reviewed evaluations (for instance in Burkhauser and Sabia, 2007; Leigh, 2007). However, approximately 60 per cent of estimates are positive: put differently, the minimum wage tends to reduce poverty if anything, despite the potential disemployment effects.

A closer look at the 12 (unweighted) estimates that are statistically significant and positive reveals that most measure the incidence of poverty among families with children. Moreover, one study uses the Foster–Greer–Thorbecke indicator with $\alpha = 1$ and 2, and one measures the change in the income-to-needs ratio, for a total of 13 findings, all of which are non-significant but positive, which suggests a reduction in the depth and the severity of poverty.

6.2.4 Conclusions

Given the available evidence, it appears reasonable to say that low minimum wages set at around one-third of the gross average wage, such as those found in the US, do not strongly reduce the *incidence* of poverty as measured by the headcount ratio. In the case of the US, then, it seems appropriate to share Nobel Laureate Joseph Stiglitz's conclusion: 'a higher minimum wage does not seem to be a particularly useful way to help the poor' (quoted in Vedder and Galloway, 2001). However, it is likely that minimum wages reduce the income gap, which in turn reduces the expenses the welfare state must incur to combat working poverty, as employers also play their part. A minimum wage set at a higher level, but low enough not to generate significant disemployment effects, could have a stronger impact on poverty.

Unfortunately, neither the evidence gathered here, nor evidence stemming from literature reviews, allows drawing conclusions as to the level at which this minimum should be set. Whereas the issue of the disemployment effects of minimum wages has drawn the attention of many (labour) economists and generated a plethoric literature in the recent past in the US, the topic of the antipoverty impact accounting for employment effects has attracted less interest in Europe.

In my view, it is relatively unfruitful to keep on publishing national studies based on well-known empirical strategies and argue about specifications of regression models; it would be certainly more useful to use comparative methods to try and estimate the level where employment effects are not significantly negative and antipoverty effects non-negligible, and the conditions under which these conclusions hold.

It should be added that, whether or not minimum wages efficiently combat working poverty, they seem to be necessary when in-work benefits are implemented; indeed, tax credits for workers in the US and the UK, which I evaluate below, work in tandem with a minimum wage. The existence of a wage floor prevents employers from paying their employees very low wages, as they might be tempted to, knowing that low-wage workers benefit from income supplements in the form of a tax credit. Last but not least, minimum wages can also be seen as useful in order to reduce the gender pay gap.

I tend to share Marx and Verbist's (2008: 275) conclusion: 'as an isolated measure, higher minimum wages – within realistically feasible ranges – cannot contribute much towards fighting in-work poverty. Which is not to say that minimum wages have no role to play … they do, but not as an isolated measure'.

6.3 TAX CREDITS FOR WORKING FAMILIES/ WORKERS

6.3.1 Existing Literature Reviews

A literature review carried out by Hotz and Scholz (2003) is mentioned by many authors of the evaluations meta-analysed here. Their review contains 13 studies of the effects of the EITC on labour force participation and hours worked, published over the period 1993–2002. There are seven studies that measure the impact of the EITC on labour force participation and six studies that measure the impact on hours worked.

The five studies measuring the impact of the EITC on single mothers' employment unanimously conclude that the impact is positive; one study concludes that overall employment increased. An evaluation of the impact of the EITC on married couples concludes that married men very slightly increased their employment levels, while married women worked less after expansions of the EITC.

The evidence pertaining to the number of hours worked is mixed: in some cases the impact is positive, in others it is negative, whereas one evaluation finds a non-significant effect. One of the evaluations deals with the situation of married couples and also points to a decrease in employment among married women. All in all, Hotz and Scholz (2003) conclude that the overall employment impact of the EITC is positive, despite disemployment effects for married women.

In what follows, the apples and oranges problem may be important, as some evaluations use a sample of single mothers, while others include married (and sometimes also cohabiting) women, and still others combine both population groups. Hence, after a global analysis, a more detailed analysis by population group is provided.

In addition, I rechecked the articles that evaluate minimum wages, in order to find further estimates of the impact of tax credit for workers, as some articles contained specifications that checked the impact of minimum wages controlling for the impact of tax credits, especially in US evaluations.

6.3.2 Overall Meta-analysis

The search for evaluations of the EITC – with the keywords 'Earned income tax credit' and 'EITC' – with the ISI Web of Knowledge search engine yielded 95 hits for the period 2000–2009, all of which were checked.

As far as the UK is concerned, the search yielded 60 hits for the period 2000–2009 (keywords: 'working tax credit' and 'working family tax credit'). Regarding the Employment Premium in France (PPE), the number of hits was minimal: 'Prime pour l'emploi' one hit, 'tax credits*France' six hits.

As indicated above, other tax credits exist, but the number of articles identified was either zero or very low, even when the specific names of these programmes were entered in the ISI Web of Knowledge search engine, except for Canada with 31 hits (keywords: 'tax credit*Canada'); however, only one article was usable. In addition, the search for articles based on provinces names was unsuccessful. Moreover, neither 'In-work tax credit', nor 'tax credit*New Zealand', nor 'Working for families', nor 'in-work benefits*New Zealand', nor 'Family income supplement', nor 'tax credit*Ireland', nor 'in-work benefits*Ireland', nor 'Earned income tax credit*Sweden', nor 'tax credit*Sweden', nor 'in-work benefits*Sweden', allowed identifying potential articles.

Hence, I made the decision to focus on the EITC, the WFTC and the PPE. The article search was furthered by using the IZA and the IFAU search engines, looking for articles about these three programmes: the first provided 190 papers for the EITC and 179 for 'working tax credit', most of which, however, had nothing to do with the EITC or the WFTC, while the second allowed identifying 62 articles for British tax credits and 77 for the EITC. Some articles were identified that had already been retrieved through the ISI Web of Knowledge. Finally, articles in French and English about the PPE and the antipoverty effects of tax credits in general were searched for with Google Scholar, with the keywords 'Tax credits poverty' and 'Prime pour l'emploi'. This allowed identifying some more articles, especially for the French PPE.

6.3.2.1 Employment effects

The overall vote count that includes the three credits, all population groups and all indicators, yields the following results for employment effects of employment-conditional tax credits (see Table 6.7).

Table 6.7 Employment effect of tax credits, based on all estimates, weighted vote count with sign test

Type of vote count	Majority	Significance of majority
Sign (regardless of significance)	113/162 positive effects	**
Significance (regardless of sign)	83/162 inconclusive	n.s.
Sign among significant effects	64/77 positive effects	**

Notes: **significant at the 1% level; n.s. not significant at the 5% level.

The employment effect appears to be positive, whereas it is impossible to conclude, based on this global analysis, whether the impact is significant or not. This may be attributable to the variety of employment indicators and samples used.

6.3.2.2 Antipoverty effects

Table 6.8 Antipoverty effect of tax credits, based on all estimates, weighted vote count with sign test

Type of vote count	Majority	Significance of majority
Sign (regardless of significance)	35/52 positive effects	*
Significance (regardless of sign)	36/51 insignificant effects	**
Sign among significant effects	14/14 positive effects	**

Notes: **significant at the 1% level; *significant at the 5% level.

As shown in Table 6.8 the global vote-counting procedure points in the direction of a positive yet insignificant antipoverty effect. As already indicated, the vote count based on significance is rather conservative, so it is not unlikely that tax credits have, overall, a slightly positive antipoverty effect.

As for the meta-analysis of the effects of minimum wages, it is important to break down results by welfare regime. Moreover, it is fundamental to distinguish single mothers from married mothers.

6.3.3 Meta-analysis by Welfare Regime and Further Considerations

6.3.3.1 Employment effects

As a first step, I want to draw conclusions about the employment effects within the liberal cluster. The three vote-counting procedures are summarized in Table 6.9.

Table 6.9 Employment effect of tax credits in the liberal welfare regime, weighted vote count with sign test

Type of vote count	Majority	Significance of majority
Sign (regardless of significance)	101/123 positive effects	**
Significance (regardless of sign)	73/124 significant effects	*
Sign among significant effects	63/74 positive effects	**

Notes: **significant at the 1% level; *significant at the 5% level.

These findings lead to an unambiguous and straightforward conclusion: tax credits in Anglo-Saxon countries have a statistically significant impact on employment and a large majority of estimates are positive. Tax credits have significantly increased employment.

Let us now have a closer look at unweighted observations. Nearly all estimates of the effects on lone mothers' employment are positive and a large majority are significant. Only two estimates are negative and regard full-time year round work (Herbst, 2008). By contrast, all articles except one find negative effects for married women or women in couples in general. The exception is an article written by Francesconi et al. (2009) in which most effects are positive but insignificant.

As far as the conservative cluster is concerned, only four studies could be identified; however, they contain 38 estimates. Two articles are evaluations of the French PPE and two are simulations of the introduction of the WFTC in Continental Europe, mainly France and Germany (there are two estimates for Finland, however, that were aggregated with France and Germany's findings).

Table 6.10 Employment effect of tax credits in the conservative corporatist welfare regime, weighted vote count with sign test

Type of vote count	Majority	Significance of majority
Sign (regardless of significance)	23/38 negative effects	n.s.
Significance (regardless of sign)	34/38 insignificant effects	**
Sign among significant effects	2/3 negative effects	n.s.

Notes: **significant at the 1% level; n.s. not significant at the 5% level.

As shown in Table 6.10 it seems that tax credits would/do not have a significant effect in Continental Europe. Strikingly, and in contrast to Anglo-Saxon countries, tax credits may even have a negative employment impact, should they have any impact at all. For this cluster, however, conclusions in terms of significance have to be drawn with great caution, as most are derived from simulations: policies are deemed to have a 'significant' impact if it amounts to a variation of at least 5 per cent. A robustness check was carried out by using 2 and 3 per cent as 'significance thresholds', rather than a variation of at least 5 per cent. With the threshold set at 2 or 3 per cent, 33 or 32 instead of 34 weighted estimates point to non-significant effect. More importantly, the three significant additional findings are negative. It is probably safe to say that employment-conditional tax credits would not have the same impact in Continental Europe as in the UK or in the US; contrary to the Anglo-Saxon world, they may not have any impact or even a slightly negative one.

A closer look at the unweighted estimates based on the simulated effect of the introduction of the WFTC in Continental Europe (plus a couple of estimates for Finland) leads to the following results: 40 out of 45 unweighted estimates are non-significant (with the 5 per cent 'significance threshold'); 12 equal zero and 15 are negative. Hence, whereas tax credits for workers have a significant positive impact in Anglo-Saxon countries, they seem to be inefficient in Continental Europe, as they appear not to have any significant effect on employment. All estimates (13) of the impact on married women or women in a couple are negative or equal zero. For single mothers, only four estimates are provided and all are positive; there are five additional estimates for single women in general that are also unanimously positive. Hence, as in Anglo-Saxon countries, the impact is positive for single mothers and single women in general, but negative for women in couples.

These are important findings, despite the fact that they are based on simulations, whereas most Anglo-Saxon evaluations are based on regression models and real situations. Continental European labour markets are very different from Anglo-Saxon markets: unemployment is usually higher, female employment is usually lower, the earnings distribution is more compressed and lone mothers are not so strongly over-represented among welfare recipients, which was one of the main concerns in Anglo-Saxon countries (Blundell, 2006; Meyer and Holtz-Eakin, 2001). Hence, it is likely that, in Continental Europe, the positive impact on single mothers would be outweighed by the negative impact on married women, should a credit such as the WFTC be implemented.

Regarding the employment impact of the PPE in France, I could only find 20 estimates (unweighted). However, conclusions are virtually unanimous: the PPE has an insignificant impact (only three unweighted estimates are significant). Moreover, three-quarters of unweighted results are negative. Hence, it is probably fair to say that the PPE does not have any impact on employment in France; should it have any impact, it might be negative. The reasons brought to the forefront in the few articles available are that the amounts are very small and the design of the programme is so complex that it is difficult for recipients to really understand it, so that the behavioural impact is necessarily limited. Moreover, the unemployment rate is high for young and unskilled workers and the PPE does not solve the problem that many unskilled workers who are willing to work face in an environment characterized by a low labour demand: the high level of the minimum wage may outprice them from the labour market, given their low level of productivity (Cahuc, 2002; Legendre et al., 2004). The latter argument seems to be in line with the few evaluations of the employment effects of the French minimum wage (SMIC) reviewed above. However, more empirical work is required to really assess the impact of the French SMIC on employment, as other factors may better explain the grim situation of unskilled workers, for instance, high social security contributions (Kenworthy, 2004).

All in all, tax credits for workers may not be the best tool in terms of employment in Continental Europe. These programmes appear to have been efficient in Anglo-Saxon countries, as they allowed a large number of lone mothers to enter the labour market without facing high marginal effective tax rates; lone mothers represented, in the 1990s, a large group of welfare recipients. This labour market entry of lone mothers more than offset the withdrawal of a group of married women, leading to an overall positive employment effect. In many Continental European countries, one of the conditions for the effectiveness of tax credits is probably missing, namely that there must be enough jobs to be had (Sawhill and Thomas, 2001; Stancanelli and Sterdyniak, 2004), so that providing incentives might not be sufficient to increase the labour force participation of low-skilled women. The Belgian experience may be revealing in this regard: a low-wage tax credit was introduced in 2002; given the limited impact it had, it was abolished in 2005 and replaced by a reduction in employee's social security contributions (Marx and Verbist, 2008).

6.3.3.2   Antipoverty effects

For the liberal cluster, 36 estimates derived from seven articles could be identified (five of them analyse the situation in the US); that is, the number of estimates of the antipoverty effect is much smaller than for employment effects. It is striking, indeed, that the main focus of evaluations of tax credits has been on employment, usually female employment, rather than on poverty, even though they are always brought to the forefront as anti-working poverty tools, especially in the US. The reason for this apparent paradox lies in the way the fight against working poverty is conceived in Anglo-Saxon countries; the main approach, especially in the US since the mid-1990s, is the maximization of labour force participation, as already indicated above.

The results of the meta-analysis are shown in Table 6.11.

Table 6.11 Antipoverty effect of tax credits in the liberal welfare regime, weighted vote count with sign test

Type of vote count	Majority	Significance of majority
Sign (regardless of significance)	25/36 positive effects	*
Significance (regardless of sign)	24/36 insignificant effects	*
Sign among significant effects	12/12 positive effects	**

Notes: **significant at the 5% level; * significant at the 1% level.

Based on the evidence gathered here, it can be said that tax credits reduce poverty in the US and the UK; yet, a significant majority of estimates point in the direction of a statistically insignificant impact (but only for $\alpha = 5$ per cent), despite numerous claims about the numbers of families escaping poverty based on descriptive, pre-transfer/post-transfer evidence. Again, the vote count based on significance may be too conservative; hence, it is not unlikely that tax credits have a slightly positive impact on the incidence of working poverty in Anglo-Saxon countries.

Here too, a more qualitative in-depth review of unweighted estimates appears necessary. First, ten of the 38 estimates stem from the same study by Gundersen and Ziliak (2004) and all of them are insignificant, which means that this evaluation weighs heavily on conclusions, even after weighting results. Second, 31 estimates stem from US studies, four from a Canadian evaluation and three from a British evaluation. This means that conclusions mainly concern the US.

All in all, it seems safe to assert that the EITC has had a slightly positive impact on working poverty in the US; many claims have been made, however, that the EITC lifts up to four million people out of poverty every year, but these claims probably do not take into account behavioural responses to tax credits, especially disemployment effects on married mothers that are systematically underlined in the evaluations meta-analysed here.

Regarding the Continental cluster, 13 estimates have been identified (unweighted), ten of which are simulations of the introduction of the WFTC, one a simulation of the introduction of the EITC and two are evaluations of the French PPE. As in the Anglo-Saxon cluster, the majority is positive; however, only a minority of estimates point in the direction of a significant effect (four estimates). As shown above, these tax credits are likely not to have any effect on employment (or even a slightly negative one); moreover, they do not seem to have a significant antipoverty impact. All in all, it is relatively safe to say that the introduction of the EITC or of the WFTC in Continental Europe would not have much of an effect.

6.3.4 Conclusions

Based on the evidence meta-analysed in this section, it appears that tax credits for workers have been successful in the UK and the US at increasing female labour force participation, as the increase in single mothers' employment appears to have outweighed the decline in married women's employment. In addition, they appear to have slightly reduced poverty among working families, although probably to a lesser extent than pre-transfer/post-transfer evidence suggests.

Moreover, it appears that the French PPE has had very little effect; if anything, it had a small redistributive impact, but the amounts at stake are too small to have a significant impact.

It is very important to note that the introduction of such credits may not have much effect in Continental Europe; the employment effect might be slightly negative or, more probably, there would not be any effect at all. The antipoverty effect would probably be modest and limited to a small reduction of the poverty gap, rather than of the incidence of poverty. The reasons of this difference are not clearly identified, although some factors mentioned by a few authors could explain these results. First, the earnings and income distributions are narrower in Continental Europe. Second, the situation British and American single mothers faced in the 1990s was particularly unfavourable; in Continental Europe, family policy is more generous, be it in terms of income transfers and of family services (with the notable exception of Southern European countries and Switzerland). Third, these employment-conditional benefits are part of a more general approach of the fight against working poverty that aims at maximizing labour force participation; a part of the system is to have a labour market in which there are enough jobs to be had, especially low-skilled service sector jobs. This is far less the case in Continental European countries than in Anglo-Saxon and Scandinavian countries.

6.4 FAMILY CASH BENEFITS

6.4.1 Existing Literature Reviews

I have not been able to identify a noteworthy literature review, nor did the review of relevant evaluations allow for identifying a research synthesis mentioned by most authors.

6.4.2 Overall Meta-analysis

Again, I used the ISI Web of Knowledge search engine first and used the following keywords:

- family cash benefits (58 hits);
- family allowance(s) (22 hits);
- child allowance(s) (82 hits);
- child benefit(s) (32 hits);
- child poverty (92 hits).

I checked all these hits; this allowed me to identify and retrieve a smaller number of articles than for the policies meta-analysed above. Again, I used the IZA's and the IFAU's search engines with the following keywords: 'child allowances', 'family benefits', 'family policy', 'child benefit', 'poverty', 'child poverty', 'family allowances', which yielded a large number of hits ranging from around 150 to more than 1000 in a few cases. The IZA search engine generated many more hits than the IFAU; for each hit, the engine provides an indicator of relevance that increases with its degree of pertinence. I started with the highest scoring articles and stopped checking abstracts when this relevance indicator amounted to around 2.5, which is the level at which articles no longer have much to do with the employment and antipoverty effects of family cash benefits.

As for previous policies, I also used Google Scholar with the keywords 'family cash policy' (without commas) and got more than 2000 hits. What is striking is that most articles and papers either pertain to the impact of family benefits on fertility or to antipoverty effects measured with a microsimulation model, such as EUROMOD, the tax and benefits simulation model for EU countries, without accounting for behavioural aspects. These simulations are very interesting in order to understand which family types get what amount of money from the state, however, they do not provide estimations of the antipoverty impact among workers, because in order to be able to formulate policy recommendations, one should also take into account possible behavioural responses (Bibi and Duclos, 2008).

Regarding the hits generated by Google Scholar, I reviewed the first 300; from that point onwards, articles and papers did not seem to have any relevance anymore with the topics dealt with in this section.

The large majority of articles regard benefits that are either universal or means-tested, but that do not have an employment condition. Two articles, however, pertain to employment-conditional benefits: one analyses child benefits for working mothers in Spain, while the other one deals with programmes that exist in some Canadian provinces and are partly employment-conditional. Results will be provided with and without these two studies, as it is obvious that employment-conditional benefits may have a different impact on parental work.

6.4.2.1 Employment effects

The overall vote count, including all policies and indicators, yields the results for employment effects shown in Table 6.12.

Table 6.12 Employment effect of family cash benefits, based on all estimates, weighted vote count with sign test

Type of vote count	Majority	Significance of majority
Sign (regardless of significance)	47/66 negative effects	**
Significance (regardless of sign)	36/66 insignificant effects	n.s.
Sign among significant effects	22/29 negative effects	**

Notes: **significant at the 1% level; n.s. not significant at the 5% level.

The employment effect appears to be negative, whereas it is not possible to conclude, based on this global analysis, whether the impact is significant or not. This majority of insignificant findings is relatively small (36 out of 66), however, such that it is probably safe to say that family benefits only have a slight negative impact on employment. As indicated above, clear negative employment effects of social transfers have mainly been observed in the US; in Europe, this trend is far less marked, which may explain this low global impact observed here, as most evaluations concern European countries. Moreover, negative impacts are usually observed for welfare benefits that often constitute an important share of recipients' household income, whereas this is not usually the case for family cash benefits.

6.4.2.2 Antipoverty effects
The number of articles I was able to identify and retrieve is limited, namely seven articles containing 29 estimates.

Table 6.13 Antipoverty effect of family cash benefits, based on all estimates, weighted vote count with sign test

Type of vote count	Majority	Significance of majority
Sign (regardless of significance)	28/29 positive effects	**
Significance (regardless of sign)	15/29 insignificant effects	n.s.
Sign among significant effects	14/14 positive effects	**

Notes: **significant at the 1% level; n.s. not significant at the 5% level.

The sample size is small ($n = 29$), but the available estimates almost unanimously show a positive effect (see Table 6.13). However, it is not possible to say whether the impact is significant or not. Family cash benefits are likely to reduce the incidence of poverty or, at least, they reduce the poverty gap; this means that their antipoverty effect appears to outweigh their slight disemployment effect.

6.4.3 Meta-analysis by Welfare Regime and Further Considerations

Contrary to the policies presented in previous sections, many studies of the impact of family cash benefits are comparative and combine data from conservative and social-democratic countries, as benefits have a similar design in many countries and exist in most EU member states, which facilitate the production of comparative studies. Hence, the analyses by welfare regimes are more limited than in previous sections, because single-country evaluations are less numerous.

6.4.3.1 Employment effects

As a first step, I want to draw conclusions about the employment effects within the liberal cluster. Three studies (two American and one Canadian) have been identified as mainly focusing on the employment effect of TANF and food stamps among families with children or the National Child Benefit in Canada. These evaluations contain 18 estimates, so that the meta-analysis presented here (see Table 6.14) must be interpreted with great caution.

Table 6.14 Employment effect of family cash benefits in the liberal welfare regime, weighted vote count with sign test

Type of vote count	Majority	Significance of majority
Sign (regardless of significance)	12/18 negative	n.s.
Significance (regardless of sign)	11/18 insignificant	n.s.
Sign among significant effects	3/6 inconclusive	n.s.

Note: n.s. not significant at the 5% level.

Unsurprisingly, given the small number of estimates, no majority is significant. The two American studies find negative effects exclusively and are statistically significant for single mothers. The Canadian study finds positive effects as it is, in the provinces under study, based on programmes that are partly employment-conditional.

This vote count can be completed with a review of the evidence found in studies devoted to the EITC and minimum wages that I have meta-analysed above, as many contained the level of TANF benefits (sometimes combined with the Food Stamp Program) as control variables; TANF benefits help low-income families with children. Five American evaluations are virtually unanimous, as 21 out of 22 (unweighted) estimates point to negative employment effects; 14 out of 21 effects are statistically significant.

Finally, one evaluation for the UK shows that the effect of the WFTC expansion was positive, as it increased single mothers' employment rate by 5.95 percentage points; however, the impact of all reforms implemented during that period (including increases in benefits that do not have an employment condition) increased employment by 3.86 points only, which shows that the other reforms reduced the positive impact of the WFTC expansion; indeed, increases in Income Support, one of the UK's main means-tested benefit, dulled the positive labour supply impact of the WFTC (Blundell, 2006).

As far as the conservative cluster is concerned, there is even less evidence available. Weighted results lead to the following conclusions: the direction of the impact is unclear if all evaluations are accounted for (six estimates are positive, six are negative). However, the six positive estimates stem from the evaluation of the Spanish employment-conditional child benefit, which means that the others are unanimously negative. Nine out of 12 findings points to an insignificant effect, but that majority could be an artefact (based on the Z-test). If the Spanish evaluation is removed, all estimates are insignificant. Hence, it is probably fair and safe to say that too little is known about Continental Europe to draw clear-cut conclusions about the employment effects of these benefits, and that more evaluations that include dynamic aspects (rather than static microsimulations) are requested. However, the results presented here suggest that the negative impact of these benefits may be insignificant in Continental Europe or at least very weak, in line with findings pertaining to cash transfers in general presented in Chapter 4. One reason could be the situation of single mothers, as already indicated; another could be the fact that, for low-skilled mothers, there may be fewer jobs to be had in many Continental European countries, as the low-skilled service sector is less developed than in Anglo-Saxon countries and Scandinavia.

Some evidence is also available for Scandinavian countries, but scarce. Of the 12 weighted estimates I could identify, five are negative and four equal zero; eight are statistically insignificant. Hence, the impact may be very slightly negative; however, it is probable that there is no effect at all. In fact, Scandinavian mothers have a very high employment rate, which is partly attributable, as will be shown below, to high work incentives, mainly in the form of available and inexpensive childcare services.

6.4.3.2 Antipoverty effects

The number of estimates is too small to draw conclusions as to the antipoverty effects of family cash benefits at the welfare regime level; moreover, most findings stem from comparative studies.

6.4.4 Conclusions

Family cash benefits, and, indeed, family policy in general, has drawn researchers' interest inasmuch as they have an impact on maternal employment and fertility decisions. They are also included in studies that use static simulation models, that is, they do not include behavioural responses. The microsimulation models used, one of the most widespread being EURO-MOD as it accounts for the tax and benefits system of many EU member states, are very sophisticated tools that provide precious and useful findings regarding the distributive impact of various tax and social policies. They do not, however, allow for policy recommendations, as the generosity of some benefits might reduce maternal employment, especially in countries in which low-skilled mothers face high employment-related and childcare costs.

Overall, these benefits appear to have a negative employment effect in Anglo-Saxon countries, whereas it is difficult to say whether this impact is signficiant or not; on the contrary, the impact appears to be insignificant in Continental Europe, despite usually more 'generous' benefits. Family cash benefits seem to have a positive antipoverty effect, even when employment effects are accounted for.

6.5   CHILDCARE SERVICES

The last policy meta-analysed in this chapter is the provision of childcare services. This policy belongs to the same group of policies as family cash benefits, obviously, in terms of target group. However, these two policy groups (services and cash benefits) differ in their positioning on the main dimensions that underpin the fight against working poverty: whereas family cash benefits are income transfers, childcare policies belong to policies that aim to maximize labour market participation, mainly female participation.

6.5.1   Existing Literature Reviews

Among the articles reviewed here, Kalb (2009) carried out a literature review that summarizes 23 evaluations of the impact of childcare costs on workforce participation published between 1992 and 2007; eight were published in the 1990s and all but one of these older evaluations deal with the American case. The evaluations published in the 2000s include a broader set of countries: the US two, Canada three, Australia three, Germany two, the Netherlands one, France one, Italy one, Japan one, Sweden one and Norway one. The vast majority of the 80 estimates deal with the situation of married mothers, some also analyse single mothers (21 estimates), while four estimates pertain to mothers in general.

The review does not provide information as to the significance of the effects, but indicates elasticities for labour force participation and average number of hours. Virtually all of the estimates are negative, but elasticities vary greatly. For employment elasticities, they range from 0 to 0.92 in absolute value: 23 estimates are smaller than 0.1 and 22 estimates are larger. Put differently, around half these elasticities predict a decrease of employment of less than 1 per cent for a 10 per cent increase in childcare costs, which is a small impact. Regarding the impact of childcare costs on the number of hours, 23 out of 35 elasticities are lower than 0.1 in absolute value: a 10 per cent increase in childcare costs reduces work by less than 1 per cent, which is a very small decrease (24 minutes for a 40-hour work week).

6.5.2   Overall Meta-analysis

The search for evaluations of the impact of childcare costs and availability for the period 2000–2010, with the ISI Web of Knowledge search engine, was based on the following keywords: 'child care' and 'childcare', which led to 744 and 325 hits respectively (I restricted the number of research fields to sociology, economic sciences, political sciences, social work, economics, public administration, social sciences and anthropology; without this restriction, the number of hits was very high and most of them completely irrelevant). I checked abstracts until I had identified around 20 articles dealing with the employment effects of childcare policies. It proved more problematic to find articles measuring the effect childcare services have on poverty. I checked 'child care poverty' (134 hits) and 'childcare poverty' (26 hits), within the same set of research fields in the ISI Web of Knowledge and even 'maternal employment' (143 hits).

Eventually, I also used the IZA and the IFAU search engines, and performed a search based on similar keywords, but also including very broad searches with keywords such as 'poverty', 'child poverty'. I stopped searching for articles when the relevance level of articles reached around 2.5 for the IZA search engine, while I checked all hits generated by the IFAU search engine. Likewise, I used similar keywords with Google Scholar, but quit searching after 400 hits, as papers, reports and articles no longer had much to do with the topic of childcare and poverty.

6.5.2.1   Employment effects
The topic of the employment effects of childcare policies is the one that yielded the highest number of estimates among the policies analysed in this chapter. The figures presented in Table 6.15 pertain both to the availability of childcare (usually the share of children in formal childcare) and its cost.

In a second step, I check if conclusions differ depending on whether it is childcare fees that are reduced or the number of childcare slots that are increased.

Table 6.15 Employment effects of the availability and cost of childcare, based on all estimates, weighted vote count with sign test

Type of vote count	Majority	Significance of majority
Sign (regardless of significance)	125/171 positive effects	**
Significance (regardless of sign)	94/171 significant effects	n.s.
Sign among significant effects	85/94 positive effects	**

Notes: **significant at the 1% level; n.s. majority is not significant at the 5% level.

This overall vote count doubtlessly points to positive employment effects of decreases in childcare fees or increases in the number of childcare slots, and the vast majority of evaluations analyse the situation of mothers. The effect may be significant, whereas the estimates I have gathered do not unambiguously show it (based on a Z-test).

Conclusions are very similar for reductions in childcare fees or increases in the number of childcare slots. Regarding fees reductions, weighted estimates are distributed as follows: 62 out of 93 are positive and 32 out of 37 significant findings are positive; however, 60 out of 97 findings are statistically insignificant. Regarding the impact of childcare availability, likewise, a large majority of estimates are positive (63 out of 72), as well as a majority of significant estimates (53 out of 55 are positive); contrary to childcare fees, however, a large majority of effects are significant (55 out of 72). Overall, it appears, then, that both decreases in childcare fees and increases in availability have a positive impact on maternal employment, and that availability, usually expressed as a percentage of young children in formal childcare, may have a bigger impact than fees.

6.5.2.2 Antipoverty effect
Evaluations of antipoverty effects are in stunning contrast to assessments of the employment impact of childcare policies: the number of estimates I managed to find and retrieve is anecdotal, namely 12 estimates

(unweighted) found in four articles. This is indeed the main conclusion that can be drawn about the antipoverty effect of childcare services: very little evidence has been published in the recent past. Needless to say, no meta-analysis broken down by welfare regime is provided below.

A closer look at unweighted estimates shows that all estimates but one are positive: childcare services, by allowing mothers to work more, probably contribute to the alleviation of poverty. However, as indicated by some authors, the level of childcare fees may contribute to an increase in disposable income inequality if there is a fees cap, as middle-class or high-income families may have to spend less on childcare, in relative terms, than lower-income families.

Chapter 7 will provide indirect evidence about the antipoverty effects of family policy in general, and childcare policy in particular, as my comparative perspective includes countries with both high and low shares of children in formal childcare, and both highly subsidized public childcare and largely private-owned facilities.

6.5.3 Meta-analysis by Welfare Regime and Further Considerations

6.5.3.1 Employment effects

Table 6.16 Employment effects of the availability and cost of childcare in the liberal welfare regime, weighted vote count with sign test

Type of vote count	Majority	Significance of majority
Sign (regardless of significance)	55/85 positive effects	**
Significance (regardless of sign)	49/85 insignificant effects	n.s.
Sign among significant effects	32/37 positive effects	**

Notes: **significant at the 1% level; n.s. not significant at the 5% level.

Estimates found in articles analysing the situation in the liberal welfare regime cluster (see Table 6.16) point to a positive effect of childcare services, but it is difficult to say whether this impact is significant or not. American evaluations mainly deal with programmes that reduce the cost of childcare, as the state is not involved in the creation of publicly funded childcare centres; this kind of evaluation clearly points to positive employment effects of a reduction of childcare fees (15 out of 20 unweighted estimates). Likewise, Australian evaluations measure the impact of fees on maternal employment. It appears that estimates are almost unanimously insignificant; however increases in childcare fees have a negative impact on maternal employment. Overall, then, childcare fees appear to have a negative impact in Australia, but the impact may be very small. One American evaluation pertains to the introduction of universal pre-kindergarten in two states and analyses the impact of eligibility, which is negative but statistically insignificant. Fitzpatrick (2010) explains this surprising result by the fact that comparable women in other states may benefit from childcare subsidies.

There were 67 estimates found in articles that analyse the situation in the province of Quebec, Canada. Quebec introduced a major family policy reform that began in 1997 with the extension of full-time kindergarten to all five-year-olds and the provision of childcare at an out-of-pocket price of CAN$5.00 for all children aged 0–4. The programme was phased in, starting with four-year-olds, then three-year-olds in 1998, followed by all two-year-olds in 1999 and all children younger than two in 2000. Moreover, the number of spaces doubled between 1997 and 2005. The estimates of this increase of coverage and reduction in fees are overwhelmingly positive, except for mothers with no children younger than six and with at least a high school diploma. It should be noted that, given the features of the family policy of the Quebec province, it is debatable whether it really belongs to the liberal cluster on this dimension.

As far as the Continental welfare regime is concerned, the number of estimates is relatively small. They are displayed in the Table 6.17.

Table 6.17 Employment effects of the availability and cost of childcare in the conservative corporatist welfare regime, weighted vote count with sign test

Type of vote count	Majority	Significance of majority
Sign (regardless of significance)	21/26 positive effects	**
Significance (regardless of sign)	19/25 significant effects	**
Sign among significant effects	18/20 positive effects	**

Note: **significant at the 1% level.

The interpretation is clear: increasing the number of childcare slots (or reducing childcare fees, but most estimates assess the impact of the availability of childcare slots) has a significantly positive impact on maternal employment. These results, however, should be interpreted with caution, as the conservative cluster is very heterogeneous here, with results from Germany, Italy and Switzerland (the latter being a rather hybrid 'liberal-conservative' model) (Bonoli, 2003c). These countries have something in common though, namely the fact that their childcare policy is limited. In other Continental countries such as France and Belgium, where childcare services are much more developed, results could have been different. Only one study is based on a Mediterranean country, namely Del Boca and Vuri's (2007) article. Interestingly, they conclude that childcare costs cannot have much effect in the Italian regions where the share of children in formal childcare is very low.

Finally, let us have a look at the social-democratic regime; Nordic countries are the countries in which the share of young children in formal public childcare is highest.

Table 6.18 Employment effects of the availability and cost of childcare in the social-democratic welfare regime, weighted vote count with sign test

Type of vote count	Majority	Significance of majority
Sign (regardless of significance)	9/18 inconclusive	n.s
Significance (regardless of sign)	15/17 insignificant	**
Sign among significant effects	1/2 inconclusive	n.s

Notes: ** majority is significant at the 1% level; n.s. not significant at the 5% level.

It may seem surprising that the impact of childcare policy on employment is not significant in Scandinavia (see Table 6.18); however, all estimates stem from studies that evaluate the impact of the introduction of a fees cap in Sweden. In fact, in a country in which maternal employment was already very high and childcare services already inexpensive, it is not surprising that the introduction of a fees cap did not have much of an impact on female employment; moreover, this measure mainly benefits middle-class and rich households, in which women tend to work more than in low-income families. As far as the direction of the impact is concerned, the evidence is inconclusive; the effect could just as well be positive or negative; it is most probably zero.

6.5.3.2 Antipoverty effect

As indicated above, the number of estimates is far too small to break down the analysis of the antipoverty effects of the cost and availability of childcare slots by welfare regime.

6.5.4 Conclusions

The evidence presented in section 6.5 unambiguously shows that the availability and affordability of childcare slots have a positive impact on maternal employment. Interestingly, the impact varies greatly across countries. In Scandinavia, where mothers have the highest labour market participation rates worldwide and childcare is heavily subsidized and inexpensive, childcare policy reforms are quite unlikely to have a big impact on both employment and poverty levels among working families. By contrast, the situation in countries or regions in which childcare coverage is low and waiting lists in public facilities are long, reforms aimed at reducing childcare fees are also quite unlikely to have any effect on employment; they may, however, improve some working families' disposable income. In these countries, on the contrary, increasing the number of childcare slots is likely to have a notable impact.

A second important conclusion is that the link between childcare policies and poverty has rarely been directly established in the empirical literature. The impact of childcare policy on child poverty is mentioned at times, but it is often taken for granted or indirectly derived from risk-group analyses rather than based on empirical estimates. This is probably due to an implicit assumption: if childcare centres allow mothers to work more and if their cost is reasonable, then, this policy must reduce poverty, one way or another. But this link has rarely been demonstrated. This is certainly an interesting avenue of research that can greatly contribute to the identification of social policies that reduce working poverty.

6.6 WHICH POLICIES WORK IN WHICH WELFARE REGIME?

The liberal cluster is characterized by the existence of minimum wages, usually enforced by law, and of tax credits for workers. These are two aspects of a more global approach often dubbed 'make work pay'. Minimum wages seem to have a limited impact on both employment levels and working poverty, given that they are set at a low level, especially in the US (and with the notable exception of Australia); moreover, their impact also depends on labour market regulations and payroll taxes. Tax credits have fulfilled one of their main goals, namely to increase employment among single mothers, and have contributed to the strategy of maximizing labour force participation. But their impact depends largely on other aspects of the welfare state. The comparison between the UK and the US is very revealing: though the British programme is around twice as generous as its American counterpart, its impact has been more limited, because its increased generosity was accompanied by an increase in other benefits that are not employment-conditional. Moreover, these 'make work pay' policies appear to have reduced poverty, whereas their real impact may have been overestimated by pre-tax and transfer/post-tax and transfer evidence. It should be noted, however, that despite these policies, actual levels of working poverty (presented in the next chapter) remain high by international comparison, which is, at least in part, explained by the relatively low levels of these benefits, especially in the US.

In the conservative corporatist, Continental European regime, the first striking element is that, apart from minimum wages, there have not been, until recently, policies that specifically target the working poor. I have shown in Chapters 2 and 3 that researchers and official bodies acknowledged this phenomenon much more recently than in Anglo-Saxon countries. Some countries, however, have introduced employment-conditional tax credits in the recent past. Yet, simulation results suggest that in Continental Europe tax credits for workers are quite unlikely to have much effect; this is probably due to the fact that the composition of the workforce is different, income inequalities less wide and family policy usually more 'generous' than in the US (and the UK to a lesser extent). Moreover, minimum wages may have a more negative employment impact than in the US, because of higher payroll taxes and a stricter regulation of hiring and firing as well as a more positive antipoverty impact on low-skilled workers, as they are set at higher levels. However, as will be shown below, working poverty is a limited problem in Continental Europe. Family cash benefits contribute to this result, as well as other social transfers, even when potential disemployment effects and negative effects on economic growth are accounted for, as already mentioned above.

Comparing the situation in the US and Canada with Europe, I have not been able to determine, however, the level at which minimum wages could be set so that they can really contribute to the fight against working poverty without creating hurdles in the labour market. I could only reach very broad conclusions: a low minimum wage set at around 35 per cent of gross average earnings combined with low payroll taxes, as is the case in the US, is unlikely to have much of an effect (on either employment or poverty); while a minimum wage set at around 45–7 per cent of gross average wage (that is, an after-tax value of 60 per cent of net average wage), in countries with high payroll taxes and strict hiring and firing regulations, such as France, is likely to have a negative employment impact on low-skilled workers, but a non-negligible antipoverty impact. Indeed, as will be shown below, France's working poor rate is very low, which cannot, however, be solely attributed to its minimum wage.

In Scandinavian countries, there are not specific policies for poor workers, except for minimum wages that are set through collective bargaining. As trade unions represent the vast majority of workers, this bargaining is unlikely to reach wage levels that constitute major obstacles in the labour market. There is, however, little evidence available. Scandinavian countries have generous and expensive family policies, especially in the shape of state-subsidized childcare centres: fees are affordable and waiting lists very short. For this reason, recent reforms, namely the introduction of fees caps, did not have much effect on female employment, for a very simple reason: it had already reached the highest level worldwide. Employment-conditional tax credits have been introduced in Scandinavia in the recent past. I was not able to find, however, any evaluation of these programmes at the time of writing this chapter. But as Scandinavian countries, like Anglo-Saxon countries, aim at maximizing labour market participation, the introduction of these credits might be more successful than in Continental Europe.

Last but not least, for all countries, it is noteworthy that the number of evaluations of the antipoverty impact of family policies that allow policy recommendations is limited, because evaluations usually do not account for dynamic aspects in the case of family cash benefits, while evaluations of the impact of childcare policies focus on their impact on employment and fertility, without paying much attention to distributional effects.

These conclusions pave the way to the next chapter, which deals with the overall impact of welfare regimes on working poverty. In Chapter 5, the main features of welfare regimes and of the four countries that epitomize them have been described. In the next chapter (Chapter 7), I analyse the composition of the working poor population as well as the relative weight of the three working poverty mechanisms across welfare regimes. In addition, the robustness of findings is assessed by using various poverty lines (50 and 60 per cent of median income and consumption levels) and various poverty indicators (headcount and poverty gap).

NOTES

1. As indicated above, some researchers advocate to weight estimates according to their accuracy: the larger the sample, the more accurate the estimate – that is, the smaller the sampling error.
2. It should be noted that, due to the weighting and the fact that numbers are rounded, the number of estimates may vary slightly for various vote counts pertaining to the same social policy (by one or two estimates).
3. This threshold has nothing to do with significance levels of 5 per cent (or 1 per cent) used when I check the assumption that the number of estimates in one category equals the number of estimates in the other category. These significance levels, usually denoted by α in statistics, correspond to the likelihood to reject a null hypothesis that is in fact true (Type I error).
4. The Kaitz index is the ratio of the minimum wage to the average wage.

7. The weight of each working poverty mechanism across welfare regimes

After having assessed the employment and antipoverty effects of each social policy tool identified in the literature as a promising instrument in the fight against working poverty, with an analysis by welfare regime, it is fundamental to measure the overall impact of each welfare regime on working poverty. As indicated above, the social policy instruments analysed in the previous chapters interact with one another; moreover, they co-vary with a broad array of institutional arrangements and their impact depends on the sectoral and sociodemographic composition of the labour market.

This chapter represents the second empirical contribution of this book. First, I provide figures pertaining to working poverty and employment performance in the four countries chosen to illustrate the welfare regimes used in this book (liberal, conservative corporatist, social-democratic and Southern European), and then carry out a 'classical' analysis of the working poor population in terms of risk groups, based on a relative poverty line and headcount ratio. Then, I re-assess my findings by using poverty indicators that account for the depth of poverty, namely the income gap and the poverty gap; finally, I check the robustness of my findings by using another poverty line derived from consumption levels by comparing the situation in three countries for which I have information on both household income and consumption expenditure, namely France, Italy and Switzerland.

Second, I measure the relative weight of each working poverty mechanism, namely getting a low wage rate, having a low degree of labour force attachment and having high needs (especially a high number of dependent children). The combination of both approaches (risk groups and poverty mechanisms) provides an in-depth insight into the topic of the main types of working poverty found in each welfare regime, as well as to the impact specific policy mixes appear to have. Hence, this chapter allows drawing robust conclusions to the following questions: which welfare regime generates which type of working poverty? Which policy mix appears to work in which country?

Two important restrictions must be underlined: first, the analysis presented here does not account for the major economic downturn of the late 2000s, as at the time of writing this book, too little is known about the possible consequences of this deep recession on welfare regimes. It will probably take a few years to allow analysts to fully understand the implications of this massive exogenous shock on welfare states, labour market regulations and the role families play in these difficult times. However, some comments are made, especially for the two countries that have been hit particularly hard, namely the US and Spain.

Second, the analyses presented below mainly describe the situation in the early 2000s and the mid-2000s and the conceptions that were dominant, and sometimes hegemonic, in each welfare regime. This does not mean, however, that every policymaker and every citizen shared these dominant perspectives on social issues, nor that the prevailing conception of the fight against working poverty has always been the same in these countries. For instance, in the US, the 'work-first' approach and explanations of poverty in terms of disincentives to work (rather than structural problems) have become overwhelmingly dominant. The fact that the 1996 welfare reform was implemented by the Democrats is very revealing in this regard. However, this rather conservative conception of social policy has not always been dominant in the US; for instance, the 1900–1919 period has been dubbed the 'progressive era' (Merrien et al., 2005), and the same could be said about the 1960s during the Kennedy and Johnson administrations, when structural explanations of poverty were dominant (Meyer and Holtz-Eakin, 2001). Moreover, welfare reform and 'make work pay' policies are understood differently: for many conservatives, the main aim is to have welfare-deterrent institutions, whereas many liberals prefer the notion of an enabling welfare state (which promotes education, childcare and other measures that allow citizens to work more). Likewise, the situation has changed in Germany since 2000; the Hartz reforms that I have described in Chapter 5 were implemented stepwise, the more recent being a reform of unemployment and social assistance benefits (dubbed Hartz IV). These reforms represent a paradigmatic shift in Germany; however, in the recent past, many have criticized these reforms and advocated, among other things, the introduction of a statutory minimum wage (Müller and Steiner, 2008).

In short, the following sections aim at understanding the impact of a welfare regime at a moment in time, not to account for the history of each welfare regime nor for the power conflicts and different viewpoints that coexisted in the early to mid-2000s. Moreover, since the beginning of the crisis in 2008, the situation has changed significantly in some of these countries, but as indicated it is probably too early to draw conclusions –

once this crisis is over, will the situation be fundamentally different or very similar to the pre-crisis situation? However, this does not play a role here. What matters is to understand the interplay of markets (especially the labour market), the welfare state and families, as well as the mechanisms that lead to working poverty at a given point in time in each regime. If this is done adequately, this provides us with an analytical framework that will allow us to understand the changes that may arise after the current recession.

7.1   THE EXTENT AND COMPOSITION OF THE WORKING POOR POPULATION

7.1.1   The Situation at the Turn of the Millennium

In order to achieve the objectives presented in the introduction of this chapter, I have used Luxembourg Income Study data, Wave V (2000) and Wave VI (mid-2000s). This database provides comparable data-sets for most OECD countries. As its name indicates, the aim of this database is to provide detailed and comparable information on household income. A complicated issue concerns the definition of disposable income, that is, the income a household has at its disposal once social security contributions and taxes have been paid and cash benefits received. As the tax and benefits system varies from country to country, this poses very challenging difficulties for comparative research. However, the Luxembourg Income Study allows this kind of analysis, because it provides a measure of disposable income that is comparable across countries. Data are derived from national surveys and the most important variables (for the analysis of the financial situation of households) are made as comparable as possible.

Moreover, the Luxembourg Income Study contains the variables that are necessary for the analysis of the three working poverty mechanisms I have presented previously: individual wage rates, the volume of work performed, household size and composition, the age of household members, as well as their status within the household (head of household, spouse, other status).

Some important and tricky empirical difficulties must be highlighted though. First, the working poor (luckily) represent a small share of the labour force in post-industrial countries. The labour force itself does not include a large minority of the population (retirees and other non-active persons). In addition, in all surveys dealing with the financial situation of households, income questions inevitably yield non-response rates that are not marginal. All this indicates is that large samples are requested; otherwise results would not be statistically reliable, due to large confidence intervals. This excludes many comparative databases from the outset; the Luxembourg Income Study, fortunately, contains national samples that are large enough.

Second, some of the Swedish data used here date back to the mid-1990s wave, because in Wave V (2000) many variables related to the volume of work were not available. As no other Scandinavian data-set contains these variables either, be it for Wave V or Wave VI, we have to settle for Sweden 1995 to calculate the degree of labour force attachment and the share of low-wage workers among the working poor, which is certainly an important drawback.

Third, the number of children under the age of 14, which is an important variable when the modified OECD equivalence scale is used, is not available in the 1995 Swedish data-set; hence, a weight of 0.3 instead of 0.5 has been attributed to children between the ages of 14 and 17 years old, which means that for a small minority of households the equivalized income might be slightly overestimated. In the analyses below, the Swedish child-to-adult ratio among the working poor is calculated with 2000 data, in which the number of children under the age of 14 is available. It should be added that the situation in Sweden in the mid-1990s was quite grim, as the unemployment rate soared and reached rates as high as 8 per cent, a very unusual level for Sweden. At the turn of the century, however, the Swedish economy was back on track (Halleröd and Larsson, 2008). Hence, Swedish results based on the 1995 data-set have to be interpreted with some caution, while the other countries' results do not cause any major concern.

I first assess the extent of working poverty (the poverty status is defined as having a household income below half of median disposable equivalized income, whereas the at-risk-of-poverty line is set at 60 per cent of median income), with two definitions of 'working', namely active at the time of the interview, which is the approach I advocate, and being active as the main activity status over the income reference period (see Table 7.1).

The evolution of the working poor rates between 2000 and the mid-2000s is shown in Table 7.5 below. These figures can usefully be completed with information on wages and employment performance (see Table 7.2).

The working poor rate in the US is approximately twice as high as in Sweden[1] and Germany, based on a relative poverty line, namely an income below 50 per cent of median equivalent disposable income. The difference between Germany and Sweden is not marked, but other calculations based on other data-sets confirm that the working poor rate is slightly lower in Germany than in Sweden (Lohmann and Marx, 2008). Spain's working poor rate is approximately halfway between the US and the tandem Sweden/Germany.

Table 7.1 Working poor rate, at-risk-of-poverty rate among workers and poverty rate, in 2000, in the US, Spain, Germany and Sweden (in per cent)

	Working poor rate (person is active at the time of the interview)	Working poor rate (personal status over reference period is 'employed')	At-risk-of-poverty rate among workers (active at time of interview)	At-risk-of-poverty rate among workers (employed over reference period)	Poverty rate (regardless of work status)
US	7.2	6.0	11.4	10.0	17.0
Spain	6.1	4.1	10.1	8.1	14.2
Germany	4.5	2.9	7.3	5.0	8.4
Sweden	n/a	3.1	n/a	5.3	6.6

Note: poverty rates in the last column from Luxembourg Income Study (LIS) Key Figures, as of 12 October 2008.

Source: Luxembourg Income Study (LIS), own calculations.

Table 7.2 Employment and unemployment rates and low-wage incidence in 2000 in the US, Spain, Germany and Sweden (in per cent)

Country	Harmonized unemployment rate	Employment rate	Low-wage incidence
US	4.0	74.1	24.7
Spain	11.1	57.4	16.2
Germany	7.5	65.6	12.9
Sweden	5.6	74.2	6.1

Source: OECD website, labour statistics and country statistical profiles, as of 6 June 2009.

As indicated in Chapter 5, however, the use of an absolute poverty line yields differences that are much less marked between North America and Europe, and the highest poverty rates are found in Mediterranean countries (Kenworthy, 1999; Notten and De Neubourg, 2007); hence, I would probably get smaller differences between the US and the tandem Germany/

Sweden in terms of working poverty should I use an absolute poverty line adjusted with purchasing power parities (PPP).

Table 7.2 clearly demonstrates that the US and Sweden exhibited, in 2000, the best labour market performances, and this was also the case in the mid-2000s (figures not shown). Yet, the incidence of low-wage employment is much higher in the US than in Europe and wide differences exist among the EU countries analysed here.

In what follows, the 60 per cent of median income threshold is used, due to the small number of cases obtained in most countries with a threshold set at 50 per cent of median income.[2] Hence, the working poor are individuals who are active at the time of the interview and live in a household with an equivalized disposable income below 60 per cent of median income.

Now that the extent of poverty among workers has been measured for each country, it is important to analyse the sociodemographic composition of the working poor population. Given the important role family policy appears to play, it seems natural to look at the differences in terms of gender, household composition and size, and age. As far as wage rates are concerned, gender, age and the educational level play a decisive role. Regarding labour force attachment, gender, age, educational level and household composition are also likely to play an important role. The incidence of working poverty among these sociodemographic groups is shown in Table 7.3.

Table 7.3 Working poor rate among various sociodemographic groups, 2000, in per cent, as well as mean/median age and household type among the working poor

	US	Germany	Spain	Sweden
Age				
16–25	17.3	18.6	11.6	17.9
26–35	12.4	7.7	7.4	5.3
36–45	11.1	5.4	12.3	4.1
46–55	7.7	3.5	11	2.7
56–65	8	3.7	10.6	2.3
Mean age	36	33.9	38.3	33.9
Median age	35	30	39	30
Gender				
Men	11	6.2	10.7	5.2

Table 7.3 continued

	US	Germany	Spain	Sweden
Women	11.9	8.6	9.3	5.3
Household type				
Single	12.9	16.1	13.4	11.6
Childless couple	5.4	3.1	5.5	2.3
Couple 1 child	7.8	4.1	9.6	2.6
Couple 2 children	11.1	4.3	14.8	3.1
Couple 3+ children	24.1	9.8	34.8	5.5
Lone parent 1 child	21.1	24.2	29.8	9.3
Lone parent 2 children	30.9	46.1	44	9.2
Lone parent 3+ children	57.3	51.1	85.7	8
Mean household size	3.6	2.2	3.8	2.1
Median household size	3	2	4	1
Educational level				
Low (ISCED 1 and 2)	27.5	13.1	16.6	6.2
Medium (ISCED 3 and 4)	11.3	6.5	5.0	5.6
High (ISCED 5 and 6)	4.1	3.6	2.5	3.7

Source: Luxembourg Income Study (LIS), own calculations.

German and Swedish poor workers are young. The median disadvantaged worker in these two countries is five years younger than in the US and nearly a decade younger than his or her Spanish counterpart. In Sweden, most low-income workers escape poverty early, as the working poor rate plummets after 25 years of age. This is also reflected in the fact that the median poor worker in Sweden lives alone, whereas the median household size amounts to two among the German working poor, despite the identical median age. This difference is probably attributable to the very high female labour market participation rate in Sweden: young adults are more likely to escape working poverty as soon as they live with a partner, which is less likely to be the case in Germany.

In the US, on the contrary, working poverty appears to be a longer lasting problem in a life-course perspective, as the rate does not decline markedly until after the age of 45 years. The Spanish case is interesting, as it displays a peculiar pattern. Teenagers and young adults are not, contrary to the other countries, harder hit by working poverty than middle-aged people. On the contrary, the working poor rate reaches its highest level between 36 and 45 years of age and hardly declines afterwards. This may be due, in part, to the very peculiar labour market integration pattern of young adults. As most of them work on short-term contracts until their thirties, they keep on living with their parents, as indicated above, until they are able to obtain an open-ended work contract. Hence, leaving the parental home as late as in their mid-thirties is not unusual.

In terms of gender, differences between men and women are slight, a relatively well-known finding (Andress and Lohmann, 2008). This may appear as a paradox at first, as women tend to be more exposed to poverty in general, as well as to low-wage employment. The reason is mainly due to the definition of the phenomenon: a working woman is much more likely to have a working partner than a male worker. In many poor families, especially in countries with lower female employment levels, the husband will be classified as a working poor whereas his non-working wife will not. In the Spanish case, indeed, men are more likely to be working poor, as the employment participation gap between men and women, despite a strong reduction in recent years, is still marked.

Regarding the working poverty risk broken down by household type, it appears that family policy in a general sense is an absolutely decisive factor. In the two countries with a limited family policy (namely the US and Spain), the working poor rate of couples strongly increases after the birth of the second and subsequent children, whereas it is lower than 10 per cent even for large families in Germany and Sweden, that is, in the two countries in which parental-leave schemes and family cash benefits are more generous. Childcare services are also more developed, whereas this is much more the case in Sweden than in Germany.

Another finding is striking: whereas a divorce or a breakup leading to lone parenthood is a decisive factor in the US and Spain, as well as in Germany despite its relatively generous family policy, it is far less the case in Sweden. Indeed, whereas working poor rates are staggeringly high among single mothers with more than one child in most countries, it does not exceed 10 per cent among Swedish single parents, due to their very high employment rates. Of course, the confidence intervals are likely to be large for these sub-groups of lone mothers with two children and more, but even a margin of error of ± 10 per cent would not affect the interpretation, as differences are extremely marked. This shows that the choice between a family policy largely based on passive income transfers as in Germany and a family policy largely based on the provision of services as is the case in Sweden leads to different outcomes.

The large difference observed between couples with children in the US and Spain, on one hand, and Germany and Sweden, on the other, is reflected in the fact that German and Swedish disadvantaged workers are notably younger and that households affected by working poverty are much larger in the US (the median working poor household has three members) and in Spain (the median size is four persons) than in Germany (the median equals two members) and Sweden (at least half of Sweden's low-income workers live alone).

Finally, and unsurprisingly, workers with a high educational level are less likely to suffer from income deprivation than persons with an intermediate, secondary level and far less likely than those with a low educational level. However differences in labour market regulation and structure are visible. In the US, a country in which hiring and firing is lightly regulated (except against discriminatory behaviours) and the sector of low-productivity, low-wage personal services large, the disadvantage of the low-skilled worker is marked, with a working poor rate 2.5 times higher than among workers with a secondary education level. In Spain, the difference is even larger than in the US, as the incidence of low income among workers with a primary educational level is three times higher than among secondary-level workers. In a country in which most women either work full-time or not at all, social endogamy might have a particularly strong impact: low-skilled workers are more likely to have a non-employed partner than higher skilled workers. Moreover, some low-wage sectors such as the tourism industry and agriculture are major employers of low-skilled workers in Spain.

The difference between educational levels is less marked in Germany, a country in which collective bargaining has led to high wage levels. Still, the risk of being a low-income worker is twice as high among the low skilled. It should be kept in mind that the data-set used here dates back to 2000; that is, before the Hartz reforms were introduced. It is not impossible that the gap between primary-level and secondary-level workers has grown larger with the development of low-wage employment (the so-called 'mini-jobs' and 'midi-jobs') encouraged by some of the reforms presented previously. In the case of Sweden, the earnings distribution is very compressed and many low-skilled employees, especially women, work for the government (Esping-Andersen, 1993), so that the group of low-skilled workers is not particularly hit by poverty or unemployment. Indeed, the working poor rate is very low among persons without a secondary or tertiary educational attainment, namely 6.2 per cent, and the difference with higher level workers is small (5.6 per cent for those with a secondary educational level and 3.7 for those who have a tertiary-level diploma).

Before moving on to robustness checks, let us see whether the situation changed between 2000 and the mid-2000s.

7.1.2 The Evolution of the Working Poor Rate Between the Turn of the Millennium and the Mid-2000s

Have things changed notably between the early and the mid-2000s? Table 7.4 contains the same figures as Table 7.1, but for the mid-2000s. However, the Swedish figures are not provided here; first, because the current employment status is still not available in the 2005 data-set and, more importantly, because the variable 'main activity status over the reference period' was modified between Wave V and Wave VI. Table 7.5 displays the evolutions in per cent.

Table 7.4 Working poor rate and at-risk-of-poverty rate among workers and poverty rate, in 2004, in the US, Spain and Germany (in per cent)

	Working poor rate (person is active at the time of the interview)	Working poor rate (personal status over reference period is 'employed')	At-risk-of-poverty rate among workers (active at time of interview)	At-risk-of-poverty rate among workers (employed over reference period)	Poverty rate (regardless of work status)
US	7.5	6.2	11.8	10.4	17.3
Spain	7	6.2	11	9.8	14.1
Germany	4	3	7.7	6.3	8.5

Note: poverty rates in the last column from Luxembourg Income Study (LIS) Key Figures, as of 12 October 2008.

Source: Luxembourg Income Study (LIS), own calculations.

Table 7.5 Evolution between 2000 and 2004

	Working poor rate (person is active at the time of the interview)	Working poor rate (personal status over reference period is 'employed')	At-risk-of-poverty rate among workers (active at time of interview)	At-risk-of-poverty rate among workers (employed over reference period)	Poverty rate (regardless of work status)
US	4%	3%	4%	4%	2%
Spain	15%	55%	9%	23%	–1%
Germany	–11%	3%	5%	26%	1%

Source: Luxembourg Income Study (LIS), own calculations.

In the US, there has been a slight increase in working poverty in the early 2000s, whatever the definition used; while the 1990s was a very prosperous decade, the first half of the 2000s has been characterized by economic stagnation. In Spain, the increase in working poverty has been much stronger, especially for those who have spent most of the reference period in employment, with an increase that ranges from 23 to 55 per cent. Interestingly, however, overall poverty has remained virtually unchanged (–1 per cent). This might be due to the relatively strong increase in median income, especially among workers; however, even absolute poverty lines, namely 50 and 60 per cent of median income (at 1990 level) kept constant in real terms with the national consumer price index, lead to similar conclusions – working poverty increased by 23 and 35 per cent respectively (own calculations). This evolution probably marks the end of what was called the 'Spanish miracle' at that time, namely the strong economic performance that characterized the period from the mid-1990s to the mid-2000s.

The German case is very interesting. The first half of the 2000s was characterized, as analysed in Chapter 5, by far-reaching reforms that aimed at the flexibilization of the labour market. A large number of 'mini jobs' and 'midi jobs' were created and earnings inequalities increased; the ratio of the fifth to the bottom earnings decile increased from 1.79 in 2000 to 1.95 in 2005 (OECD website, labour statistics). The Gini coefficient increased from 0.27 to 0.3. Interestingly, this evolution did not affect those with a very low income (below 50 per cent of the median), whereas the share of workers with an income below the 60 per cent cut-off did increase, especially among workers who have a high labour force attachment (+26 per cent in four

years). Despite this increase, German working poverty rates remained low
by international comparison.

So far, my analysis has relied on the headcount ratio; the next section is
based on an alternative poverty indicator.

7.2   DEPTH OF POVERTY

As indicated in Chapter 2, the present work focuses on monetary definitions of poverty, as they appear to be more useful for social policy purposes.
So far, I have only used the headcount ratio. It is, however, advisable to use
alternative monetary indicators. Important dimensions must be added to
the analysis, namely the income gap and the poverty gap: not only is it
important to know how many workers have an income below the poverty
line in a given year, but it also matters a great deal whether disadvantaged
workers have, on average, an income that is slightly below the threshold or,
on the contrary, way below it. Moreover, taking into account the depth of
poverty may affect country rankings.

In short, not only is it important to know how many people are poor, but
also how poor they are. The mean and median income gap ratios are shown
in Table 7.6.

*Table 7.6 Mean and median income gap ratios, expressed as a percentage of
the poverty line, 2000*

	US	Germany	Spain	Sweden
Mean income gap	29%	27%	29%	27%
Median income gap	24%	21%	24%	24%

Source: Luxembourg Income Study (LIS), own calculations.

The mean income gap ratio is highest in the US: on average, poor workers in
the US have an income 29 per cent lower than the poverty line. Put
differently, not only is the incidence of working poverty highest in the US,
but the income gap is also deepest. The mean and median income gap are
similar in Spain, but as the incidence of working poverty is lower than in the
US, the poverty gap – that is, the product of the headcount ratio and the
income gap ratio – is lower in Spain. The mean income gap ratio is identical

in Germany and Sweden, whereas the median is lower in Germany. Overall, the country ranking is unaffected by the inclusion of the depth of poverty, but the distance between countries grows bigger, as the countries with the highest incidence of working poverty display the highest income gap.

Looking at income gaps, and, hence, at poverty gaps, does not fundamentally affect conclusions regarding the distribution of the poverty risk among various sub-groups of workers (see Table 7.7).

Table 7.7 Income gap (average income of poor workers as a share of the poverty line) and poverty gap (headcount ratio*income gap), 2000

	US		Germany		Spain		Sweden	
	Income gap	Poverty gap	Income gap	Poverty gap	Income gap	Poverty gap	Income gap	Poverty gap
Age								
16–25	29%	5	30%	5.6	31%	3.6	27%	4.8
26–35	28%	3.5	32%	2.5	28%	2.1	27%	1.4
36–45	28%	3.1	22%	1.2	29%	3.6	22%	0.9
46–55	27%	2.1	22%	0.8	31%	3.4	25%	0.7
56–65	33%	2.6	23%	0.9	30%	3.2	42%	1
Gender								
Men	28%	3.1	28%	1.7	27%	2.9	28%	1.5
Women	29%	3.5	26%	2.2	33%	3.1	26%	1.4
Household type								
Single	32%	4.1	35%	5.6	42%	5.6	32%	3.7
Childless couple	30%	1.6	21%	0.7	23%	1.3	29%	0.7
Couple 1 child	26%	2	17%	0.7	30%	2.9	23%	0.6
Couple 2+ children	26%	4.1	20%	1.1	30%	5.4	19%	0.7
Single parent 1 child	28%	5.9	27%	6.5	32%	9.5	22%	2
Single parent 2+ children	32%	13	24%	11.2	33%	17.5	12%	1.1

	US		Germany		Spain		Sweden	
	Income gap	Poverty gap	Income gap	Poverty gap	Income gap	Poverty gap	Income gap	Poverty gap
Educa-tional level								
Low	30%	8.3	26%	3.4	29%	4.8	27%	1.7
Medium	28%	3.2	27%	1.8	27%	1.4	27%	1.5
High	27%	1.1	29%	1	39%	1	27%	1

Source: Luxembourg Income Study (LIS), own calculations.

The ranking of sociodemographic groups based on the poverty gap is identical to the ranking derived from the headcount ratios in the US and Germany. In Spain, the difference between men and women is reversed: whereas the incidence of working poverty is higher among men, women have a notably deeper income gap, and, hence, a larger poverty gap. In Sweden, men and women display a virtually identical working poor rate, but the income gap for women is slightly narrower. A closer look at age groups shows that, as young people display above average income gaps and poverty rates, their disadvantage is even more marked when the poverty gap is used as a poverty indicator.

Regarding household type, not only are lone parents much more likely to be hit by poverty, they also have above-average income gaps, which means that they appear to be the most disadvantaged household type in terms of poverty gaps. It is noteworthy, however, that Swedish lone mothers display below-average income gaps, probably due to their very high labour market participation rates. Single people also display high poverty gaps in all countries. Conclusions pertaining to couples with children vary widely across welfare regimes: in Germany and Sweden, thanks to generous family policies, these households have notably below-average income gaps; it is also the case in the US, despite a limited family policy, probably owing to a high labour market participation among parents, but the difference is less marked. In Spain, on the contrary, parents living in a couple display income gap ratios that are close to those of single parents.

As to the impact of the educational level, low-skilled workers have above-average income gaps in the US and Spain, which increases their disadvantage, whereas this is not the case in Sweden and Germany.

All in all, conclusions drawn from the analysis of headcount ratios are not fundamentally altered when the depth of poverty is accounted for; however, some disadvantaged groups that have an above-average working-poverty risk appear even worse off in terms of the poverty gap.

7.3   ROBUSTNESS CHECKS WITH A CONSUMPTION POVERTY LINE

Another way to set a monetary poverty line is to use consumption expenditures rather than income. Studies have shown that the overlap between income poverty and consumption poverty is only partial; in the case of Australia, for instance, the correlation coefficient between income and consumption expenditures is only $r = 0.52$ (Headey et al., 2009). Unfortunately, none of the national data-sets used in the previous sections contains consumption expenditure data. Hence, an attempt has been made to find countries that are more or less comparable to the four countries analysed so far for which consumption data are available. It proved impossible to find a Scandinavian country filling this criterion. For the Southern European cluster, Italy contains the necessary variables for the purpose at hand. For the Continental conservative cluster, French data are available. Within the liberal cluster, the US database does not contain consumption expenditure data, nor do the Canadian, Australian, UK and Irish databases. A country that has at least some features in common with Anglo-Saxon countries is Switzerland, with its lightly regulated labour market (according to the OECD, Switzerland is the non-Anglo-Saxon country with the least regulated labour market), its reliance on public-private partnerships (pensions, healthcare and so on) and its low level of spending on family policy. However, many aspects of Switzerland's welfare regime are rather comparable to other Continental countries. Hence, Switzerland can be seen as an in-between, 'liberal-conservative' case (Bonoli, 2003c).

In what follows, due to common data limitations in the Luxembourg Income Study data-sets, the current labour force status was used to identify the French and the Swiss working poor; in the Italian database, however, this variable does not exist and the main labour force status during the income reference period was used. Being poor is defined as having an income or consumption expenditures below 60 per cent of the median level; both values are standardized with the modified OECD scale. Table 7.8 shows the incidence of income and consumption poverty in the three countries analysed in this section.

Table 7.8 Working poverty rates according to the type of monetary poverty threshold used, 2000

	Consumption poverty			Income poverty		
	France	Italy	Switzer-land	France	Italy	Switzer-land
At-risk-of-poverty among workers (60%)	8.5	8.7	8.7	5.6	9.7	6.5
Working poverty (50%)	4.6	4.6	4.2	2.5	6.2	4.3

Source: Luxembourg Income Study (LIS), own calculations.

In Switzerland and France, the working poor rate is higher when a consumption poverty line is used. This may mean that the distribution of consumption expenditure is more unequal than the income distribution in Continental Europe; the opposite appears to be true of the Southern European country analysed here (Italy), as the incidence of working poverty is slightly lower when based on consumption expenditures. Italy's figures are based on those who were active in the labour market for most of the reference period, which means that consumption poverty would be higher if workers with a looser connection to the labour market were included.

Let us now have a closer look at the sociodemographic composition of the group of low-consumption workers and compare it to that of low-income workers, in order to assess the robustness of the findings presented in previous sections. Table 7.9 contains working poor rates measured with an income threshold, whereas Table 7.10 contains the same risk-group analysis based on consumption poverty.

Table 7.9 Income poverty risk among workers, broken down by age, gender, household type and educational level, 2000, in per cent

	France	Italy	Switzerland
Age			
16–25	9.7	10.9	7.9
26–35	4.7	7.2	6.1
36–45	5.7	10.7	6.5
46–55	5.1	10.9	5.5
56–65	4.5	9.7	7.8
Gender			
Men	6.1	12.6	6.9
Women	5.1	4.8	6
Household type			
Single	7.5	3.7	5.6
Childless couple	2.9	3.4	2.4
Couple 1 child	5	10.2	4
Couple 2 children	5.6	15.8	7.9
Couple 3+ children	10.8	33.8	20.9
Lone parent 1 child	9.5	7.1	7.6
Lone parent 2 children	19.1	12.8	21.9
Lone parent 3+ children	17.4	–	40.5
Educational level			
Low	9.6	16.4	11.2
Medium	5.1	5.4	6.3
High	2.2	1.8	4.1
Total	5.6	9.7	6.5

Source: Luxembourg Income Study (LIS), own calculations.

In all three countries, younger workers have an above-average poverty risk. Switzerland displays a peculiar pattern: workers aged 55 years and over are more exposed to poverty than middle-aged workers. Couples with at least two children are more exposed to poverty – but much less so in France, which is probably attributable to a generous family policy – as well as single parents. The difference between men and women is not very marked in Switzerland and France, but surprisingly large in Italy.

Let us now see if these conclusions in terms of risk groups are robust to the use of a poverty line derived from consumption expenditures, by comparing Table 7.9 and Table 7.10.

Table 7.10 Consumption poverty among workers, broken down by age, gender, household type and educational level, 2000, in per cent

	France	Italy	Switzerland
Age			
16–25	8.9	12.9	11.1
26–35	7.7	6.7	6.5
36–45	9.2	9.2	8
46–55	8.2	8.2	8.6
56–65	10	10.2	10.1
Gender			
Men	9.2	10.5	9.4
Women	7.7	5.6	7.8
Household type			
Single	9.7	8.9	4.3
Childless couple	5.4	2.8	4.8
Couple 1 child	4.9	8.8	8.1
Couple 2 children	9.8	10.3	10.3
Couple 3+ children	13.3	21.2	22.8
Lone parent 1 child	13.7	5.7	12
Lone parent 2 children	14.6	24.7	12.4

Table 7.10 continued

	France	Italy	Switzerland
Lone parent 3+ children	28.2	–	34.4
Educational level			
Low	15.9	13.6	14.4
Medium	7.5	5.9	9.1
High	2.4	2.2	3.7
Total	8.5	8.7	8.7

Source: Luxembourg Income Study (LIS), own calculations.

Most findings are comparable to the conclusions obtained with income-based poverty lines. Gender differences are hardly modified; in Italy, however, the gender gap is narrower with a consumption-based poverty threshold. Regarding the situation of household types, there is never more than a one-rank change between the income-based and consumption-based rankings, except for single people in Switzerland and lone mothers with children in Italy, who both move two ranks. The ranking of educational levels is unaffected, whereas differences are less marked with income than with consumption levels.

There is, however, a factor that is affected by switching from an income threshold to a consumption poverty line, namely the impact of age. In terms of rankings, in all three countries, the groups most affected by consumption poverty are people under 26 years and over 55 years; whereas the younger age group is also the hardest hit by income poverty, older workers appear to be among the least affected by income poverty in France and Italy. In Switzerland, older workers are more affected by working poverty both in terms of income and consumption levels; however, the difference is less marked when measured with consumption levels.

Overall, then, using a consumption poverty line does not fundamentally modify conclusions about most risk groups in Continental European and Mediterranean countries, as well as in countries with a lightly regulated labour market and a limited family policy. However, the extent of the phenomenon is affected by this definitional change, which appears to be largely due to changes among age groups.

The difference is marked for older workers, who appear to spend less than middle-aged workers; this may not reflect, however, lower living standards. Indeed, most workers aged 55 years and over have had at least 30 years to build-up savings, to buy a house and other durables; this could explain their lower consumption expenditures. In this regard, it is certainly advisable to carry out the same analysis with non-monetary indicators to better understand the situation of senior workers. Unfortunately, Luxembourg Income Study data do not contain indicators that allow a direct measurement of living conditions, but this is doubtlessly an interesting avenue for future working poverty analyses.

Finally, a cautionary note is of order here: consumption measurement is not, obviously, the core of the Luxembourg Income Study and indicators may be less comparable than income variables. Moreover, it is more difficult to collect expenditure data, as it is not possible to do it in a standard survey format (Headey et al., 2009). Swiss and French consumption data are derived from household budget surveys, whereas Italian data stem from a survey on income and wealth, which may partly explain differences between France and Switzerland on the one hand, and Italy on the other hand.

7.4 WORKING POVERTY MECHANISMS ACROSS WELFARE REGIMES

The sociodemographic composition of the population affected by working poverty varies from country to country, as shown above. This is due to the fact that the weight of each mechanism that leads to working poverty differs from one country to another; measuring these variations is the object of this section.

Based on the analysis of the four countries presented in Chapter 5, I formulate the following hypotheses: in social-democratic welfare states I do not expect any of the three mechanisms to be particularly strong. Working poverty should be a quantitatively limited phenomenon. In Anglo-Saxon countries, I expect working poverty to be mostly the result of low wages and high children to adult ratios. Low labour force attachment should play a less important role. In conservative corporatist welfare states (Continental Europe), working poverty will be mostly the result of low labour force attachment, and working poverty should also be less widespread. In Southern European welfare states, working poverty should mostly be the result of low labour force attachment and high children to adult ratio.

7.4.1 The Relative Weight of the Three Mechanisms Leading to Working Poverty across Welfare Regimes

My first aim is to assess the relative weight of the three mechanisms outlined above and to verify whether the impact of each factor differs from one welfare regime to the other, by comparing the situation of poor and non-poor workers in each country under review. Second, the main features of each welfare regime that explain, at least partly, the weight and impact of each working poverty mechanism will be identified. I compare the mean and median values of labour force attachment and child-to-adult ratio, as well as the incidence of (hypothetical) low full-time year-round earnings as a proxy for the remuneration rate of a wage-earner. The three mechanisms are operationalized as follows.

1.   *Low hourly earnings.* The most intuitive mechanism leading to work-ing poverty is the fact of being badly paid. However, several research-ers have pointed out that low wages alone are seldom the cause of working poverty (Andress and Lohmann, 2008; Nolan and Marx, 2000; Peña-Casas and Latta, 2004; Strengmann-Kuhn, 2003). How-ever, few will object that being paid a low wage vastly increases the risk of ending up in working poverty. I operationalize the notion of low wages by taking into account the number of hours usually worked, as well as the number of weeks spent in the labour market over the income reference period, leading to the calculation of hypo-thetical 'full-time year round earnings' (FTYRE). Half median FTYRE is used as a low-wage threshold. This indicator (low pay in full-time year round equivalents) is calculated for all household members who are wage-earners.

2.   *Low labour force attachment.* This mechanism is proteiform and hits underemployed and intermittent workers, as well as persons, usually women, who cannot or are not willing to work more due the presence of children in the household. The rise in double earnership observed in most OECD countries puts families with a non-working spouse in a relatively more difficult situation than during the post-war years, when single-earnership was the norm. I focus on heads of households (according to the Luxembourg Income Study's terminology) and their spouses (if any) aged between 18 and 65. In most cases, this corresponds exactly to the number of potential workers in a house-hold. In some cases, however, there may be working adult children who are not taken into account. This should not lead to a large distortion of results for the US, Germany and Sweden, but could be problematic for Spain, as most Spaniards live with their parents until they are in their thirties. I get back to this point below, when discuss-ing country profiles.

     For example, a couple with children where one parent works full-time and the other one has a half-time job will have a labour force attachment of 0.75 (1.5 full-time equivalents/two adults = 0.75).

3. *High needs, especially a large number of dependent children in the household.* Most studies show that having many children can lead to poverty. Having a third or a fourth child is a dangerous choice for a couple to make, in terms of poverty risk. The same number of children is more likely to lead to poverty for one-parent families than for two-parent families. In fact, after a breakup or a divorce, even just two children may become problematic, because the needs of the two resulting households (usually the ex-husband who lives alone and the mother with the children, most of the time) increase significantly. What matters, as a result, is not the absolute number of children in a household, but rather the ratio of children to adults. For this reason, I operationalize this mechanism by dividing the number of children by the number of working-age adults (18–65 years). A family of four (two parents and two children) will have a child-to-adult ratio of one, just like a single parent with one child. A family of five (two parents and three children) will have a child-to-adult ratio of 1.5.

7.4.1.1 Low-wage rate

Even if low earnings spontaneously appear as the main, if not the only, cause of working poverty, many researchers have highlighted the fact that these two phenomena differ. It is, hence, fundamental to evaluate the weight of this factor. Figure 7.1 is very revealing in this regard.

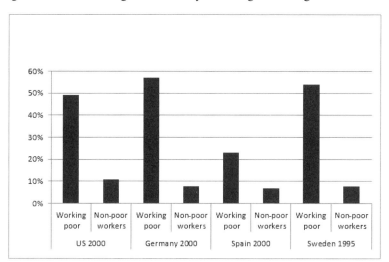

Source: Luxembourg Income Study (LIS), own calculations.

Figure 7.1 Share of workers with 'full-time year round earnings' below 50 per cent of the median

Even if the relationship between low-wage employment and working poverty is far from straightforward, my conclusion is clear-cut: being on low wage-rate employment seems to be an important factor everywhere, whereas the difference is less marked in Spain. Interestingly, the incidence of low FTYRE is not higher in the US than in Sweden, for instance, despite a much higher incidence of low-wage employment in the US. However, as the incidence of working poverty is much higher in the US than in Sweden, the share of the workforce made up of poor workers on low-wage employment is noticeably higher. In addition, the working poor in Sweden and Germany are notably younger, that is, in age brackets in which the incidence of low-wage employment is high.

7.4.1.2   Low labour force attachment

The labour force attachment at the household level is expressed as the ratio of the volume of work performed by the head of household and his or her spouse (if any) to their full work potential, namely a full-time job for each partner. Figure 7.2 compares poor and non-poor workers, both in terms of median and mean work attachment.

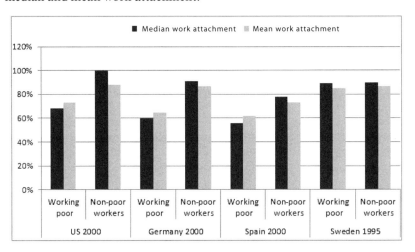

Source: Luxembourg Income Study (LIS), own calculations.

Figure 7.2 Median and mean work attachment expressed in per cent of the full work potential

The level of labour force attachment seems to be a mechanism of working poverty everywhere, except in Sweden, where poor and non-poor workers have similar employment levels, which at first may seem counterintuitive. I get back to this fact in the section devoted to country profiles. Sweden and the US are the countries in which low-income active persons work the most (Sweden exhibiting the highest levels) while the labour force attachment is lower in Germany and lowest in Spain. In all countries but Sweden, mean labour force attachment is slightly higher than the median, the difference being largest in Spain.

7.4.1.3   High number of children relative to the number of working-age adults

This indicator produces more surprising results at first sight. It should be noted that in all four countries the median non-poor worker does not have children – more precisely at least half of them do not live with children (a divorced father who does not live with his children, for instance, has a child-to-adult ratio of zero).

Let us now consider the mean number of children per adult. In the US and in Spain, it is an important working poverty factor, as the mean value is notably higher among the working poor (more than twice as high in the US, 86 per cent higher in Spain; see Figure 7.3). In Germany the mean is hardly higher among poor workers, due to very generous family cash benefits, among other factors, and in Sweden the average ratio is even higher among non-poor workers. This is very counterintuitive, but understandable if one considers that in Sweden poor workers are mostly younger people

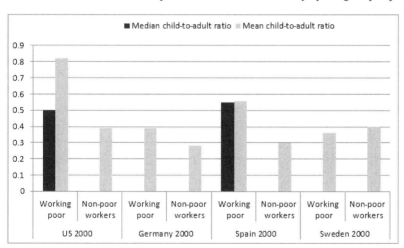

Source: Luxembourg Income Study (LIS), own calculations.

Figure 7.3 Median and mean child-to-adult ratio

who have left the parental home early and because family policy is generously designed. The fact of having children is clearly not a factor of poverty in that country.

Before turning my attention to country profiles, I have to account for the interplay of these three mechanisms. It is probable that employees whose work volume is low are more exposed to low-wage employment (a low-wage rate); moreover, families with children are likely to have a lower labour force participation than childless households. In order to assess these interactions, a logistic regression model has been calculated: the logarithm of the odds of being a poor worker was regressed on the three variables analysed in this chapter. As these three variables represent the channels through which all working poverty factors have a bearing on working households, the models presented in Table 7.11 do not include control variables. However, as age appears to play a very different role from one country to another and is strongly correlated with being badly paid, especially in Sweden and Germany, regression models controlling both for age and age-squared, not shown here for the sake of clarity and brevity, were carried out.

Each variable has a statistically significant impact, *ceteris paribus*, on the odds of working poverty in each of the analysed countries (the *p* values are always smaller than 0.001), and controlling for age and age-squared does not change this result. Moreover, I checked whether there is a multicolinearity problem in the model. None of the variance inflation factors exceeds 1.1, which is way below the customary threshold in social sciences of VIF = 5. Hence the correlations between the three mechanisms do not bias the estimates presented in Table 7.11, which contains the odds ratios of the four regression models.

The odds ratios indicate that an increase in employment has the largest antipoverty impact in Spain and Sweden and the smallest impact in the US: an increase of 0.1 unit increase in the work volume (for instance, a 10 percentage point increase, if the potential is measured in per cent) performed by the head of the household and his or her spouse reduces the odds of being a poor worker by 33 per cent in Spain ($\ln(0.077) = -2.56$ and $\exp(-0.256) = 0.77$) and by 28 per cent only in the US ($\ln(0.13) = -2.042$ and $\exp(-0.2042) = 0.82$). An increase of one child per adult (hence of two children for a couple) has the strongest impact in Spain, as the odds of being a working poor are multiplied by 5.7, whereas they are multiplied by three in the US and are lowest in Sweden and Germany (the odds are multiplied by 2.1 and 1.8 respectively). Having a low earning potential (that is, low FTYRE) has the worst effect in Germany, where the odds of

Table 7.11 Odds of being a working poor in the US, Sweden, Germany and Spain

	Odds ratio (Exp(B))			
	US	Sweden	Germany	Spain
Share of full labour potential actualized	0.13	0.094	0.099	0.077
Child-to-adult ratio	2.967	2.135	1.832	5.712
Dummy low wage employment	9.106	7.653	15.612	7.257
Nagelkerke R^2	0.281	0.095	0.249	0.192

Source: Luxembourg Income Study (LIS), own calculations.

working poverty are multiplied by 15, whereas they are multiplied by 9.1 in the US, by 7.6 in Sweden and by 7.3 in Spain. These findings are largely in line with the descriptive evidence presented above. Last but not least, based on Nagelkerke's pseudo-R^2, it can be said that these three mechanisms have the strongest explanatory power in the US, followed by Germany and Spain; as expected, it is smallest in Sweden.

7.4.2 Country Profiles

I have already given a certain number of indications on why these mechanisms vary from one country to another. I will now discuss country profiles in relation to my hypotheses in a more systematic fashion.

7.4.2.1 The US
The three mechanisms play an important role, even if low labour force participation is a less decisive factor than in Germany and Spain, as the US working poor have a relatively high labour force attachment. This is not surprising because increasing labour market participation of disadvantaged groups was the main aim of the welfare reform brought about by the Personal Responsibility and Work Opportunity Reconciliation Act of 1996

(Clinton Administration) and the repeated increases in the generosity of the Earned Income Tax Credit (EITC). Indeed, working poverty has been a growing concern since the reform was implemented (Joassart-Marcelli, 2005). The fact that the incidence of low FTYRE is not higher than in Germany and Sweden can be surprising, given that the incidence of low-wage employment is notably higher in the US. However, even if the share is similar among poor workers in these three countries, the fact that the incidence of working poverty is higher in the US means that the percentage of the workforce on low-wage employment living in poverty is significantly higher.

Having children is also a significant poverty factor, which is not very surprising given that working parents have to buy childcare services in the market, which can be a financial burden for low-income families even in the presence of a large low-wage personal services sector; in addition, there are no child benefits in cash (Esping-Andersen et al., 2002). Yet, the EITC has been strongly expanded since the early 1990s and its main beneficiaries are working families with children. In fact, it is generally considered by American scholars that many families are lifted out of poverty by the EITC – out of poverty by American standards. This means that these families are not necessarily lifted above 60 per cent of median equivalized disposable income – not even above 50 per cent, probably. The following example is revealing in this regard: a microsimulation was carried out by Swiss researchers in order to assess the poverty reduction potential of the EITC in Switzerland, using PPP to set the boundaries of the various ranges (phase-in, plateau, phase-out) that characterize the design of the EITC. The authors conclude that the EITC is not generous enough to significantly reduce working poverty in Switzerland, using Swiss poverty standards amounting to approximately 55 per cent of median income (Gerfin et al., 2002; Swiss Federal Statistical Office, 2007).

Another factor that has not been stressed so far deserves attention, namely the fact that household size is similar among poor and non-poor workers (the median value is three for both groups according to own calculations based on the same database). This may seem surprising as poor workers tend to have more children, but this is in line with the finding that poverty incidence among single-parent families is extremely high in the US: according to Luxembourg Income Study (LIS)-based own calculations shown in Table 7.3, the working poor rate is much higher among single parents than among couples.

7.4.2.2 Sweden

This is probably the country for which I have obtained the most puzzling findings. First, there is virtually no difference in terms of mean and median labour force attachment between poor and non-poor workers. The overall high work attachment of poor workers is not surprising in a country with a very high labour market participation rate. My results are in line with others; for instance, Halleröd and Larsson (2008) note that a vast majority of the working poor in Sweden work more than 30 hours per week. Another, at first sight, surprising feature is the fact that non-poor workers have more children than the working poor. This is due to the fact that childcare services are largely available and affordable in Sweden and that parental-leave schemes are very generous (Fagnani and Math, 2008); put differently, the opportunity cost of having children in Sweden is very low by international comparison (Armingeon and Bonoli, 2006). Indeed, child poverty is very low in Sweden (Whiteford and Adema, 2007). But perhaps a more revealing indication is that the median Swedish low-income worker lives alone (own calculations based on the same data-set), while the median among non-poor workers amounts to 2.1 household members: in a country in which two-earner couples constitute the very dominant form of household arrangement and set the level of median income, being single is a disadvantage. Moreover, many Swedish poor workers are young and single (Halleröd and Larsson, 2008); young Swedes tend to leave the parental home early in international comparison.

In Sweden, having a relatively low wage seems to be a precondition to working poverty (Halleröd and Larsson, 2008), which is a widespread characteristic of young employees, not only in Sweden. In this regard, working poverty in Sweden, in a social investment perspective, is probably a less problematic social issue, as it often concerns young, single and childless adults. Working poverty, then, does not massively affect children, nor does it seem to have a long-lasting character: the working poor rate drops after age 25 (see Table 7.3). However, the problem of working poverty should not been ignored, as it is a growing problem among Swedish employees (Halleröd and Larsson, 2008).

The 1995 Swedish figures on low wage rates and labour force attachment, however, should be interpreted with some caution, as they rely on family units rather than households (contrary to the 2000 data), which leads to an overestimation of the number of households by some 12 per cent. It is estimated that around 50 per cent of family units in the first decile of equivalized disposable income are children between 18–29 years who are considered as independent units. Hence the average volume of work among low-income workers is probably underestimated in 1995.

7.4.2.3   Germany

A significant poverty factor among workers is the degree of labour market participation, as the difference between low-income workers and the rest of the workforce is marked. Indeed, poverty among full-time workers who benefit from standard employment conditions (*Normalarbeitsverhältnis*) is very low: as of 2004, only 3.3 per cent had an income below 60 per cent of median income (Andress and Seeck, 2007). Unemployment was high at the turn of the millennium in Germany and the female employment rate quite low, owing to the fact that the German welfare regime reflects a modified male-breadwinner model that does not aim at maximizing women's participation in employment. It is still expected that women leave the labour market for some years when they become mothers (Andress and Seeck, 2007; Giesselmann and Lohmann, 2008). If male partners have relatively low earnings, this can then easily lead to financial difficulties; however, child poverty is low in Germany, due in large part to significant increases in tax credits for families with children and child allowances in late 1990s and the early 2000s (Andress and Seeck, 2007). The other mechanism that plays a significant role is to have low earnings per unit of time. In fact, this is the main difference between poor and non-poor workers. This mechanism probably plays a bigger role in the Eastern part of the country, as low-wage workers are much more likely to be the main, if not the sole, wage-earner of the family, while most low-paid employees in Western Germany usually are 'secondary earners' – mostly women – whose earnings allow the household to escape poverty (Giesselmann and Lohmann, 2008).

Another factor is certainly important: as mentioned above, the working poor are usually young, as they have virtually the same age as the Swedish working poor. According to Giesselmann and Lohmann (2008), based on another indicator and another database, four out of ten workers with an income below 60 per cent of median income are under 31 years of age. This is also reflected by the fact that the median working poor live in a smaller household than his or her non-poor counterpart (2 versus 2.7 members, own calculations based on the Luxembourg Income Study (LIS) 2000 data-set).

The fact of having children in Germany is not a decisive poverty factor, even if poor workers tend to have more children than the rest of the labour force, but the difference is not as striking as in the US or Spain. In fact, this is due to very generous cash benefits for families with children: child allowances represented 11.8 per cent of the income of a family with two children relying on the earnings of a full-time industrial worker, while this share amounted to 4.7 per cent in 1995 (Andress and Seeck, 2007). Interestingly, Germany's generous family policy (more than 3 per cent of GDP is spent on family policy around the mid-2000s, according to the social spending database of the OECD, a level only slightly lower than Sweden's) largely prevents child poverty and contributes to the reduction of poverty among working parents. However, as it is largely based on cash transfers and far less on childcare services than in Sweden (Fagnani and Math, 2008), the outcomes are perceivable in terms of maternal employment levels.

7.4.2.4   Spain

In Spain, low labour force participation seems to be an important poverty factor, even if the impact of this mechanism is less marked than in the other 'Bismarckian'[3] country reviewed here, namely Germany. Interestingly, the difference between the mean and the median is largest in Spain, probably owing to the fact that part-time jobs only represent a small share of available positions. Hence, women either work full-time or not at all when they have children (Eurofound, 2007; Moreno, 2002). Put differently, single-earner couples are more widespread than in most countries (Gutiérrez Palacios et al., 2009). This all-or-nothing phenomenon among mothers probably explains the dissymmetric distribution of labour market participation of the heads of households and their spouses in Spain. All in all, the Spanish working poor display the lowest mean and median work attachment, due to a higher unemployment rate and a lower female participation rate; however, these factors have changed significantly in Spain since the mid-1990s, with an increasing female workforce participation (Guillén and Alvarez, 2002). Between 2000 and the beginning of the late-2000s crisis, the female participation rate has skyrocketed (OECD website, labour statistics), which may contribute to a decline in working poverty, but also to an increasing gap between single-earner and dual-earner couples.

Having children can also be a poverty factor, as the mean as well as the median child-to-adult ratio is higher among the working poor, which is not completely surprising in a country with a low level of spending on family policy (Fagnani and Math, 2008). However, due to the importance of the family, one of the most characteristic traits of the Spanish welfare regime (Garrido and Gutiérrez, 2009; Moreno, 2002), the effect of the limited provision of childcare services is reduced.

These results are in line with those obtained by García Espejo and Ibáñez Pascual (2007) with a logistic regression of the working poor rate on various poverty factors (in terms of risk groups), such as occupational profiles, household type and other demographic factors; the authors conclude that the main factors are labour market attachment and the number of dependants.

An important remark is of order here, namely the fact that the median household is larger in Spain than in the other countries analysed in this chapter (Gutiérrez Palacios et al., 2009); my calculations indicate a median household size of four persons among poor workers and three among the rest of the workforce. This is due to the fact that, among other factors, a large majority of young Spaniards leave the parental home in their thirties, in striking contrast with Sweden for instance. This factor is important, because the labour force attachment calculated in this chapter is based on the situation of the head of the household and his or her spouse/partner. Hence, the conclusions drawn may be slightly distorted for the Spanish case; young adults' income is accounted for, but not their labour force participation. So the reader should always keep in mind that we are talking about the head of the household and his or her spouse when analysing labour market participation.

Finally, a rather surprising finding is the relatively low incidence of low pay among poor workers, when both the hours per week and the weeks per year are accounted for, as available data do not seem to suggest that wage dispersion is more compressed in Spain than in Sweden for instance – the opposite is true. As indicated, the role played by the Spanish families in the provision of welfare is fundamental, by allowing economies of scales in consumption. The aforementioned research carried out by García Espejo and Ibáñez Pascual (2007) also concludes that the incidence of low pay is not very high among poor workers in Spain. This is largely attributable, in my view, to the fact that the working poor rate is low among young workers (see Table 7.3).

In fact, the incidence of low-wage jobs (below two-thirds of median hourly gross wage) in 2000 was much higher among workers on fixed-term contracts (approximately 30 per cent) than among workers with a permanent contract (less than 10 per cent) (Blázquez Cuesta, 2008). This corresponds to the fact that the share of non-permanent contracts falls sharply with age (Garrido and Gutiérrez, 2009), and that the incidence of low-wage jobs is high among young and prime-age workers (73 per cent of low-wage workers are under the age of 40) and much lower in their parents' age brackets.

7.4.3   Preliminary Conclusions: Working Poverty Mechanisms and Policy Factors

It is undisputable that working poverty is by far not merely a matter of low earnings and that the relationship between individual earnings and house-hold income is loose, as has been shown by many authors. However, it seems to be an important factor that should not be downplayed in social policy analysis. It is noteworthy that the explanations of the incidence of low-wage employment among poor workers differ from country to country: in Sweden and Germany, it is mainly the young age of poor workers, whereas in the US it is mainly the high incidence of low-wage employment in general. These explanations point to the impact of labour market regulations, among other factors.

However, being badly paid is not the sole working poverty mechanism: other factors are also very important, notably household size and composi-tion as well as labour market participation, as has already been demon-strated by others in terms of the composition of the working poor population (see for instance Andress and Lohmann, 2008).

Family policy broadly understood, that is including family cash benefits, but also parental leave schemes and the provision of childcare services, seems to be the most important welfare state related factor – in terms of the relative weight of the three mechanisms leading to working poverty. This factor plays a decisive role in terms of the cross-sectionally measured levels of working poverty, but also in a social-investment, life-course perspective, as it allows working parents to have a lower likelihood of falling into poverty, and, hence, reduces the share of children of working parents who grow up in poverty.

This leads us to another conclusion, namely that working poverty in Sweden and Germany is a less detrimental social problem than in Spain and the US: first, because the incidence is weaker, but also because many working poor are young and childless workers who may well escape poverty once they start living with a partner who also works; second, they will benefit from generous family-policy schemes should they have children.

Let us now assess whether some of the policy reforms and economic changes described in Chapter 5 have had an impact on the working poverty mechanisms during the first half of the 2000s.

7.4.4   The Evolution of the Working Poverty Mechanisms: 2000–2004

Section 7.2 has shown that the working poor rate has fluctuated between 2000 and 2004. There was a slight increase in working poverty in the US, whatever the definition of 'working' and the poverty cut-off used, while working poverty rose markedly in Spain, which did not translate into an overall increase in poverty; in Germany, working poverty did not increase when measured with the 50 per cent cut-off, contrary to the trend obtained with 60 per cent of median income, which may show that the flexibilization of the labour market induced by the Hartz reforms had a differentiated impact on the lower end of the labour market. However, the ranking of countries remains unaffected. Unfortunately, as indicated in section 7.2, the Swedish figures cannot be reliably updated.

In addition to the overall evolution of working poor rates, it is also interesting to have a closer look at the evolution of each working poverty mechanism. Tables 7.12, 7.13 and 7.14 describe the evolution of the three working poverty mechanisms between 2000 and 2004.

Table 7.12 Evolution of the incidence of low pay (in full-time equivalents) among the working poor and non-poor workers in the US, Germany and Spain, 2000–2004

	US 2000		Germany 2000		Spain 2000	
	Working poor	Non-poor workers	Working poor	Non-poor workers	Working poor	Non-poor workers
Per cent with low earnings (<50% median)	49.0%	11.0%	57.0%	8.0%	23.0%	7.0%

	US 2004		Germany 2004		Spain 2004	
	Working poor	Non-poor workers	Working poor	Non-poor workers	Working poor	Non-poor workers
Per cent with low earnings (<50% median)	51.8%	11.1%	55.7%	8.9%	23.0%	5.1%

Source: Luxembourg Income Study (LIS), own calculations.

As shown in Table 7.12, this first mechanism, low pay, has hardly evolved between 2000 and 2004 in the three countries for which a comparison is possible. The German case is interesting, because the incidence of low-wage employment has increased, but not its incidence among the working poor. This reminds us of another at first surprising result: countries that have very different levels of low-wage employment may have similar shares of low-wage workers among the working poor (see Figure 7.1 above).

As far as the labour force attachment is concerned (see Table 7.13), some changes are perceivable, due to the fact that unemployment increased in the US and Germany, while it decreased in Spain (OECD website, labour statistics, harmonized unemployment rates).

Table 7.13 Evolution of the labour force attachment among the working poor and non-poor workers, in the US, Germany and Spain, 2000–2004

	US 2000		Germany 2000		Spain 2000	
	Working poor	Non-poor workers	Working poor	Non-poor workers	Working poor	Non-poor workers
Median work attachment	0.68	1	0.6	0.91	0.56	0.78
Mean work attachment	0.73	0.88	0.65	0.87	0.62	0.73
	US 2004		Germany 2004		Spain 2004	
	Working poor	Non-poor workers	Working poor	Non-poor workers	Working poor	Non-poor workers
Median work attachment	0.56	1	0.56	0.88	0.57	0.78
Mean work attachment	0.69	0.87	0.64	0.84	0.68	0.74

Source: Luxembourg Income Study (LIS), own calculations.

Interestingly, the work attachment of non-poor workers did not change much over this period, while that of the working poor decreased in the US and Germany, and increased in Spain. Eventually, this mechanism had a larger weight in the mid-2000s than at the turn of the millennium. The difference between poor and non-poor workers grew markedly in the US, due to both an increase in unemployment and a decrease in the employment rate (OECD website, labour statistics and country statistical profile).

The third working poverty mechanism is a high child-to-adult ratio. Table 7.14 summarizes its evolution.

Table 7.14 Evolution of the child-to-adult ratio among the working poor and non-poor workers in the US, Germany and Spain, 2000–2004

	US 2000		Germany 2000		Spain 2000	
	Working poor	Non-poor workers	Working poor	Non-poor workers	Working poor	Non-poor workers
Median child-to-adult ratio	0.5	0	0	0	0.55	0
Mean child-to-adult ratio	0.82	0.39	0.39	0.28	0.56	0.3

	US 2004		Germany 2004		Spain 2004	
	Working poor	Non-poor workers	Working poor	Non-poor workers	Working poor	Non-poor workers
Median child-to-adult ratio	0.5	0	0	0	0.5	0
Mean child-to-adult ratio	0.75	0.4	0.42	0.28	0.55	0.3

Source: Luxembourg Income Study (LIS), own calculations.

The evolutions of these ratios are very slight. In all three countries, the number of children per working-age adult remains an important working poverty mechanism and its relative weight has hardly changed.

In summary, the only notable change regards the role of the work volume among the working poor. It seems that when unemployment increases and/or employment decreases, this mechanism is reinforced. This suggests that the downturn that started in 2008, which has translated into an unemployment upswing in the US and Spain, a moderate increase in

Sweden and a slight increase in Germany, has probably given this mechanism a larger weight; unfortunately, however, Luxembourg Income Study data for the end of the 2000s are not yet available and no other data-set allows a comparison of the situation in the US and Europe. Hence, analysing the evolution of working poverty mechanisms during the global crisis is an important goal for future analysis.

7.5 CONCLUSIONS: WORKING POVERTY MECHANISMS AND RISK GROUPS ACROSS WELFARE REGIMES

This chapter has shown that despite the massive exogenous shocks that occurred in the 1970s and the 1980s, differences across welfare regimes in terms of the approaches that allow combating working poverty are still marked, even though a certain degree of convergence has been perceivable since the late 1990s/early 2000s. These differences translate into the fact that each working poverty mechanism has a different weight in each welfare regime, which explains the differences in the extent and composition of the working poor population.

In the liberal cluster, all three mechanisms play a role, but labour market participation less so. In conservative corporatist countries, a low degree of labour force attachment is an important factor, as well as having a low wage, due to the fact that most working poor are young; children are not an important risk factor. In Southern European countries, too, low workforce participation is a significant determinant, as well as having children; low-wage employment is not fundamental due to the very specific patterns of labour market integration of youths. In Scandinavia, no factor appears to be decisive, except for low wages, as the Swedish working poor are very young. The extent of working poverty is highest in the liberal and Southern European clusters and noticeably lower in Scandinavia and in corporatist European countries. In terms of employment, until the beginning of the crisis of the late 2000s, the best performers were Anglo-Saxon and Scandinavian countries, whereas Germany's perspectives look less grim today than they did at the turn of the millennium.

In terms of risk groups, the main differences across regimes concern families with children. The case of single mothers is particularly striking. These findings confirm that family policies are extremely important public policy variables, as maternal employment rates appear to play a fundamental role. Differences are also striking for workers under 30 years of age; in

Sweden and Germany, the median working poor is 30 years old; he or she is about five years older in the US and nearly a decade older in Spain.

These findings are robust to the use of alternative poverty lines and poverty indicators. The situation of senior workers remains somewhat unclear, though. In income terms, they appear to be better off workers, whereas they seem more disadvantaged when consumption expenditures are accounted for. This may, however, reflect lower needs and higher savings and wealth rather than deprivation. Hence, the use of non-monetary indicators could prove very useful for further researches on the financial situation of senior workers.

Between 2000 and the mid-2000s, working poverty has tended to rise in the US, Germany and Spain, while overall poverty remained more or less constant. One of the three working poverty mechanisms changed over this period, namely the degree of labour force attachment; its weight increases in times of increased unemployment and/or decreased employment. Given the recent evolution of labour markets due to the worldwide downturn of the late 2000s, it is quite likely that this mechanism has more weight at the end of the decade than in the mid-2000s.

NOTES

1. The current labour force status is not available in the Swedish data-set 2000, hence the use of the labour force status over the income reference period in the second and fourth columns of Table 7.1.
2. Otherwise, I would have used both 50 and 60 per cent of median income. One the one hand, using the 60 per cent threshold yields poverty rates that are very high: for instance, one in six people are deemed to be poor in the average EU member state (regardless of the employment status). On the other hand, using this poverty line yields working poor rates that are more comparable to those found in the few European studies that have been carried out and in official statistics.
3.   The expression 'Bismarckian welfare state' is often used in the literature and includes the conservative corporatist and the Mediterranean welfare states. As indicated in Chapter 5, Southern European welfare states share many features with other Continental European welfare states.

8. There is no such thing as 'the working poor' or a one-size-fits-all solution

I can now draw conclusions regarding the three arguments presented in the introduction of this book and answer the question that has been at the heart of my analysis: is it possible to combat working poverty without generating hurdles in the labour market? The main findings are grouped into three sections. Each section corresponds to one of the arguments formulated in the introduction. The results presented here open up interesting avenues of research.

8.1 ARGUMENT 1: THERE IS NO SUCH THING AS 'THE WORKING POOR'

Given the evidence presented in this book, this first thesis is clearly established. There are three working poverty mechanisms through which economic, sociodemographic and public policy factors have a bearing on working households, and, hence, three basic types of working poverty. The evidence is synthesized in the following sections.

8.1.1 There Are Three Basic Types of Working Poverty

A striking feature of mainstream research has been, until very recently, a definitional chaos. In many cases, some groups of poor workers (whatever the poverty line used) are not classified as 'working' for reasons that are, more often than not, implicit. These implicit assumptions might be connected to personal values as to what really 'being in work' means. They could also pertain to social policy implications: the situation of workers with a low labour force attachment requires other types of policy interventions. I think that this chaos is potentially harmful to social policy analysis and would like to suggest some solutions.

Throughout the first part of the present work, my idea was to take a step back and think about what 'being in work' means and if it is a good idea to exclude some groups of workers from the outset. Another central element is the definition of poverty, a problem that has kept social scientists busy ever

189

since the first poverty analyses were published in the nineteenth century; unfortunately, no consensus has been found to this date.

Regarding the first element, I suggest that a very encompassing definition of 'working' poverty should be used. Sure enough, a respondent who has been working one day per week during the month prior to the interview and was unemployed before is in a completely different situation than a respondent who has worked full-time over the whole period. However, if this person is in work and has an income below a given poverty line, why exclude him or her from the group of the working poor? Not classifying this person in this category means, as a consequence, including him or her in the category of the non-working poor; however, his or her situation is also very different from that of a person who did not work in the year prior to the interview and who is not looking for a job. It is also different from that of an unemployed person who has been actively looking for a job, but could not find one.

The approach I advocate is the following: based on a very encompassing definition of 'working', it is then possible to draw a typology of poor workers. I have shown that there are three working poverty mechanisms, namely: being badly paid, having a low degree of labour force attachment and high needs (especially the number of children per working-age adult). These mechanisms are the channels through which macrolevel factors have a direct bearing on working households. Starting from these three mechanisms and, hence, from the three basic types of working poverty, it is possible to draw a typology of poor workers in order to allow a 'fine tuning' of social policy. It is indeed possible to draw a more refined typology, because the three working poverty mechanisms partly overlap, for instance, in the case of workers who have a low labour force attachment and more than two children or workers who combine a low-wage rate and part-time employment. This could be achieved by setting thresholds in terms of the number of children per adult, the work volume at the household level and the wage rate; at this point, setting arbitrary values is less problematic, because no low-income worker has been excluded from the analysis. Another, and arguably better, possibility is to use a statistical classification technique, for instance a cluster analysis. The main drawback of this approach is methodological, namely that it requires large samples. Using a cluster analysis, however, allows choosing the number of clusters wanted at the end of the procedure; hence, a researcher can adjust the number of clusters to the number of poor workers in the sample in order to get reliable figures.

Another approach can be useful, though, namely to use official definitions, especially in comparative research. These definitions are usually arbitrary, but at least they have the advantage of increasing the comparability of analyses by limiting each researcher's subjectivity. Researchers specialized in comparative social policy analysis are partly dependent on the studies and figures produced by other researchers and official bodies; as an increasing number of European researchers use Eurostat's definition, for instance, it might be advisable to use it too in order to get comparable results for European studies. Ideally, a European researcher should use both definitions, namely the most encompassing definition of 'working' as well as Eurostat's criterion of having spent at least six months in the labour market and compare results, which I have done in Chapter 7 (Table 7.1) by using both the current labour force status and the main activity status over the income reference period.

Regarding the definition of poverty, there is no answer out there waiting to help clear up the confusion. Poverty lines vary from around 40 per cent of median income up to 60 per cent, which represents a very broad spectrum. Moreover, even if it is true that the vast majority of researchers dealing with working poverty rely on income thresholds and the headcount ratio, other possibilities exist. Accounting for the depth of poverty (poverty gap) or the severity of poverty (squared poverty gap) are also useful approaches, and the former has been used in the present work. In addition, other monetary indicators are conceivable, consumption expenditure in particular, an approach used in Chapter 7. Non-monetary indicators could also prove useful.

The absence of a consensus regarding poverty lines does not, in my view, constitute a major problem for social policy analysis. All poverty definitions in rich countries entail a certain degree of arbitrariness, as those who are considered to be 'poor' do not face difficulties that threaten their survival, because famines and death from easily curable diseases have largely been eradicated in post-industrial societies.[1] A pragmatic solution to definitional problems can be the use of a poverty definition that corresponds to a social policy objective. In every country, social policy defines a minimum income level any citizen is entitled to; these thresholds are often found in social assistance programmes. This is not advisable, however, for comparative purposes; in this case, poverty lines set by a supranational body can be used, especially if the purpose of the indicator is to monitor the progress of a policy goal.

8.1.2 Economic, Sociodemographic and Policy Factors have an Impact on Working Households Through the Three Working Poverty Mechanisms

Regarding the main determinants of poverty among workers in post-industrial economies, the following conclusions have been drawn.

- Economic development per se is a good thing, especially in the early stages of the development process. In advanced economies, however, further development can lead to more inequality and relative poverty. Hence, in post-industrial countries, economic growth can help reduce poverty in the short run, but its impact depends on the evolution of the income distribution.
- Concerns about globalization and North–South trade have sometimes been exaggerated. Nonetheless, should North–South trade represent a higher share of total trade in the future, that is, if there is less trade among OECD countries and more between OECD countries and emerging economies, the situation could become a greater preoccupation for the low-skilled labour force in high-income countries. Moreover, endogenous mutations, especially skill-biased technological changes, have had a pervasive impact.
- The evolution of productivity growth could be a potential danger, as many service occupations suffer from the cost-disease problem identified by Baumol; some authors, however, relativize this phenomenon. Moreover, the assumption that increased productivity will lead to increased national prosperity may no longer hold, due to automation and technological changes that could leave a large share of workers in lower-paid service jobs.
- There have been pervasive demographic and social changes in high-income countries over the past four decades: families are less stable and divorce rates have skyrocketed. Single parenthood is a significant poverty factor. Moreover, in a society still characterized by social endogamy, increased female labour force participation furthers inequalities in terms of income and employment.
- Risks have shifted towards young adults, as they are more affected by problems to find and hold a stable job, to reconcile work and family life in a society in which dual-earner couples have become the norm and by the existence of much higher obstacles for low-skilled and inexperienced workers.
- The welfare state reduces poverty, in a static sense, thanks to its redistributive effect, but also in the longer run. It seems that worries pertaining to the potential poverty-generating effect of welfare state

benefits are not verified empirically. It is reasonable to think, however, that a very heavy tax burden generated by welfare expenses could impede the economy to be running at full speed.

- More generally, public policy factors appear to play a pervasive role. The economic and demographic changes that took place over the last three to four decades have been broadly the same in all post-industrial countries; yet, great variations in terms of outcomes are striking and virtually all authors acknowledge the impact of institutional factors, such as labour market regulations and welfare state benefits and services. Public policy factors shape the socio-economic and demographic composition of the working poor population and have a different impact on each type of working poverty in each welfare regime.

One of the main contributions of the present work is to show that these economic, demographic and public policy factors have a bearing on households through three channels, namely the remuneration rate, the degree of labour force attachment and the level of needs, especially the number of children per adult. Figure 8.1 summarizes the main findings presented in Chapters 3 and 4.

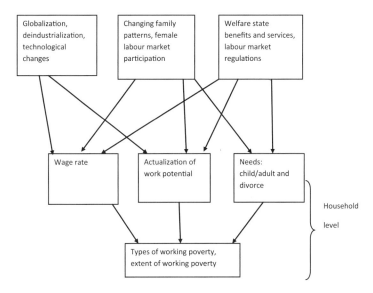

Source: own representation.

Figure 8.1 Economic, sociodemographic and public policy factors and the three working poverty mechanisms

Figure 8.1 simply aims at summarizing the findings of Chapters 3 and 4; it is not meant to show all possible causal relationships between each set of causal factors. Moreover, the dynamic dimension is deliberately absent.

The factors summarized in Figure 8.1 affect various sociodemographic groups, defined in terms of the following listed below.

- *Age*: youths have a higher risk of being unemployed or badly paid, as they lack experience in the labour market. Prime working-age adults, that is, most young parents, are more exposed to working poverty in many countries because the presence of children increases household needs, especially if they divorce, as the poverty rate of single-parent households is significantly above average in most countries.
- *Gender*: women are more likely to be badly paid than their male counterparts and are over-represented in unskilled service sector jobs, while many unskilled males work in the manufacturing sector. Women are also more likely to be unemployed or involuntarily in part-time employment and much more likely to be the heads of lone-parent households. Hence, they are more at risk of poverty. However, they are not necessarily more exposed to working poverty, especially married women, because disadvantaged female workers are more likely to have a working partner than their male counterparts; this raises the question, however, of their economic independence.
- *Education*: low-skilled workers, especially people with no post-compulsory education, are more likely to be low paid and unemployed, as the educational level has become the most hegemonic determinant of life chances. Social endogamy reinforces the disadvantage of low-skilled workers, both in terms of income and of employment.
- *Household type*: single parents and large families are more exposed to poverty because of high needs and also because, in many cases, labour force participation must be reduced.
- *Immigrant or minority status*: whereas there are very mobile and cosmopolitan elites made up of CEOs, executives, academics, high-ranking officials, and the like, persons with a migration background as well as other minorities tend to have a lower educational level (or their diplomas are not accepted by the host country) and less desirable positions in the labour market, as they are over-represented in low-wage sectors. Moreover, they are more exposed to unemployment. However, it is often difficult to distinguish class-related factors (skills, diplomas and so on) from 'ethnic'/'racial' disadvantages, such as statistical discrimination (Becker, 1971; Bonoli and Hinrichs, 2010; Crettaz, 2011). Limited linguistic skills of non-native speakers are

also an obvious barrier to employment and vertical mobility. For children, having parents who are not native speakers is an obstacle to educational achievement. Moreover, some immigrant groups tend to have a larger family, which increases their needs.

Risk factors such as belonging to a visible minority or having a migration background have not been analysed thus far, because they are mainly reflected in the three working poverty mechanisms, due to differences in skill levels, diplomas, language proficiency, family size and composition, among other factors. However, there may be elements that are specific to these groups, such as for instance, statistical discrimination; this phenomenon, likewise, mainly translates into lower wage rates and less employment opportunities.

I briefly review some figures I have not presented in Chapter 7, namely the incidence of working poverty broken down by nationalities or minority groups, based on Luxembourg Income Study data for the year 2000. I do not review this evidence extensively, but the main findings illustrate the heterogeneity of minorities and of the population with a migrant background.

In 2000 in the US, natives born in the US made up 87 per cent of non-poor workers but only 74 per cent of the working poor; one out of eight working poor (12.3 per cent) arrived in the US between 1990 and 2000. In the same year, German nationals made up 93 per cent of non-poor workers and only 82 per cent of poor workers; interestingly, other EU-15 citizens have a lower working poor rate than Germans. The difference between nationals and other workers is less marked in Sweden, probably owing to the relatively small size of the migrant population in 2000. Swedes represent 96 per cent of non-poor workers and 92 per cent of poor workers; as in Germany, some groups of European non-nationals have a lower working poor rate than Swedes, especially other Scandinavians and Finns (4.3 per cent versus 5.1 per cent among Swedes). In Spain, in 2000, the presence of non-nationals was still limited; however, this has changed in the recent past, as indicated above, with a 900 per cent increase between the mid-1990s and the late 2000s. But in 2000, Spaniards made up 99 and 98 per cent of non-poor workers and poor workers, respectively. These figures show, unsurprisingly, that non-nationals and other persons with a migration background are more exposed to working poverty. However, in each country, some groups are less affected than native-born nationals; in Europe, it is often the case of persons coming from old EU member states. It should be kept in mind that any form of discrimination or difficulties due to the non-acceptance of diplomas does not constitute a working poverty mechanism per se; it translates into lower wage rates and greater difficulties finding a job.

8.2 ARGUMENT 2: DIFFERENT WELFARE REGIMES GENERATE DIFFERENT TYPES OF WORKING POVERTY

The three working poverty mechanisms have a different weight in each welfare regime. I was able to show in Chapter 7 that all three factors have an impact in the US, whereas workforce participation has a lower weight than the wage rate and the child-to-adult ratio. In Germany the main mechanisms are low workforce participation and being badly paid, whereas the latter has much to do with the young age of the median working poor as well as with specific problems in the Eastern part of the country (the former German Democratic Republic). In Spain, having children and a low workforce participation are the main determinants of working poverty, while holding a low-paying job is not a pervasive factor. In Sweden, none of the mechanisms appear to play a fundamental role, whereas having a low wage is very widespread due to the fact that most Swedish working poor are very young and live alone. Chapter 7 also demonstrates that the sociodemographic distribution of the working-poverty risk varies considerably across countries. I can conclude that the second thesis is clearly established, in terms of mechanisms and of risk groups.

Hence, it comes as no surprise that specific policies appear to be more efficient in some countries than in others. Family policies appear to play a particularly important role in shaping working poverty; their generosity as well as their emphasis on either cash benefits of family services are decisive factors.

In addition, the present work allows an understanding of how existing policy mixes shape the three types of working poverty (extent and composition), and that any reform aiming at reducing working poverty will have to identify the types of working poverty that are not efficiently combated, as well as the negative side-effects a policy that efficiently combats one type of working poverty can have on the other working poverty mechanisms. Though I have already analysed working poverty mechanisms in each welfare regime, I still have to provide a succinct depiction of the functioning of each welfare regime in systemic terms.

The liberal cluster is mainly characterized by legally enforced minimum wages and tax credits for workers, which are both components of a 'make work pay' strategy (MWP). In the US, this MWP approach is accompanied by a welfare-to-work orientation, and caseloads have markedly decreased since the welfare reform of 1996. The US case, as it is today, is based on a 'work-first' approach. The UK is somewhat different in this regard, as means-tested social assistance benefits were made more generous at the same time as the Working Family Tax Credit (WFTC) was expanded, because the reduction of child poverty was also an important goal of the proponents of the 'third way'. The functioning of the work-first approach is the following: the goal is to maximize workforce participation. Labour markets are lightly regulated, the minimum wage is set at a relatively low level in relative terms (the latter comment does not apply to the Antipodes), and welfare recipients are strongly encouraged, and sometimes forced, to accept any job available. A large low-skilled service sector exists. Moreover, efforts have been made in the field of childcare policies, in order to further help low-skilled mothers in general, and lone mothers in particular, to participate in the labour market. Hence, there are many workers who need a public intervention in order to be able to make ends meet. If a person holds a low-paying job, then he or she is granted financial support through the tax system, which is less stigmatizing than going to a welfare agency, mainly through earned income and childcare tax credits. It is hoped that, by keeping low-skilled workers in the labour market, they will climb the earnings ladder after some time and become financially more autonomous and will not be back on welfare. This approach requires, on the part of voters/taxpayers, the acceptance of large income inequalities and is associated with a reluctance to see the state heavily involved in the economy in general, and the labour market in particular.

In the social-democratic cluster the approach to the fight against working poverty is fundamentally different. The central goal is also to have high employment rates and low unemployment levels, but another fundamental aim is to keep income and earnings inequality as low as possible. Active labour market policies, generous parental leaves and childcare policies, combined with the existence of a very large public sector, ensure that enough jobs are available and that all groups of citizens can have a high employment rate, including mothers of young children and senior workers. Earning inequalities are kept at a low level through collective agreements; public employment also plays an important role, as many low-productivity jobs are provided by the state and are, hence, relatively well-paid. Income inequalities are also combated through generous income transfers towards unemployed and inactive citizens. Moreover, household expenses on childcare services and healthcare are low. In the Swedish case, for instance, this combination of factors ensures that households who are in the bottom decile of the income distribution are better off than their counterparts in most OECD countries, especially US low-income families. The Scandinavian model requires a fundamental condition: voter/taxpayers must be ready to pay high taxes and to accept a heavy involvement of authorities in many aspects of everyday life, such as employment and family matters, and they must have a relatively egalitarian ethos. This appears to be more or less the opposite of the prerequisites of the liberal model.

The conservative corporatist European model constitutes a largely different world of social policy efforts than both the liberal and the social-democratic model. Until the late 1990s/early 2000s, the goal was not to maximize employment, but to ensure good quality jobs for those who are in the labour market. Early retirement, low female labour force participation and labour shedding were perceived as appropriate measures, that is, the reduction of labour supply. The core labour force is well protected, both through employment protection regulations and collective bargaining, whereas the relative weight of each component varies largely across countries. For instance, regulation by law plays the main role in France, while in Germany collective bargaining is the main component. While the situation of the core workforce has remained stable in recent years, flexibility has been obtained by deregulating the labour market at its margins in many countries since the 1980s. Short-term employment, temp agency work, lower payroll taxes for low-paying jobs and similar other measures have been used to this end, thereby generating a certain degree of dualization in the labour market. In addition, exception clauses have increasingly been accepted in collective agreements. Working poor rates are low in Continental Europe, and can be even lower than in Scandinavia, thanks to a combination of relatively high wages with generous social transfers. However, whereas Scandinavian countries combine both low working poor rates and a good employment performance, Continental European countries appear to be subject to a complex trade-off. For instance, both better employment performances and larger inequalities characterize Germany in the late 2000s compared to the early 2000s. The trade-off seems to be reinforced by the fact that voter/taxpayers are reluctant to see inequalities increase: some authors think, for instance, that the perceived unfairness of some of the Hartz reforms explain the electoral loss of the Red–Green coalition in 2005.

The Southern European cluster has many features in common with other Continental European countries, mainly its heavy reliance on passive income transfers to support those who are not in the labour force and the fact that employment maximization has never been a priority. This cluster has, however, distinctive features, mainly the role that families play. The main pillars of the fight against working poverty are generous social transfers combined with a very strict regulation of the labour market: Spain and Portugal are the two European countries with the strictest employment protection legislations. Hence, workers who are in the core labour force are very well protected and in the event of a layoff, severance pay is very expensive for employers. In Spain, young workers have a long and relatively hectic pattern of labour force integration and alternate between unemployment and short-term employment. In periods of economic slump, their unemployment rate shoots up and can reach staggeringly high levels: around four out of ten Spanish workers under 25 years of age are unemployed at the time of writing. Unemployment in Spain is, hence, strongly cyclical. However, the working poor rate is relatively low among workers in their late twenties and early thirties, as a large majority live with their parents, who hold well protected jobs; in addition, unemployed household members get 'generous' unemployment benefits. Most Spaniards leave the parental home when they are in their thirties, once they obtain an open-ended work contract.

Finally, I can draw conclusions as to the efficiency of the fight against working poverty in each welfare regime. It is probably fair to say that Scandinavian countries are the best-equipped in the fight against new social risks in general and working poverty in particular. These countries demonstrate that there is not necessarily a trade-off between unemployment and working poverty, but they display a very specific constellation of institutional factors. Anglo-Saxon countries appear to be relatively well prepared to face post-industrial challenges; after the culmination of neoliberal policies in the 1980s, which led to a strong increase in social exclusion and poverty in general, and working poverty in particular, these countries have largely expanded tax credits for workers, reduced the impact of childcare costs and, in the US, expanded healthcare coverage. Despite these efforts, relative poverty levels remain high by international comparison. Continental European countries have had many difficulties in facing the challenges posed by post-industrial mutations; in the 1990s and early 2000s, they appeared to be unable to tackle high unemployment levels and were perceived as a 'frozen landscape'. However, according to many authors, they seem to be in the midst of a paradigmatic shift, with a gradual transformation of the model. Understanding and analysing this evolution will certainly be a key component of European social policy analysis in the near future; researchers are currently analysing this 'long goodbye to Bismarck' (Palier, 2010). Finally, it does not seem unfair to say that Southern European countries are the less well-equipped to adjust to new social risks. However, it should be kept in mind that they are young democracies who until recently had closed economies and, given this point of departure, many improvements they have made in recent years are quite impressive. In Spain, female labour force participation has increased massively, the average educational level is much higher than it was 15 years ago and the welfare state has been expanded to unprecedented levels. However, Spain's labour market probably needs far-reaching reforms.

8.3   ARGUMENT 3: THERE IS NO 'ONE-SIZE-FITS-ALL' POLICY MIX: EACH COUNTRY MUST FIND ITS OWN COMBINATION OF POLICIES

This thesis is largely confirmed by the meta-analyses presented above; they show that most policies do not have the same impact across welfare regimes. The risk-group analysis clearly shows that the composition of the working poor population varies across countries, which further confirms that it is not possible to determine a single policy mix that would work everywhere.

8.3.1   Different Social Policy Instruments Affect Different Types of Working Poverty (in Different Welfare Regimes)

I have shown that the fight against working poverty relies on three basic approaches, namely minimum wages, social transfers and an employment-maximizing strategy, and that each approach can be broken down into two main subcategories. The first and the third approach mainly combat one type of working poverty (poverty due to a low-wage rate and that caused by a weak labour force attachment, respectively), whereas social transfers can support each type of poor worker, by providing benefits that supplement low earnings, by supporting 'high-need' households with family cash benefits and by providing incentives to work if they are employment-conditional.

It is possible to draw a typology of welfare regimes according to the two main subcategories that underpin the fight against working poverty: a rather coercive employment-maximization approach combined with complementing cash transfers in the US; an employment-maximizing strategy based on incentives and minimum wages set through collective bargaining in Sweden; substitution income transfers mainly aimed at non-working persons and collectively bargained wages in Germany; and legal minimum wages and substitution income transfers in Spain.

I have then meta-analysed in Chapter 6 the impact of specific policy instruments usually brought to the forefront in the literature, namely minimum wages, be they legally enforced or collectively bargained, employment-conditional tax credits, namely the US EITC, the UK's WFTC and the French PPE (*prime pour l'emploi*), as well as family cash benefits, be they universal or means-tested and policies that aim at reducing the fees or increasing the availability of childcare services. These meta-analyses have been accompanied by qualitative interpretations that focused on subsamples of estimates.

The main conclusions I have been able to draw on the basis of the meta-analyses are the following: low *minimum wages* set at around one-third of gross average wage, such as the US federal minimum wage, are unlikely to efficiently reduce working poverty and they seem to have little disemployment effects, if any. In countries with higher minimum wages, such as France with a legal minimum set at 45–7 per cent of average gross wage, they are more likely to reduce working poverty; but they also appear to have a more negative impact on employment performance, whereas it may not be as negative as is often assumed in 'textbook' labour economics. Moreover, even if minimum wages set at a level that does not harm employment do not strongly reduce the incidence of working poverty, they reduce its depth and, hence, the welfare state expenses that are needed in order to fill the poverty gap. However, neither the evidence I have gathered, nor the evidence stemming from literature reviews, has allowed me to draw conclusions as to the level at which these minimum levels should be set.

It is fundamental to note that this optimal level will vary from country to country, because minimum wages interact with other labour market regulations and taxation. The same minimum wage in purchasing power parities (PPP) will not have the same impact in countries with high payroll taxes and strict employment regulations as in countries that have a lightly regulated labour market and low social security contributions. Finally, minimum wages appear to be necessary complements to employment-conditional benefits, in order to prevent employers from lowering wages after the introduction of these work-conditional programmes.

Employment-conditional tax credits for workers appear to have efficiently contributed to employment increases in Anglo-Saxon countries, but these conclusions apply to very specific contexts. First, single mothers had very low employment rates and made up a large share of welfare recipients before the expansion of these credits. Second, the UK and the US have lightly regulated labour markets and a large low-skilled service sector, with a high degree of wage dispersion and a high incidence of low-wage employment. Third, both the UK during Tony Blair's era and the US during Bill Clinton's era experienced very good economic performances; this is particularly true for the US with one of the most prosperous decades in its history. Fourth, in the case of the US, the increased generosity of the EITC was accompanied by a fundamental welfare reform which led to a massive decrease in caseloads, contrary to the UK, a country in which means-tested benefits were also increased as the reduction of child poverty was high on the political agenda. This fundamental difference between the US and the British reform helps to explain a pronounced puzzle, namely that the WFTC, which was twice as generous as its US counterpart, was roughly half as efficient in employment terms. In both countries, it was mainly lone mothers who were reactive to the positive incentives provided by the EITC and the WFTC; on the contrary, married women reduced their labour force participation following the expansions of the tax credits. Nonetheless, the increase in single mothers' employment appears to have outweighed the decline in married women's employment. These tax credits also appear to have slightly reduced the incidence of poverty among working families.

Interestingly, simulations of the introduction of similar programmes in Continental Europe lead to different conclusions, as it appears that these credits would have little effect, if any. The employment effect may even be slightly negative, with disincentive effects for married women outweighing the positive impact on lone mothers' employment. A few explanations are plausible: first, the distribution of earnings and income is more compressed and the incidence of low wages smaller in Continental Europe. Second, the situation of single mothers appears to be less grim, due to more generous family policies; in countries in which family policy mainly takes the form of cash benefits, the employment effect of tax credits might be dulled by relatively generous benefits. Third, the number and types of jobs available in Continental European labour markets probably do not allow a large influx of low-skilled (single) mothers. Some attempts have been made in Continental Europe and led to disappointing results. A tax credit introduced in Belgium was suppressed after a few years only and virtually all evaluations of the PPE in France also conclude that its impact is very limited and only redistributive. It will be interesting to see whether the tax credits that have been introduced in Scandinavia in the very recent past will be more successful; this could be the case, because Scandinavian welfare systems actively promote maternal employment.

Family policy appears to be a more promising tool for European countries, whereas this conclusion largely varies from one instrument to another. First and foremost, providing *affordable childcare slots in sufficient numbers* has a positive impact on maternal employment in countries in which the supply of childcare slots is still quite limited and/or prices high. In countries in which childcare slots are already largely available and not expensive, mainly in Scandinavia, reforms implemented in the 2000s have not had, logically, a large impact, as the vast majority of mothers were already in work and in-work poverty was low. It should be noted, however, that this approach works in Scandinavia because there are enough jobs to be had, even for low-skilled mothers, because there is a large pool of public sector jobs in personal services, including the employees of publicly funded and subsidized childcare facilities. Moreover, this servicing strategy is articulated with other employment-maximizing policies, mainly active labour market policies and 'generous' parental leave schemes. It might not be necessary, however, to have a similar institutional environment as Scandinavian countries for childcare policies to be successful. If unemployment is reasonably low, as is the case in some Continental European countries, increasing the number of subsidized childcare slots and decreasing childcare fees may contribute to the fight against working poverty, because this would create a virtuous circle, due to the multiplier effect of female employment in post-industrial economies.

Interestingly, while the impact of childcare policy on maternal employment and on fertility has been evaluated by many authors, its antipoverty impact has rarely been quantified. This might be due to the implicit assumption I have often read between the lines of many articles, namely that an increase in maternal employment leads to a reduction of poverty. This is probably true, overall, but in many cases, as indicated by Whiteford and Adema (2007), the servicing strategy alone is not sufficient. Hence, I think that investigating the anti-working poverty effect of an increase in the availability of childcare slots and/or a decrease in childcare fees is probably an important avenue for future research on potential efficient policies in the fight against working poverty.

Another approach to family policy is possible, namely supporting families with children through *cash benefits*. Their antipoverty impact has often been assessed and sophisticated evaluations based on static microsimulations are available. Yet, they do not take into account the fact that low-skilled mothers may reduce their labour force participation after an increase in family cash benefits. Evidence stemming from Anglo-Saxon countries, in which family benefits are mostly means-tested, tends to indicate a negative employment effect. On the contrary, disemployment effects appear to be only marginal in European countries. This may be due to the fact that there are, as already indicated, probably less low-skilled jobs available in the service sector in Continental Europe; in addition, due to the more compressed wage distribution and the lower incidence of low-wage jobs, mothers who hold a job may be less likely to leave the labour market in the event of an increase in family cash benefits. Family benefits appear to have a positive antipoverty impact; however, this conclusion is only tentative. As in the case of childcare policies, the number of estimates of their antipoverty effect is limited – estimates that take into account the potential negative employment effects. Another clue is provided by Moller et al. (2003); in their regression models, family cash benefits have a positive antipoverty impact, even when economic growth and employment are controlled for.

In hindsight, I realize that, as social policy instruments cannot be expected to have the same impact in all socio-economic contexts and all groups of working poor, it would be ideal to follow my model and to evaluate the impact of social policies on each working poverty mechanism, in each welfare regime. This, of course, is not the case in evaluations, except for the employment effects of various policies; moreover, a few evaluations also measure the impact of various policies on earnings. As the first prong of my empirical contribution is a meta-analysis, that is, a statistical analysis of estimates produced by others, this would require an in-depth re-analysis of these findings and would prove impossible in most cases. Still, I will shortly analyse, in retrospect, the impact of the instruments I have meta-analysed on different types of working poverty.

Minimum wages, obviously, have an impact on the fact of being badly paid, by preventing wage rates becoming too low. As the wage a worker gets is not a function of his or her household's size and composition, then, minimum wages cannot fight working poverty when it is caused by high household needs. If minimum wages are set at a high level that may affect the employment opportunities of low-skilled and/or inexperienced workers or, on the contrary, if they help low-wage workers without creating hurdles in the labour market because they are set at an optimal level, they can have an impact on the second working poverty mechanism, namely the degree of labour force attachment at the household level. Hence, the impact of a minimum wage will depend on the share of badly paid workers among the working poor, on their sociodemographic characteristics and on how low their wages are. Finally, it appears that minimum wages set through collective bargaining, by allowing more flexibility, may allow taking into account the characteristics of economic sectors (especially low-productivity industries, such as hotels, catering, tourism, retail and the like) and of specific groups of workers (for instance workers under 25 years of age), thereby reducing the risk of creating hurdles in the labour market. However, the coverage of minimum wages set in collective agreements is never universal, and in some countries, it is far from universal, which means that many workers still have the risk to be paid a 'poverty wage'.

Tax credits for workers mainly have an impact on two mechanisms. First, they were mainly designed to increase the labour force participation of low-skilled workers, especially lone mothers, and reduce welfare dependency. In Anglo-Saxon countries, they have had a positive employment impact and have, hence, helped workers who were poor because of a low labour force attachment. Second, as the level of the maximum credit depends on the number of children, they have also contributed to combat poverty among those who were in a difficult situation due to high needs. As minimum wages exist in countries in which these employment-conditional credits are more developed (notably in the UK and the US), it can be said that the tandem EITC/minimum wage dulls the effect of the three working poverty mechanisms. In the US, however, as the benefits are relatively limited and mainly aim at preventing workers from falling into extreme poverty (the official poverty line, which is low by international comparison, is about where the EITC starts phasing out), they do not lift many workers above the usual poverty thresholds used in mainstream comparative social policy analysis.

Cash benefits for families mainly affect two mechanisms. First, of course, they help workers who are poor because they have higher needs due to the presence of children in their household, by providing them with cash benefits; however, they may reduce the workforce participation of mothers (mainly in Anglo-Saxon countries and less so in Continental European countries), which in turn could have a negative impact on the second working poverty mechanism. Childcare services, if they are largely available and affordable, allow parents of young children to work more. They reduce the type of working poverty that is generated by a low degree of labour force attachment, but this approach is quite unlikely to have striking results if job opportunities are scarce, especially for low-skilled mothers. In Scandinavia, there is a large public low-skilled service sector (and it is noteworthy that public employment accounts for about one-third of employment in Sweden); this allows mothers to work more if they wish to, which in turn generates more personal-service jobs due to the multiplier effect of maternal employment. In other countries, especially in Continental Europe, mothers have less employment opportunities. Still, even in these countries, mothers who have a job will also be better off if the availability of childcare slots is increased and fees reduced. Moreover, as already indicated, employers may be more inclined to pay better wages and invest more on mothers' human capital if they think that the birth of children will not strongly decrease their productivity.

These are the main answers I can give to the question: which policy mixes have an impact on which kind of working poverty in which welfare regime? This leads me now to another empirical contribution of the present work, namely the overall impact welfare regimes have on various types of working poverty.

8.3.2 The Trade-off between the Quality and the Quantity of Jobs is Dealt with in Various Ways across Welfare Regimes

In the introduction of the present work, I suggested that policymakers are held hostage by a trade-off between combating (working) poverty and establishing an employment-friendly environment. However, the fact that there is no trade-off between working poverty and employment performance is illustrated by Scandinavian countries, but this welfare regime combines very specific features that probably make this model difficult to export, mainly the very large size of the public sector and taxpayers who have an egalitarian ethos and do not rebel against high tax rates.

And what about the trade-off between the quantity and the quality of jobs[2] in the other welfare regimes? In Anglo-Saxon countries, the trade-off exists but is not very marked. Employment performance remains the number one priority and the existence of high levels of income inequality is not perceived as a major problem, especially in the US. However, as indicated above, the large increase in working poverty that took place during the Reagan era seemed to undermine a core US belief: that a commitment to the work ethic will provide a road out of poverty (Levitan and Shapiro, 1988). After the peak of the neoliberal era, measures aiming at helping low-income working families have been largely expanded in the 1990s, especially the EITC; many states have implemented an EITC that 'piggybacks' on its federal counterpart as well as minimum wages that are more generous than the one set at the federal level. Healthcare coverage for children has been expanded through the State Children's Health Insurance Program (SCHIP) (which is not employment-conditional), and at the time of writing, a global healthcare reform is being debated. It is noteworthy, though, that the access to financial support has become more restricted for non-working persons, especially since the 1996 reform.

Continental Europe appears to be the region in which this trade-off is the most pronounced. The German case is very interesting in this regard. In the 1990s, Germany was regarded as the 'sick man of Europe' due to its difficulties to perform well in macroeconomic terms, especially its high unemployment levels. Now that the Hartz reforms have been introduced, some of which increased the number of jobs supplied, especially in the low-wage segment, Germany has achieved better employment performances – of course, there are other factors than the Hartz reforms that also explain this improvement, for instance overall economic performance, as the German industrial sector has performed really well between 2004 and 2007, and exports have been very good since 2009. Evaluation results show that the Hartz reforms have contributed to the creation of many low paying jobs and to an increased efficiency of public employment services. However, both earnings inequality and the poverty risk have been on the increase in Germany over the 2000s, and many voices have expressed their concern, despite the fact that earnings inequality and poverty remain low in international comparison. After the electoral defeat of the government that implemented the Hartz reforms, subsequent administrations have adopted a more moderate stance towards labour flexibilization. Moreover, many politicians have advocated the introduction of a minimum wage to stop this trend towards increased inequalities.

In Southern European countries, there is a trade-off between protecting the core labour force (by means of very strict employment protection legislation) and preventing a strong dualization of the labour market, because the majority of young workers hold a fixed-term contract. In my view, national debates on in-depth reform of the labour market cannot be avoided. In Spain, since 1994, four reforms have been implemented. These reforms included the introduction of a new type of open-ended contract with lower layoff costs for certain groups of workers, reductions in payroll taxes for employers who sign open-ended contracts and rules that limit the use and the accumulation of open-ended contracts. These reforms have not been very successful so far, though, and many scholars call for a more far-reaching reform of the labour market (Conde-Ruiz et al., 2010). As unemployment levels are currently very high and public debt abysmal, however, the priority may well be given to reducing unemployment and cutting welfare state expenses, especially pensions, thereby relegating poverty reduction to the role of a secondary goal for some years.

In conclusion, I would like to underline the fact that what could work in each welfare regime in the fight against working poverty largely depends on the existing policy mix, which has an impact on the relative weight of each working poverty mechanism. It is necessary to identify which of the poverty mechanisms are not efficiently combated in order to broaden the scope of the fight against working poverty.

In addition, it seems reasonable to conclude that the trade-off between the quality and the quantity of jobs can be overcome, but that it probably takes a costly policy mix to achieve this goal: for instance, countries like Sweden and Denmark spend around 1.5 per cent of their GDP on family services (mainly childcare services); moreover, Denmark, Sweden and the Netherlands spend at least 1.4 per cent of their GDP on active labour market policies (Kluve, 2006).

8.4   WHERE DO WE GO NOW? CHALLENGES FOR WORKING POVERTY RESEARCH

The findings summarized in this chapter open up interesting and important avenues of research: further theoretical developments are necessary and some empirical challenges should be tackled.

8.4.1   Theoretical Developments

This work combines a sociological analysis of welfare regimes and social inequalities with a political economy that aims at the identification of best practice models. Each part relies on a theoretical and conceptual framework that is coherent, for instance conceptual reflections about the nature and the definition of the problem, and about the dimensions that underpin the welfare regime typology used in this work, a causality model based on exogenous factors and mechanisms and so on. However, having two distinct parts makes the development of a global theoretical framework more difficult.

A fundamental question would be at the heart of this theoretical framework: to what extent is it possible to compare models and regimes? This model should be three-pronged.

The role of social norms and cultural values: there are many indications of the importance of cultural values and social norms scattered throughout the text. I have underlined the role of the family in Southern European countries; it is also noteworthy that young Swedes leave the parental home very early and that one of the main aims of the Scandinavian welfare regime is that people are not dependent on their family. I also underlined the fact that Scandinavians do not rebel against high tax rates nor against the strong intervention of the state in many aspects of everyday life and that they have an egalitarian ethos, while most Americans are not appalled by the high level of income inequality found in the US and are distrustful towards government interventions. Moreover, the impact of what people think about what 'good mothers' should do is measured in some of the studies I have meta-analysed. The fact that Germany displays a 'modified male-breadwinner model' and that mothers are still expected to leave the labour market for a few years after childbirth is pivotal in the section on this country. In addition, it may not be a coincidence that the maximization of labour force participation is an important dimension of the fight against working poverty in countries with a strong protestant ethos (the US and Sweden). In the literature presented in this book, such aspects are also mentioned, but not in a systematic fashion; more often than not, it is economic conditions and institutional factors that are analysed when the 'exportability' of a model is discussed.

Such a coherent theoretical model should include the following dimensions: the perceptions of the role of the family and of the distribution of roles within the family; the conception of solidarity and of the relationship between citizens and the state; the role that is attributed to gainful employment and even the impact of the religious tradition found in a country. Again, some of these aspects are found in the literature; however, the idea would be to have a systematic modelization. Such a systematic analysis of these factors would greatly enhance our understanding of the 'exportability' of policy mixes.

The specific context in which a model was implemented: all the conclusions drawn in this work pertain to specific points in time and space. In the comparative social policy literature, many models and 'employment miracles' are brought to the forefront, and they are often seen as a coordinated model that was the object of conscious decisions, such as the 'Dutch miracle', flexicurity in Denmark, family policies in Sweden or the expansion of the EITC in the US, to name a few examples. In hindsight, however, these models can be questioned. In some cases, one could even ask: was it really cleverness or was it luck? Was it really a coordinated effort? In the case of flexicurity in Denmark, for instance, social partners and the government probably never had a clear and systematic model in mind; it was the result of a stepwise negotiation and adaptation to adverse economic conditions; the same can be said about the Netherlands (Viebrock and Clasen, 2009). In the case of family policies in Sweden, they were not meant to fight (working) poverty and were introduced at a time when the financing of pensions was not yet a pressing problem (Bonoli, 2007). In the US, the expansion of the EITC combined with the welfare reform has been hailed as successful by many authors, as shown in the meta-analysis: the employment of low-skilled mothers increased and poverty decreased; moreover, Temporary Assistance for Needy Families (TANF) caseloads plummeted. However, some American authors have underlined that these reforms took place in a very specific context, namely one of the most prosperous decades in US history (Sawhill and Thomas, 2001).

On the contrary, some cases were presented as obvious failures. Germany was seen as the 'sick man of Europe' until recently and as a 'frozen landscape', while the massive impact of the reunification of Germany was largely left out of the analysis. However, a few years later, in the midst of one of the worst recessions since the Great Depression, Germany is performing well and has a reasonably low level of unemployment compared to other OECD countries in 2009; moreover, this country has been able to undergo important labour market reforms in the recent past.

In summary, the success stories and alleged failures presented in the literature depend on a very specific context and some successes may have been somewhat lucky. In addition, the current worldwide crisis may well question some models, for example the US 'work-first' approach, as the poverty rate among the working-age population is at its highest level since the 1960s (US Census Bureau, 2010): when unemployment strongly increases in a country that mainly relies on the maximization of labour force participation, poverty skyrockets.

The differences between a large country like the US, with its federalist institutions and its great diversity and a small country like Sweden with its relatively homogenous population may constitute a major obstacle to comparative analysis. Hence, the differences in terms of *size of the country*, *heterogeneity* and *political institutions* should also be problematized in this model.

Apart from this global theoretical model aiming to modelize the conditions under which sound comparisons can be made, two other theoretical avenues could contribute to a better understanding of the conditions under which best practices can be exported. Such theories already exist in the literature, especially in the field of political science, but specific models could be developed for the analysis of working poverty.

A first theoretical element would be an analysis of the dynamic aspects of working poverty. The present work largely relies on a static analysis of welfare regimes and the types of working poverty they generate, but a longitudinal perspective would add to our understanding of the situation in various welfare regimes. Theoretical models are already available, such as the path dependency model in political science; interestingly, however, as indicated by many authors, some recent successes took place in countries in which policymakers and social partners walked away from the path and found original solutions (Kenworthy, 2004; Viebrock and Clasen, 2009). Another important dimension of a dynamic analysis would include a longitudinal analysis of the financial situation of working households; I get back to this point below.

A second important contribution would be a theory of the role of various actors (politicians, social partners, policymakers and other stakeholders) and the conditions under which they successfully impose their views on how to best combat working poverty and contribute to social policy reforms. General models pertaining to social policy in general already exist, such as neo-institutionalist models, the power resources model, the garbage can model, the rational choice model, just to name a few. The idea would be to develop a specific model dealing with the fight against working poverty.

8.4.2 Empirical Challenges

Apart from the theoretical models discussed above, the results presented in this work also open up interesting avenues in terms of empirical work.

8.4.2.1 Dynamic aspects and longitudinal analyses

As indicated above, I have focused on a static and transversal analysis of working poverty in this book. It would be equally important, however, to include dynamic aspects. The situation of a worker whose household lived on a low income for one or two years and then managed to escape poverty is fundamentally different from that of a working household that is in the midst of a long poverty spell. In addition, the choice of a social policy instrument to help a group of disadvantaged workers may depend on the duration of the problem before the policy intervention. For instance, in the case of the working poor who have a low degree of labour force attachment, it is fundamental to know whether they have been in this situation for a long time or not; this has an impact on the choice of social policy instruments and on the cost of the policy intervention.

However, analysing the situation of the workforce at the microlevel over a period of five to ten years poses very tricky empirical challenges, not least in terms of the availability of panel data and of sample size. Indeed, the working poor (luckily) represent a small share of the workforce; in addition, any panel is subject to attrition over time. This means that the sample size shrinks rapidly. Indeed, many analyses focus on overall poverty rather than working poverty; in addition, the number of years analysed is usually small, typically three to five years, due to data limitations (García et al., undated).

8.4.2.2 Meta-regressions

Despite the difficulties faced by the meta-analyst, this technique is doubtlessly a useful tool. Meta-analysis goes beyond traditional literature reviews in which the selection criteria are rarely explicit and the conclusions drawn as to the efficiency of a policy left to the subjective appreciation of the researcher. Meta-analysis is, hence, less exposed to subconscious biases and more rigorous than traditional literature reviews, as shown in Chapter 6. In addition, the method I have used does not exclude any evaluation a priori: even if I excluded some evaluations or estimates from the meta-analysis in a second step, the decision was based on explicit criteria (sample size, the use of economic controls in the econometric models and so on). Moreover, all the studies I have identified and retrieved are summarized in tables (see Appendix), even those that have not been included in the meta-analysis, so that the reader can draw his or her own conclusions.

One of the main difficulties of meta-analysis is the famous 'apples and oranges problem': how is it possible to draw general conclusions on the basis of evaluations that analyse different countries, different risk groups, and rely on different poverty and employment measures? A first way to proceed is to take into account the fact that each policy is intertwined with a large set of public policies and that its impact depends on the sociodemographic composition of the population in general, and of the workforce in particular, as well as on the degree of economic performance of a given country or region. For this reason, all meta-analyses presented in Chapter 6 were broken down by welfare regimes; as far as I know, this is a relatively original solution to the problem of meta-analysis applied to social policy

212 Fighting working poverty in post-industrial economies

analysis. Moreover, after the meta-analysis, I had a more in-depth look at the evidence and tried to answer the following questions: are conclusions different for various risk groups? Do they depend on the evaluation methods and the indicators used?

In summary, I would say that meta-analysis deserves more attention by social scientists and that its benefits outweigh its drawbacks. In many cases, a meta-analysis can be more fruitful than yet another evaluation of the impact of given social policy on a specific group of workers in a given country, especially when the corpus of available evaluations is relatively large. Moreover, meta-regressions would probably be more useful than the kind of meta-analysis I have carried out; however, this approach requires being able to find a common metric for all estimates, which is far from a trivial task for multiple regression results, especially for generalized linear models (logit, probit and so on). A promising avenue of research would be to expand the pool of evaluations of the employment and antipoverty effects of the policies I have analysed in this work and, for each policy, to carry out a meta-regression of the outcomes on the policy variable, controlling for the population group analysed (all workers, single mothers, unskilled female workers and so on), for various institutional factors, such as a measure of the strictness of the employment protection legislation and the level of payroll taxes, for sociodemographic controls such as the share of unskilled workers in the labour force or the share of single mothers among welfare recipients. It remains to be seen whether economic controls should be included or not in the model, because most estimates stem from econometric evaluations that rely on specifications that include economic controls, the most usual being GDP growth and the unemployment rate.

This would largely solve the problem of comparing apples and oranges, as the effect measured by the coefficient of the policy variable would be the 'pure effect' of the programme, all other things being equal.

NOTES

1. Unfortunately, however, some cases of extreme poverty still exist: for instance, homeless people die of hypothermia in many North American and European cities every winter.
2. Of course, defining the quality of a job is complex and goes beyond income considerations (Guillén Rodríguez et al., 2009); I have, however, focused on monetary aspects in the present work for reasons developed in Chapter 2.

Appendix: summary tables and data-sets used for the meta-analyses

The articles that have been identified and retrieved are summarized in various tables that can be downloaded at the following address:

http://www.eric-crettaz.net

Some evaluations have not been included in the meta-analyses; yet, their summary can also be found in these tables, with a justification of their non-inclusion.

The data-sets (in pdf format) used for the meta-analyses can also be downloaded at this address.

References

Articles used for the meta-analyses are listed separately below

Anderson, Karen M. and Traute Meyer (2006), 'New Social Risks and Pension Reform in Germany and Sweden: The Politics of Pension Rights for Child Care', in Armingeon, Klaus and Giuliano Bonoli (eds), *The Politics of Post-Industrial Welfare States*, London: Routledge.

Andress, Hans-Jürgen and Gero Lipsmeier (1995), 'Was gehört zum notwendigen Lebensstandard und wer kann ihn sich leisten? Ein neues Konzept zur Armutsmessung', *Aus Politik und Zeitgeschichte, Bd*: 31–2.

Andress, Hans-Jürgen and Henning Lohmann (eds) (2008), *The Working Poor in Europe: Employment, Poverty and Globalization*, Cheltenham, UK and Northampton, MA, USA: Edward Elgar.

Andress, Hans-Jürgen and Till Seeck (2007), 'Ist das Normalarbeitsverhältnis noch Armutsvermeidend?', *Kölner Zeitschrift für Soziologie und Sozialpsychologie*, **59**(3): 459–92.

Antille, Gabrielle, Hedia El May, David Miceli and Jacques Silber (1997), 'L'analyse multidimensionnelle des conditions de vie: méthodologie et application à la Suisse', Série de publications du LEA No. 14, Université de Genève.

Arai, Mahmood, Rita Asplund and Erling Barth (1998), 'Low Pay, a Matter of Occupation', in Asplund, Rita, Peter J. Sloane and Ioannis Theodossiou (eds), *Low Pay and Earnings Mobility in Europe*, Cheltenham, UK and Lyme, NH, USA: Edward Elgar.

Arellano, Manuel and Samuel Bentolila (2009), 'La burbuja inmobiliaria: causas y responsables', in *La Crisis de la Economía Española. Lecciones y Propuestas*, Fundación de Estudios de Economía Aplicada (FEDEA).

Armingeon, Klaus (2006), 'Reconciling Competing Claims of the Welfare State Clientele. The Politics of Old and New Social Risk Coverage in Comparative Perspective', in Armingeon, Klaus and Giuliano Bonoli (eds), *The Politics of Post-Industrial Welfare States: Adapting Post-War Social Policies to New Social Risks*, London: Routledge.

Armingeon, Klaus and Giuliano Bonoli (eds) (2006), *The Politics of Post-Industrial Welfare States: Adapting Post-War Social Policies to New Social Risks*, London: Routledge.

Arriba González de Durana, Ana and Begoña Pérez Eransus (2007), 'La última red de protección social en España: prestaciones asistenciales y su activación', *Política y Sociedad*, **44**(2): 115–33.

Atkinson, Anthony B. (1989), *Poverty and Social Security*, New York, London: Harvester Wheatsheaf.

Atkinson, Anthony B. (1998), *Poverty in Europe*, Oxford: Wiley-Blackwell.

Atkinson, Anthony B. (2008), *The Changing Distribution of Earnings in OECD Countries*, New York: Oxford University Press.

Bäcker, Gerhard (2000), 'Armut und Unterversorgung im Kindes- und Jugendalter: Defizite der sozialen Sicherung', in Butterwegge, Christoph (ed.), *Kinderarmut in Deutschland. Ursachen, Erscheinungsformen und Gegenmassnahmen*, Frankfurt/Main: Campus Verlag.

Baumol, William J., Alan S. Blinder and William M. Scarth (1990), *L'économie, principes et politiques*, Montréal: Ed. Études vivantes.

Bazen, Stephen (2000), 'Minimum Wages and Low-Wage Employment', in Gregory, Mary, Wiemer Salverda and Stephen Bazen (eds), *Labour Market Inequalities: Problems and Policies of Low-Wage Employment in International Perspective*, Oxford: Oxford University Press.

Becker, Gary S. (1971), *The Economics of Discrimination*, 3rd edn, Chicago: Chicago University Press.

Becker, Gary S. (1981), *A Treatise on the Family*, Cambridge, MA: Harvard University Press.

Becker, Howard S. (1998), *Tricks of the Trade*, Chicago: University of Chicago Press.

Bergmark, Ake (2000), 'Solidarity in Swedish Welfare – Standing the Test of Time?', *Health Care Analysis*, **8**(4): 395–411.

Bergmark, Ake and Olof Backman (2004), 'Stuck with Welfare? Long-Term Social Assistance Recipiency in Sweden', *European Sociological Review*, **20**(5): 425–43.

Bibi, Sami and Jean-Yves Duclos (2008), 'A Comparison of the Poverty Impact of Transfers, Taxes and Market Income across Five OECD Countries', IZA Discussion Paper No. 3824, Forschungsinstitut zur Zukunft der Arbeit (IZA).

Blank, Rebecca M. (2000), 'Fighting Poverty: Lessons from Recent US History', *The Journal of Economic Perspectives*, **14**(2): 3–19.

Blank, Rebecca M., David Card and Philipp K. Robins (1999), *Financial Incentives for Increasing Work and Income Among Low-Income Families*, Paper prepared for the Joint Center for Poverty Research Conference 'Labor Markets and Less Skilled Workers', 5–6 November, 1998.

Blázquez Cuesta, Maite (2008), 'Low-Wage Employment and Mobility in Spain', *Labour* **22**(Special Issue: The Evolution of Labour Market Inequalities): 115–46.

Blundell, Richard (2006), 'Earned Income Tax Credit Policies: Impact and Optimality: The Adam Smith Lecture, 2005', *Labour Economics*, **13**(4): 423–43.

Bonoli, Giuliano (1997), 'Classifying Welfare States: A Two-Dimension Approach', *Journal of Social Policy*, **26**(3): 351–72.

Bonoli, Giuliano (2003a), 'Social Policy through Labor Markets: Understanding National Differences in the Provision of Economic Security to Wage Earners', *Comparative Political Studies*, **36**(9): 1007–30.

Bonoli, Giuliano (2003b), 'Aider les working poor: une perspective comparée', Université de Fribourg, Départment Travail social et politiques sociales, Chaire francophone.

Bonoli, Giuliano (2003c), 'The Welfare State in Switzerland', in Aspalter, Christian (ed.), *Welfare Capitalism Around the World*, Hong Kong, Taipei, Seoul: Casa Verde Publishing.

Bonoli, Giuliano (2006), 'New Social Risks and the Politics of Post-Industrial Policies', in Armingeon, Klaus and Giuliano Bonoli (eds), *The Politics of Post-Industrial Welfare States*, London: Routledge.

Bonoli, Giuliano (2007), 'Time Matters: Postindustrialization, New Social Risks, and Welfare State Adaptation in Advanced Industrial Democracies', *Comparative Political Studies*, **40**(5): 495–520.

Bonoli, Giuliano and Fabio Bertozzi (2008), *Les Nouveaux défis de l'État social*, Lausanne: PPUR presses polytechniques.

Bonoli, Giuliano and Karl Hinrichs (2010), 'Statistical Discrimination and Employers' Recruitement Practices for Low-Skilled Workers', RECWOWE, Working Papers on the Reconciliation of Work and Welfare in Europe 10/2010, RECWOWE Publication, Dissemination and Dialogue Centre.

Bonoli, Giuliano and Frank Reber (2010), 'The Political Economy of Childcare in OECD Countries: Explaining Cross-National Variation in Spending and Coverage Rates', *European Journal of Political Research*, **49**(1): 97–118.

Boos-Nünning, Ursula (2000), 'Armut von Kindern aus Zuwandererfamilien', in Butterwegge, Christoph (ed.), *Kinderarmut in Deutschland. Ursachen, Erscheinungsformen und Gegenmassnahmen*, Frankfurt/Main: Campus Verlag.

Booth, Charles (1888), 'Conditions and Occupations of the People of East London and Hackney, 1887', *Journal of the Royal Statistical Society*, **51**(2): 276–339.

Bourdieu, Pierre (1979), *La distinction: critique sociale du jugement*, Paris: Ed. de Minuit.

Bourdieu, Pierre (ed.) (1993), *La misère du monde*, Paris: Seuil.

Bourgois, Philip (2003), *In Search of Respect: Selling Crack in El Barrio*, New York: Cambridge University Press.

Boyer, Robert and Jean-Pierre Durand (1998), *L'après-fordisme*, Paris: Syros.

Brady, David (2004), 'The Welfare State and Relative Poverty in Rich Western Democracies, 1967–1997', *Social Forces*, **83**(3): 1329–64.

Brewer, Mike (2001), 'Comparing In-Work Benefits and the Reward to Work for Families with Children in the US and the UK', *Fiscal Studies* **22**(1): 41–77.

Bryner, Gary and Ryan Martin (2007), 'Innovation in Social Policy: Evaluating State Efforts to Reform Welfare, Promote Work, and Help Low-Income Families', in Russel, Crane D. and Tim B. Heaton (eds), *Handbook of Families and Poverty*, Thousand Oaks: Sage Publications.

Burkhauser, Richard V., Kenneth A. Couch and Andrew J. Glenn (1995), 'Public Policies for the Working Poor: The Earned Income Tax Credit versus Minimum Wage Legislation', Institute for Research on Poverty, Discussion Paper No. 1074-95, University of Wisconsin-Madison.

Burniaux, Jean-Marc, Flavio Padrini and Nicola Brandt (2006), 'Labour Market Performance, Income Inequality and Poverty in OECD Countries', OECD Economics Department Working Papers, OECD.

Bushman, Brad J. (1994), 'Vote-Counting Procedures in Meta-Analysis', in Cooper, Harris and Larry V. Hedges (eds), *The Handbook of Research Synthesis*, New York: Russell Sage Foundation.

Butterwegge, Christoph (ed.) (2000), *Kinderarmut in Deutschland: Ursachen, Erscheinungsformen und Gegenmaßnahmen*, Frankfurt/Main: Campus.

Cahuc, Pierre (2002), 'A quoi sert la Prime Pour l'Emploi?', *Revue française d'économie*, **16**(3): 3–61.

Calmfors, Lars and John Driffill (1988), 'Bargaining Structure, Corporatism and Macroeconomic Performance', *Economic Policy*, **3**(6): 13–62.

Card, David and Alan B. Krueger (1995), *Myth and Measurement: The New Economics of the Minimum Wage*, Princeton: Princeton University Press.

Carrasco, Raquel, Juan J. Jimeno and Ana Carolina Ortega (2004), 'The Effect of Immigration on the Employment of Native-Born Workers: Some Evidence for Spain', Documentos de trabajo 2004-17, Fundación de Estudios de Economía Aplicada (FEDEA).

Castel, Robert (1995), *Les métamorphoses de la question sociale. Une chronique du salariat*, Paris: Fayard.

Christoph, Bernhard (2008), 'Was fehlt bei Hartz IV? Zum Lebensstandard der Empfänger von Leistungen nach SGB II', *Informationsdienst Soziale Indikatoren*, **40**: 7–10.

Citro, Constance F. and Robert T. Michael (1995), *Measuring Poverty: A New Approach*, Washington: National Academy Press.

Clasen, Jochen and Daniel Clegg (2006), 'New Labour Market Risks and The Revision of Unemployment Protection Systems in Europe', in Armingeon, Klaus and Giuliano Bonoli (eds), *The Politics of Post-Industrial Welfare States*, London: Routledge.

Clayton, Richard and Jonas Pontusson (2000), 'Welfare State Retrenchment Revisited', in Pierson, Christopher and Francis G. Castles (eds), *The Welfare State: A Reader*, Cambridge: Polity Press.

Conde-Ruiz, Ignacio J., Florentino Felgueroso and José Ignacio García Pérez (2010), 'Las reformas laborales en España: un modelo agotado', Colección Estudios Económicos 11-2010, Fundación de Estudios de Economía Aplicada (FEDEA).

Conger, Rand D. and Katherine Jewsbury Conger (2007), 'Understanding the Processes Through Which Economic Hardship Influences Families and Children', in Russel, Crane D. and Tim B. Heaton (eds), *Handbook of Families and Poverty*, Thousand Oaks: Sage Publications.

Cooper, Harris M. (1998), *Synthesizing Research: A Guide for Literature Reviews*, Thousand Oaks, CA and London: Sage Publications.

Cooper, Harris M. and Larry V. Hedges (eds) (1994), *The Handbook of Research Synthesis*, New York: Russell Sage Foundation.

Crettaz, Eric (2011), 'Working poverty among immigrants and "ethnic minorities": theoretical framework and empirical evidence across welfare regimes', MAPS Working Papers Series 3/2011, University of Neuchâtel.

Crettaz, Eric and Jérémie Forney (2010), 'Situation financière des agriculteurs: mieux comprendre en croisant les perspectives', *Yearbook of Socioeconomics in Agriculture*, 255–84.

Crompton, Rosemary and Michaela Brockmann (2006), 'Class, Gender and Work-Life Articulation', in Perrons, Diane, Colette Fagan, Linda McDowell, Kath Ray and Kevin Ward (eds), *Gender Divisions and Working Time in the New Economy. Changing Patterns of Work, Care and Public Policy in Europe and North America*, Cheltenham, UK and Northampton, MA, USA: Edward Elgar.

Daguerre, Anne (2006), 'Childcare Policies in Diverse European Welfare States: Switzerland, Sweden, France, and Britain', in Armingeon, Klaus and Giuliano Bonoli (eds), *The Politics of Post-Industrial Welfare States*, London: Routledge.

Danziger, Sheldon and Peter Gottschalk (1996), *America Unequal*, New York: Russell Sage Foundation.

Darity, William A. Jr and Samuel L. Myers (1987), 'Do Transfer Payments Keep the Poor in Poverty?', *American Economic Review*, **77**(2): 216–22.

Delgado-Rodriguez, Miguel (2001), 'Glossary on Meta-Analysis', *Journal of Epidemiology and Community Health*, **55**(8): 534–6.

Dilnot, Andrew and Julian McCrae (2000), 'The Family Credit System and the Working Families Tax Credit in the United Kingdom', OECD Economic Studies No. 31, OECD.

Droz, Yvan (1998), 'De la monoculture de la vache à l'auto-exploitation: quelle économie pour quelle agriculture?', Institut Universitaire d'Études du Développement (Itinéraires No. 52), Université de Genève.

Eardley, Tony, Jonathan Bradshaw, John Ditch, Ian Gough and Peter Whiteford (1996), 'Social Assistance in OECD Countries', Department of Social Security Research Report No. 46, OECD.

Ebbinghaus, Bernhard (2006), 'Trade Union Movements in Post-Industrial Welfare States: Opening Up to New Social Interests?', in Armingeon, Klaus and Giuliano Bonoli (eds), *The Politics of Post-Industrial Welfare States*, London: Routledge.

Eichhorst, Werner and Paul Marx (2009), 'Reforming German Labor Market Institutions: A Dual Path to Flexibility', IZA Discussion Papers No. 4100, Forschungsinstitut zur Zukunft der Arbeit (IZA).

Erikson, Robert and John H. Goldthorpe (1992), *The Constant Flux: A Study of Class Mobility in Industrial Societies*, Oxford: Clarendon Press.

Esping-Andersen, Gosta (1990), *The Three Worlds of Welfare Capitalism*, Princeton: Princeton University Press.

Esping-Andersen, Gosta (ed.) (1993), *Changing Classes: Stratification and Mobility in Post-Industrial Societies*, London: Sage Publications.

Esping-Andersen, Gosta (1999), *Social Foundations of Postindustrial Economies*, Oxford: Oxford University Press.

Esping-Andersen, Gosta (2000), 'Who is Harmed by Labour Market Regulation?', in Esping-Andersen, Gosta and Marino Regini (eds), *Why Deregulate Labour Markets?*, Oxford: Oxford University Press.

Esping-Andersen, Gosta (2002a), 'Towards a Good Society, Once Again?', in Esping-Andersen, Gosta, Duncan Gallie, Anton Hemerijck and John Myles (eds), *Why We Need a New Welfare State*, Oxford: Oxford University Press.

Esping-Andersen, Gosta (2002b), 'A Child-Centered Social Investment Strategy', in Esping-Andersen, Gosta, Duncan Gallie, Anton Hemerijck and John Myles (eds), *Why We Need a New Welfare State*, Oxford: Oxford University Press.

Esping-Andersen, Gosta (2002c), 'A New Gender Contract', in Esping-Andersen, Gosta, Duncan Gallie, Anton Hemerijck and John Myles (eds), *Why We Need a New Welfare State*, Oxford: Oxford University Press.

Esping-Andersen, Gosta and Marino Regini (eds) (2000), *Why Deregulate Labour Markets?*, Oxford: Oxford University Press.

Esping-Andersen, Gosta, Duncan Gallie, Anton Hemerijck and John Myles (eds) (2002), *Why We Need a New Welfare State*, New York: Oxford University Press.

European Commission (2006), 'EU-SILC user database description', EU-SILC/BB D(2005).

European Foundation for the Improvement of Living and Working Conditions (Eurofound) (2007), 'First European Quality of Life Survey. Time Use and Work-Life Options over the Life Course', Office for Official Publications of the European Communities.

Eurostat (2002), 'European Social Statistics. Income, Poverty and Social Exclusion, 2nd Report', Office for Official Publications of the European Communities.

Eurostat (2005), 'Income Poverty and Social Exclusion in the EU25', Statistics in Focus, Issue 13/2005, Office for Official Publications of the European Communities.

Eysenck, Hans J. (1994), 'Systematic Reviews: Meta-Analysis and Its Problems', *British Medical Journal*, **309**(6957): 789–92.

Fagnani, Jeanne and Antoine Math (2008), 'Family Packages in 11 European Countries: Multiple Approaches', Saraceno, Chiara and Arnlaug Leira (eds), *Childhood: Changing Contexts*, Comparative Social Research, Vol. 25, Bingley: Emerald Group.

Falter, Jean-Marc (2006), 'Equivalence Scales and Subjective Data in Switzerland', *Swiss Journal of Economics and Statistics*, **142**(2): 263–86.

Falter, Jean-Marc and Yves Flückiger (2004), '"Bas salaires" et "working poors" en Suisse', Working Papers de l'Observatoire universitaire de l'emploi, Université de Genève.

Felgueroso, Florentino and Sergi Jiménez (2009), 'Sobre crisis, retrasos y reforma laboral. Dos pasitos para adelante, uno para atrás: un, dos, tres', in *La Crisis de la Economía Española*. Lecciones y Propuestas, Fundación de Estudios de Economía Aplicada (FEDEA).

Felgueroso, Florentino and Pablo Vázquez (2009), 'Inmigración y crisis: aciertos, desaciertos y políticas complementarias', in *La Crisis de la Economía Española*. Lecciones y Propuestas, Fundación de Estudios de Economía Aplicada (FEDEA).

Ferro Luzzi, Giovanni, Yves Flückiger and Sylvain Weber (2008), 'Multidimensional Poverty: Factor and Cluster Analysis', in Kakwani, Nanak and Jacques Silber (eds), *Quantitative Approaches to Multidimensional Poverty Measurement*, New York: Palgrave MacMillan.

Fischer, Birgit (2000), 'Statt eines Vorwortes: Mit einer tief gespaltenen Gesellschaft ins 3. Jahrtausend?', in Butterwegge, Christoph (ed.), *Kinderarmut in Deutschland. Ursachen, Erscheinungsformen und Gegenmassnahmen*, Frankfurt/Main: Campus Verlag.

Fishman, Michael E. and Harold Beebout (2001), 'Supports for Working Poor Families: A New Approach', Princeton, NJ: The Lewin Group and Mathematica Policy Research, Inc.

Foster, James, Joel Greer and Erik Thorbecke (1984), 'A Class of Decomposable Poverty Measures', *Econometrica*, **52**(3): 761–6.

Fraser, Neil, Rodolfo Gutiérrez and Ramón Peña-Casas (eds) (2011), *Working Poverty in Europe. A Comparative Approach*, Basingstoke: Palgrave Macmillan.

Freeman, Richard B. (1995), 'The Large Welfare-State as a System', *American Economic Review*, **85**(2): 16–21.

Fundación de Estudios de Economía Aplicada (2009), 'La Crisis de la Economía Española. Lecciones y Propuestas', Fundación de Estudios de Economía Aplicada (FEDEA).

Furman, Jason (2006), 'Tax Reform and Poverty', Center on Budget and Policy Priorities.

Gallie, Duncan (2002), 'The Quality of Working Life in Welfare Strategy', in Esping-Andersen, Gosta, Duncan Gallie, Anton Hemerijck and John Myles (eds), *Why We Need a New Welfare State*, Oxford: Oxford University Press.

García Espejo, Isabel and Marta Ibáñez Pascual (2007), 'Los trabajadores pobres y los bajos salarios en España: un análisis de los factores familiares y laborales asociados a las distintas situaciones de pobreza', *EMPIRIA revista de Metodología de Ciencias Sociales*, **14**: 41–67.

García, Isabel, Rodolfo Gutiérrez, Marta Ibáñez and Aroa Tejero (undated), 'A Comparative Perspective on the Dynamics of In-Work Poverty', RECWOWE papers, Network of Excellence Reconciling Work and Welfare in Europe.

Garrido, Luis and Rodolfo Gutiérrez (2009), 'More Quantity and Better Quality. Occupational Change in 21st Century Spain', Paper prepared for the conference 'The Dualisation of European Societies?', 24–25 April, Green Templeton College, University of Oxford.

Gerfin, Michael, Heidi Stutz, Thomas Oesch and Silvia Strub (2009), 'Kinderkosten in der Schweiz', Neuchâtel: Bundesamt für Statistik.

Gershuny, Jonathan (1985), 'Economic Development and Change in the Mode of Provision of Services', in Redclift, Nanneke and Enzo Mingione (eds), *Beyond Employment: Household, Gender, and Subsistence*, New York: Basil Blackwell.

Giddens, Anthony (2000), 'Positive Welfare', in Pierson, Christopher and Francis G. Castles (eds), *The Welfare State: A Reader*, Cambridge: Polity Press.

Giesselmann, Marco and Henning Lohmann (2008), 'The Different Roles of Low-Wage Work in Germany: Regional, Demographical and Temporal Variances in the Poverty Risk of Low-Paid Workers', in Andress Hans-Jürgen and Henning Lohmann (eds), *The Working Poor in Europe. Employment, Poverty and Globalization*, Cheltenham, UK and Northampton, MA, USA: Edward Elgar.

Glennerster, Howard, John Hills, David Piachaud and Jo Webb (eds) (2004), *One Hundred Years of Poverty and Policy*, York: The Joseph Rowntree Foundation.

Glyn, Andrew and Wiemer Salverda (2000), 'Employment Inequalities', in Gregory, Mary, Wiemer Salverda and Stephen Bazen (eds), *Labour Market Inequalities: Problems and Policies of Low-Wage Employment in International Perspective*, Oxford: Oxford University Press.

Goodin, Robert E., Bruce Headey, Ruud Muffels and Henk-Jan Dirven (2000), 'The Real Worlds of Welfare Capitalism', in Pierson, Christopher and Francis G. Castles (eds), *The Welfare State: A Reader*, Cambridge: Polity Press.

Gottschalk, Peter and Mary Joyce (1995), 'The Impact of Technological Change, Deindustrialization, and Internationalization of Trade on Earnings Inequality: An International Perspective', in McFate, Katherine, Roger Lawson and William J. Wilson (eds), *Poverty, Inequality and the Future of Social Policy. Western States and the New World Order*, New York: Russell Sage Foundation.

Greenstein, Robert (2005), 'The Earned Income Tax Credit: Boosting Employment, Aiding the Working Poor', Center on Budget and Policy Priorities.

Gregory, Mary and Stephen Machin (2000), 'Trade or Technological Change? Which is Working against the Low Skilled?', in Gregory, Mary, Wiemer Salverda and Stephen Bazen (eds), *Labour Market Inequalities: Problems and Policies of Low-Wage Employment in International Perspective*, Oxford: Oxford University Press.

Guillén, Ana M. and S. Alvarez (2002), 'Southern European Welfare States Facing Globalization: Is there Social Dumping?', in Sigg, Roland and

Christina Behrendt (eds), *Social Security in the Global Village*, International Social Security Association (ISSA), Transaction Publishers.

Guillén Rodríguez, Ana Marta, Rodolfo Gutiérrez Palacios and Sergio González Begega (eds) (2009), *Calidad del trabajo en la Unión Europea. Conceptos, tensiones y dimensiones*, Madrid: Thomson Civitas.

Gupta, Anjali E., Jessica Thornton Walker and Aletha C. Huston (2007), 'Working Families Should Not Be Poor: The New Hope Program', in Russel, Crane D. and Tim B. Heaton (eds), *Handbook of Families and Poverty*, Thousand Oaks: Sage Publications.

Gutiérrez Palacios, Rodolfo, Ana Guillén Rodríguez and Ramón Peña-Casas (2009), 'Earnings Inequality and In-Work-Poverty', RECWOWE Working Papers on the Reconciliation of Work and Welfare in Europe 07/2009, RECWOWE Publication, Dissemination and Dialogue Centre.

Halleröd, Björn (1994), 'A New Approach to the Direct Consensual Measurement of Poverty', Social Policy Research Centre Discussion Paper 50, Social Policy Research Centre (SPRC).

Halleröd, Björn (2006), 'Sour Grapes: Relative Deprivation, Adaptive Preferences and the Measurement of Poverty', *Journal of Social Policy*, **35**: 371–90.

Halleröd, Björn and Daniel Larsson (2008), 'In-Work Poverty in a Transitional Labour Market: Sweden, 1988–2003', in Andress, Hans-Jürgen and Henning Lohmann (eds), *The Working Poor in Europe. Employment, Poverty and Globalization*, Cheltenham, UK and Northampton, MA, USA: Edward Elgar.

Hamilton, Gayle, Stephen Freedman, Lisa Gennetian, Charles Michalopoulos, Johanna Walter, Dianna Adams-Ciardullo and Anna Gassman-Pines (2001), 'National Evaluation of Welfare-to-Work Strategies', US Department of Health and Human Services and US Department of Education.

Headey, Bruce, Peter Krause and Gert G. Wagner (2009), *Poverty Redefined as Low Consumption and Low Wealth, not just Income: Its Psychological Consequences in Australia and Germany*, Joint OECD-University of Maryland Conference: Measuring Poverty, Inequality and Social Exclusion: Lessons from Europe.

Heclo, Hugh (1995), 'The Social Question', in McFate, Katherine, Roger Lawson and William J. Wilson (eds), *Poverty, Inequality and the Future of Social Policy. Western States and the New World Order*, New York: Russell Sage Foundation.

Heinrich, Georges (2003), 'More Is Not Necessarily Better: An Empirical Analysis of the Inequality-Growth Tradeoff Using the Luxembourg

Income Study', Luxembourg Income Study Working Paper Series, Working Paper No. 344, Luxembourg Income Study (LIS).

Hemerijck, Anton (2002), 'The Self-Transformation of the European Welfare Model(s)', in Esping-Andersen, Gosta, Duncan Gallie, Anton Hemerijck and John Myles (eds), *Why We Need a New Welfare State*, Oxford: Oxford University Press.

Hemerijck, Anton and Werner Eichhorst (2009), 'Whatever Happened to the Bismarckian Welfare State?', IZA Discussion Paper No. 4085, Forschungsinstitut zur Zukunft der Arbeit (IZA).

Hills, John and Jane Waldfogel (2004), 'A "Third Way" in Welfare Reform? Evidence from the United Kingdom', *Journal of Policy Analysis and Management*, **23**(4): 765–88.

Howard, Christopher (1994), 'Happy Returns: How the Working Poor Got Tax Relief', *American Prospect*, No. 17: 46–53.

Hoynes, Hilary (2007), 'The EITC Disincentive: A Reply to Paul Trampe', *Econ Journal Watch*, **4**(3): 321–5.

Huber, Evelyne and John D. Stephens (2006), 'Combating Old and New Social Risks', in Armingeon, Klaus and Giuliano Bonoli (eds), *The Politics of Post-Industrial Welfare States*, London: Routledge.

Husby, Ralph D. (2000), 'A Policy for the Employed Poor: Minimum Wages, Wage Subsidies and Earning Tax Credits', Distributional Analysis Research Programme, Papers EEA8-2000, London School of Economics and Political Science.

Immervoll, Herwig (2007), 'Minimum Wages, Minimum Labour Costs and the Tax Treatment of Low-Wage Employment', OECD Social, Employment and Migration Working Papers No. 46, Organisation for Economic Cooperation and Development.

Immervoll, Herwig and David Barber (2005), 'Can Parents Afford to Work? Childcare Costs, Tax-Benefit Policies and Work Incentives', OECD Social, Employment and Migration Working Papers No. 31, Organisation for Economic Cooperation and Development.

Immervoll, Herwig and Mark Pearson (2009), 'A Good Time for Making Work Pay? Taking Stock of In-Work Benefits and Related Measures across the OECD', OECD Social, Employment and Migration Working Papers No. 81, Organisation for Economic Cooperation and Development.

International Labour Organization (2008), 'Global Wage Report 2008/09: Minimum Wages and Collective Bargaining: Towards Policy Coherence', International Labour Organization.

Iversen, Torben and Anne Wren (1998), 'Equality: Employment, and Budgetary Restraint – The Trilemma of the Service Economy', *World Politics*, **50**(4): 507–46.

Jacobi, Lena and Jochen Kluve (2007), 'Before and after the Hartz reforms: The Performance of Active Labour Market Policy in Germany', *Journal for Labor Market Research (Zeitschrift für Arbeitsmarktforschung)*, **40**(1): 45–64.

Jäntti, Markus and Sheldon Danziger (2000), 'Income Poverty in Advanced Countries', in Atkinson, Anthony B. and François Bourguignon (eds), *Handbook of Income Distribution*, Amsterdam: Elsevier.

Jones, Chris, Bo Burström, Anneli Marttila, Krysia Canvin and Margaret Whitehead (2006), 'Studying Social Policy and Resilience to Adversity in Different Welfare States: Britain and Sweden', *International Journal of Health Services*, **36**(3): 425–42.

Kalb, Guyonne (2009), 'Children, Labour Supply and Child Care: Challenges for Empirical Analysis', *Australian Economic Review*, **42**(3): 276–99.

Kamerman, Sheila B. (1995), 'Gender Role and Family Structure Changes in the Advanced Industrialized West: Implications for Social Policy', in McFate, Katherine, Roger Lawson and William J. Wilson (eds), *Poverty, Inequality and the Future of Social Policy. Western States and the New World Order*, New York: Russell Sage Foundation.

Kananen, Johannes, Peter Taylor-Gooby and Trine P. Larsen (2006), 'Public Attitudes and New Social Risk Reform', in Armingeon, Klaus and Giuliano Bonoli (eds), *The Politics of Post-Industrial Welfare States*, London: Routledge.

Kenworthy, Lane (1999), 'Do Social-Welfare Policies Reduce Poverty? A Cross-National Assessment', *Social Forces*, **77**(3): 1119–39.

Kenworthy, Lane (2004), *Egalitarian Capitalism*, New York: Russell Sage Foundation.

Kluve, Jochen (2006), 'The Effectiveness of European Active Labor Market Policy', IZA Discussion Paper No. 2018, Forschungsinstitut zur Zukunft der Arbeit (IZA).

Krugman, Paul (1990), *The Age of Diminished Expectations: US Economic Policy in the 1990s*, Cambridge, MA: MIT Press.

Lawson, Roger and William Julius Wilson (1995), 'Poverty, Social Rights, and the Quality of Citizenship', in McFate, Katherine, Roger Lawson and William J. Wilson (eds), *Poverty, Inequality and the Future of Social Policy. Western States and the New World Order*, New York: Russell Sage Foundation.

Legendre, François, Jean-Paul Lorgnet, Ronan Mahieu and Florence Thibault (2004), 'La prime pour l'emploi constitue-t-elle un instrument de soutien aux bas revenus?', *Revue de l'OFCE*, **88**(1): 43–58.

226 *Fighting working poverty in post-industrial economies*

Leibfried, Thomas (2000), 'Towards a European Welfare State?', in Pierson, Christopher and Francis G. Castles (eds), *The Welfare State: A Reader*, Cambridge: Polity Press.

Leu, Robert E., Stefan Burri and Tom Priester (1997), *Lebensqualität und Armut in der Schweiz*, Bern: Haupt.

Levitan, Sar A. and Isaac Shapiro (1988), *Working but Poor: America's Contradiction*, Baltimore: John Hopkins University Press.

Levitis, Jason A. and Nicholas Johnson (2006), 'Together, State Minimum Wages and State Earned Income Tax Credits Make Work Pay', Center on Budget and Policy Priorities.

Lindbom, Anders and Bo Rothstein (2004), 'The Mysterious Survival of the Swedish Welfare State', Paper presented at the Annual Meeting of the American Political Science Association, Chicago.

Lipsey, Mark W. and David B. Wilson (2001), *Practical Meta-Analysis*, Thousand Oaks, CA: Sage Publications.

Lohmann, Henning and Ive Marx (2008), 'The Different Faces of In-Work Poverty across Welfare State Regimes', in Andress, Hans-Jürgen and Henning Lohmann (eds), *The Working Poor in Europe. Employment, Poverty and Globalization*, Cheltenham, UK and Northampton, MA, USA: Edward Elgar.

Loprest, Pamela (2001), 'How Are Families Who Left Welfare Doing over Time? A Comparison of Two Cohorts of Welfare Leavers', *Economic Policy Review*, **7**(2): 9–19.

Luxembourg Income Study (LIS) Database (undated), available at: http://www.lisproject.org/techdoc.htm.

Luxembourg Income Study (LIS) Key Figures (undated), available at: http://www.lisproject.org/keyfigures.htm.

Mack, Joanna and Stewart Lansley (1985), *Poor Britain*, London: George Allen and Unwin.

MaCurdy, Thomas and Frank McIntyre (2004), 'Helping Working-Poor Families. Advantages of Wage-Based Tax Credits over the EITC and Minimum Wages', Employment Policies Institute.

Martin, Claude (1996), 'Trajectoires post-divorce et vulnérabilité', in Paugam, Serge (ed.), *L'exclusion. L'état des savoirs*, Paris: La Découverte.

Martin, John P. and David Grubb (2001), 'What Works and for Whom: A Review of OECD Countries' Experiences with Active Labour Market Policies', Working Paper 2001/14, Institutet för arbetsmarknadspolitisk utvärdering (IFAU).

Marx, Ive (2008), 'Minimum Income Protection in Postindustrial Economies: On Getting the Balance Right Between Incrementalism and Innovation. The Case of In-Work Poverty', Paper prepared for the 15th FISS International Research Seminar, 13–15 June, Sigtuna, Sweden.

Marx, Ive and Gerre Verbist (1998), 'Low-Paid Work and Poverty: a Cross-country Perspective', in Bazen, Stephen, Mary Gregory and Wiemer Salverda (eds), *Low Wage Employment in Europe*, Cheltenham, UK and Lyme, NH, USA: Edward Elgar.

Marx, Ive and Gerlinde Verbist (2008), 'Combating In-Work Poverty in Europe: The Policy Options Assessed', in Andress, Hans-Jürgen and Henning Lohmann (eds), *The Working Poor in Europe. Employment, Poverty and Globalization*, Cheltenham, UK and Northampton, MA, USA: Edward Elgar.

Mayer, Susan (1995), 'A Comparison of Poverty and Living Conditions in the United States, Canada, and Germany', in McFate, Katherine, Roger Lawson and William J. Wilson (eds), *Poverty, Inequality and the Future of Social Policy. Western States and the New World Order*, New York: Russell Sage Foundation.

McCubbin, Janet (2001), 'Noncompliance with the Earned Income Tax Credit: The Determinants of the Misreporting of Children', in Meyer, Bruce D. and Douglas Holtz-Eakin (eds), *Making Work Pay. The Earned Income Tax Credit and Its Impact on America's Families*, New York: Russell Sage Foundation.

McFate, Katherine (1995a), 'Introduction: Western States in the New World Order', in McFate, Katherine, Roger Lawson and William J. Wilson (eds), *Poverty, Inequality and the Future of Social Policy. Western States and the New World Order*, New York: Russell Sage Foundation.

McFate, Katherine (1995b), 'Trampolines, Safety Nets, or Free Fall? Labor Market Policies and Social Assistance in the 1980s', in McFate, Katherine, Roger Lawson and William J. Wilson (eds), *Poverty, Inequality and the Future of Social Policy. Western States and the New World Order*, New York: Russell Sage Foundation.

McFate, Katherine, Roger Lawson and William J. Wilson (eds) (1995), *Poverty, Inequality, and the Future of Social Policy: Western States in the New World Order*, New York: Russell Sage Foundation.

McLanahan, Sara and Irwin Garfinkel (1995), 'Single-Mother Families and Social Policy: Lessons for the United States from Canada, France, and Sweden', in McFate, Katherine, Roger Lawson and William J. Wilson (eds), *Poverty, Inequality and the Future of Social Policy. Western States and the New World Order*, New York: Russell Sage Foundation.

McLaughlin, Eithne, Janet Trewsdale and Naomi McCay (2001), 'The Rise and Fall of the UK's First Tax Credit: The Working Families Tax Credit 1998–2000', *Social Policy and Administration*, **35**(2): 163–80.

Merrien, François-Xavier (2002), 'Etats-providence en devenir: Une relecture critique des recherches récentes', *Revue française de sociologie*, **42**(2): 211–42.

Merrien, François-Xavier, Raphaël Parchet and Antoine Kernen (2005), *L'Etat social: une perspective internationale*, Paris: Armand Colin.

Meyer, Bruce D. and Douglas Holtz-Eakin (eds) (2001), *Making Work Pay: the Earned Income Tax Credit and Its Impact on America's Families*, New York: Russell Sage Foundation.

Moller, Stephanie, Eveline Huber, John D. Stephens, David Bradley and François Nielsen (2003), 'Determinants of Relative Poverty in Advanced Capitalist Democracies', *American Sociological Review*, **68**(1): 22–51.

Moreno, Luis (2002), 'Mediterranean Welfare and "Superwomen"', Unidad de Políticas Comparadas Working Paper 02-02, Consejo Superior de Investigaciones Científicas (CSIS).

Murray, Charles (2000), 'The Two Wars Against Poverty', in Pierson, Christopher and Francis G. Castles (eds), *The Welfare State: A Reader*, Cambridge: Polity Press.

Nagle, Ami and Nicholas Johnson (2006), 'A Hand Up. How State Earned Income Tax Credits Help Working Families Escape Poverty in 2006', Center on Budget and Policy Priorities.

Neumark, David and William Wascher (2007), 'Minimum Wage and Employment', IZA Discussion Paper No. 2570, Forschungsinstitut zur Zukunft der Arbeit (IZA).

Nielsen, François and Arthur S. Alderson (2002), 'Globalization and the Great U-Turn: Income Inequality Trends in 16 OECD Countries', *American Journal of Sociology*, **107**(5): 1244–99.

Nolan, Brian (1998), 'Low Pay, the Earnings Distribution and Poverty in Ireland, 1987–1994', in Bazen, Stephen, Mary Gregory and Wiemer Salverda (eds), *Low Wage Employment in Europe*, Cheltenham, UK and Lyme, NH, USA: Edward Elgar.

Nolan, Brian and Ive Marx (2000), 'Low Pay and Household Poverty', in Gregory, Mary, Wiemer Salverda and Stephen Bazen (eds), *Labour Market Inequalities: Problems and Policies of Low-Wage Employment in International Perspective*, Oxford: Oxford University Press.

Notten, Geranda and Chris De Neubourg (2007), 'Relative or Absolute Poverty in the US and EU? The Battle of the Rates', MPRA Paper No. 5313, Munich Personal RePEc Archive.

Nyberg, Anita (2006), 'Economic Crisis and the Sustainability of the Dual-Earner, Dual-Carer Model', in Perrons, Diane, Colette Fagan, Linda McDowell, Kath Ray and Kevin Ward (eds), *Gender Divisions and Working Time in the New Economy. Changing Patterns of Work, Care and Public Policy in Europe and North America*, Cheltenham, UK and Northampton, MA, USA: Edward Elgar.

OECD (1997), 'Employment Outlook', Paris: Organisation for Economic Cooperation and Development.

OECD (1998a), 'Employment Outlook', Paris: Organisation for Economic Cooperation and Development.

OECD (1998b), 'OECD Economic Outlook', Paris: Organisation for Economic Cooperation and Development.

OECD (2003), 'Employment Outlook', Paris: Organisation for Economic Cooperation and Development.

OECD (2006), 'Employment Outlook', Paris: Organisation for Economic Cooperation and Development.

OECD (2008), 'Growing Unequal? Income Distribution and Poverty in OECD Countries', Organisation for Economic Cooperation and Development.

Offermann, Volker (2000), 'Kinderarmut als Ausdruck sozialer Heterogenisierung in den östlichen Bundesländern: das Beispiel Brandenburg', in Butterwegge, Christoph (ed.), *Kinderarmut in Deutschland. Ursachen, Erscheinungsformen und Gegenmassnahmen*, Frankfurt/Main: Campus Verlag.

Okwuje, Ifie and Nicholas Johnson (2006), 'A Rising Number of State Earned Income Tax Credits Are Helping Working Families Escape Poverty', Center on Budget and Policy Priorities (CBPP).

Oxley, Howard, Thai Thanh Dang and Pablo Antolin (2000), 'Poverty Dynamics in Six OECD Countries', OECD Economic Studies No. 30, Organisation for Economic Cooperation and Development.

Pahl, Ray and Claire Wallace (1985), 'Household Work Strategies in Economic Recession', in Redclift, Nanneke and Enzo Mingione (eds), *Beyond Employment: Household, Gender, and Subsistence*, New York: Basil Blackwell.

Palier, Bruno (ed.) (2010), *A Long Good Bye to Bismarck. The Politics of Welfare Reforms in Continental Welfare States*, Amsterdam: Amsterdam University Press.

Palme, Joakim, Ake Bergmark, Olof Backman, Felipe Estrada, Johan Fritzell, Olle Lundberg, Ola Sjoberg and Marta Szebehely (2002), 'Welfare Trends in Sweden: Balancing the Books for the 1990s', *Journal of European Social Policy*, **12**(4): 329–46.

Paugam, Serge (ed.) (1996), *L'exclusion, l'état des savoirs*, Paris: Ed. La Découverte.

Paugam, Serge (2005), *Les formes élémentaires de la pauvreté*, Paris: Presses Universitaires de France.

Pearson, Mark and Stefano Scarpetta (2000), 'An Overview: What Do We Know about Policies to Make Work Pay?', OECD Economic Studies No. 31, Paris: Organisation for Economic Cooperation and Development.

Peña-Casas, Ramón and Mia Latta (2004), 'Working Poor in the European Union', European Foundation for the Improvement of Living and Working Conditions.

Pérez Eransus, Begoña, Ana Arriba González de Durana and José Manuel Parrilla Fernández (2009), 'Transformaciones de las políticas autonómicas de inclusión social: ¿Reforma o cambio de imagen?', in Moreno, Luis (ed.), *Reformas de las políticas de bienestar en España*, Madrid: Siglo XXI.

Piachaud, David and Jo Webb (2004), 'Changes in Poverty', in Glennerster, Howard, John Hills, David Piachaud and Jo Webb (eds), *One Hundred Years of Poverty and Policy*, York: The Joseph Rowntree Foundation.

Pierson, Paul (1994), *Dismantling the Welfare State?*, Cambridge: Cambridge University Press.

Ravallion, Martin (2003), 'The Debate on Globalization, Poverty and Inequality: Why Measurement Matters', World Bank Policy Research Working Paper 3038, World Bank.

Ravallion, Martin (2007), 'Inequality Is Bad for the Poor', in Jenkins, Stephen P. and John Micklewright (eds), *Inequality and Poverty Re-Examined*, New York: Oxford University Press.

Rosenthal, Robin and M. Robin DiMatteo (2001), 'Meta-Analysis: Recent Developments in Quantitative Methods for Literature Reviews', *Annual Review of Psychology*, **52**: 59–82.

Rowntree, B. Seebohm (1980 [1901]), *Poverty: A Study of Town Life*, New York and London: Garland Publishing.

Ruesga, Santos M. (2007), 'El mercado de trabajo', in García de la Cruz, José Manuel and Santos M. Ruesga Benito (eds), *Economía española. Estructura y regulación*, Madrid: International Thomson Editors Spain.

Sawhill, Isabel and Adam Thomas (2001), 'A Hand Up for the Bottom Third, Toward a New Agenda for Low-Income Working Families', The Brookings Institution.

Scholz, John K. (1994), 'The Earned Income Tax Credit – Participation, Compliance, and Antipoverty Effectiveness', *National Tax Journal*, **47**(1): 63–87.

Schulman, Karen (2000), 'The High Cost of Child Care Puts Quality Care Out of Reach for Many Families', Children's Defense Fund.

Sen, Amartya K. (1981), *Poverty and Famines. An Essay on Entitlement and Deprivation*, Oxford: Clarendon Press.

Sen, Amartya K. (1983), 'Poor, Relatively Speaking', *Oxford Economic Papers – New Series*, **35**(2): 153–69.

Sen, Amartya K. (1999), *Development as Freedom*, Oxford: Oxford University Press.

Sherman, Arloc, Shawn Fremstad and Sharon Parrott (2004), 'Employment Rates for Single Mothers Fell Substantially During Recent Period of Labor Market Weakness', Center on Budget and Policy Priorities.

Simón, Hipólito J. (2003), '¿Qué determina la afiliación a los sindicatos en España?', Revista del Ministerio de trabajo y asuntos sociales, Economía y socciología, **41**: 69−87.

Smeeding, Timothy (2005), 'Government Programmes and Social Outcomes. The United States in Comparative Perspective', Luxembourg Income Study Working Papers Series, Paper No. 426, Luxembourg Income Study (LIS).

Stancanelli, Elena G.F. and Henri Sterdyniak (2004), 'Un bilan des etudes sur la prime pour l'emploi', *Revue de l'OFCE*, **88**: 17–41.

Standing, Guy (1995), 'Labor Insecurity through Market Regulation: Legacy of the 1980s, Challenge for the 1990s', in McFate, Katherine, Roger Lawson and William J. Wilson (eds), *Poverty, Inequality and the Future of Social Policy. Western States and the New World Order*, New York: Russell Sage Foundation.

Stiglitz, Joseph E. (2002), *Globalization and its Discontents*, New York: W.W. Norton.

Strengmann-Kuhn, Wolfgang (2003), *Armut trotz Erwerbstätigkeit: Analysen und sozialpolitische Konsequenzen*, Frankfurt/Main: Campus Verlag.

Suter, Christian and Denise Paris (2002), 'Ungleichheit und Deprivation: Die Schweiz im Drei-Länder Vergleich', *Swiss Journal of Sociology*, **28**(2): 217–40.

Swiss Conference of Welfare Institutions (2003), 'Richtlinien für die Ausgestaltung und Bemessung der Sozialhilfe', Bern: Schweizerische Konferenz für Sozialhilfe (SKOS).

Swiss Federal Statistical Office (2007), 'La pauvreté des personnes en âge de travailler', Neuchâtel: Office fédéral de la statistique.

The Canberra Group, Expert Group on Household Income Statistics (2001), 'Final Report and Recommendations', United Nations Statistics Divison.

Townsend, Peter (1974), 'Poverty as Relative Deprivation: Resources and Style of Living', in Wedderburn, Dorothy (ed.), *Poverty, Inequality and Class Structure*, Cambridge: Cambridge University Press.

Townsend, Peter (1979), *Poverty in the United Kingdom: A Survey of Household Resources and Standards of Living*, London: Penguin.

US Bureau of Labor Statistics (2003), 'A Profile of the Working Poor 2001', US Department of Labor.

US Census Bureau (2010), 'Income, Poverty, and Health Insurance Coverage in the United States: 2009', Current Population Reports, US Department of Commerce.

US Department of Health and Human Services (undated), 'Characteristics and Financial Circumstances of TANF Recipients. October 1999 – September 2000', Administration for Children and Families.

Van der Veen, Romke (2009), 'The Transformation of the Welfare State. What is left of public responsibility?', in Schinkel, Willem (ed.), *Globalization and the State. Sociological Perspectives on the State of the State*, New York: Palgrave MacMillan.

Van Oorschot, Wim (1991), 'Non-Take-Up of Social Security Benefits in Europe', *Journal of European Social Policy*, **1**(1): 15–30.

Van Praag, Bernard and Ada Ferrer-i-Carbonell (2008), 'The Subjective Approach to Multidimensional Poverty Measurement', in Kakwani, Nanak and Jacques Silber (eds), *Quantitative Approaches to Multidimensional Poverty Measurement*, New York: Palgrave MacMillan.

Van Praag, Bernard, Theo Goedhart and Arie Kapteyn (1980), 'The Poverty Line – A Pilot Survey in Europe', *Review of Economics and Statistics*, **62**(3): 461–5.

Ventry, Dennis J. Jr (2001), 'The Collision of Tax and Welfare Politics: The Political History of the Earned Income Tax Credit', in Meyer, Bruce D. and Douglas Holtz-Eakin (eds), *Making Work Pay. The Earned Income Tax Credit and Its Impact on America's Families*, New York: Russell Sage Foundation.

Viebrock, Elke and Jochen Clasen (2009), 'Flexicurity – A State-of-the-Art Review', RECWOWE Working Papers on the Reconciliation of Work and Welfare in Europe, 01/2009, RECWOWE Publication, Dissemination and Dialogue Centre.

Whiteford, Pete and Willem Adema (2007), 'What Works Best in Reducing Child Poverty: A Benefit or Work Strategy?', OECD Social, Employment and Migration Working Papers No. 31, Organisation for Economic Cooperation and Development.

Wilson, William Julius (1996), *When Work Disappears. The World of the New Urban Poor*, New York: A.A. Knopf.

Wood, Adrian (1994), *North–South Trade, Employment and Inequality. Changing Fortunes in a Skill-Driven World*, Oxford: Clarendon Press.
Zubiri, Ignacio (2007), 'Social Protection and Social Security Contributions in Spain', in Martinez-Vasquez, Jorge and José Felix Sanz-Sanz (eds), *Fiscal Reform in Spain*, Cheltenham, UK and Northampton, MA, USA: Edward Elgar.

ARTICLES USED FOR THE META-ANALYSES

Abowd, John M., Francis Kramarz, David N. Margolis and Thomas Philippon (2000), 'The Tail of Two Countries: Minimum Wages and Employment in France and the United States', IZA Discussion Paper No. 203, Forschungsinstitut zur Zukunft der Arbeit (IZA).
Addison, John T., McKinley L. Blackburn and Chad D. Cotti (2009), 'Do Minimum Wages Raise Employment? Evidence from the US Retail-Trade Sector', *Labour Economics*, **16**(4): 397–408.
Bäckman, Olof and Tommy Ferrarini (2010), 'Combating Child Poverty? A Multilevel Assessment of Family Policy Institutions and Child Poverty in 21 Old and New Welfare States', *Journal of Social Policy*, **39**: 275–96.
Baker, Michael, Jonathan Gruber and Kevin Milligan (2008), 'Universal Child Care, Maternal Labor Supply, and Family Well-Being', *Journal of Political Economy*, **116**(4): 709–45.
Bargain, Olivier (2009), 'The Distributional Effects of Tax-benefit Policies under New Labour: A Shapley Decomposition', IZA Discussion Paper No. 4296, Forschungsinstitut zur Zukunft der Arbeit (IZA).
Bargain, Olivier and Kristian Orsini (2006), 'In-Work Policies in Europe: Killing Two Birds with One Stone?', *Labour Economics*, **13**(6): 667–97.
Bargain, Olivier and Isabelle Terraz (2003), 'Évaluation et mise en perspective des effets incitatifs et redistributifs de la Prime pour l'Emploi', *Economie & prévision*, **4–5**(160–161): 121–47.
Bartik, Timothy J. (2004), 'Thinking about Local Living Wage Requirements', *Urban Affairs Review*, **40**(2): 269–99.
Bazen, Stephen (2000), 'The Impact of the Regulation of Low Wages on Inequality and Labour-Market Adjustment: A Comparative Analysis', *Oxford Review of Economic Policy*, **16**(1): 57–69.
Berninger, Ina (2009), 'Welche familienpolitischen Massnahmen fördern die Arbeitsmarktpartizipation von Müttern?', *Kölner Zeitschrift für Soziologie und Sozialpsychologie*, **61**(3): 355–85.
Blau, David and Erdal Tekin (2007), 'The Determinants and Consequences of Child Care Subsidies for Single Mothers in the USA', *Journal of Population Economics*, **20**(4): 719–41.

Bloemen, Hans G. and Elena G.F. Stancanelli (2007), 'A Model with Endogenous Programme Participation: Evaluating the Tax Credit in France', IZA Discussion Paper No. 2607, Forschungsinstitut zur Zukunft der Arbeit (IZA).

Blundell, Richard (2000), 'Work Incentives and "In-Work" Benefit Reforms: A Review', *Oxford Review of Economic Policy*, **16**(1): 27–44.

Blundell, Richard (2006), 'Earned Income Tax Credit Policies: Impact and Optimality: The Adam Smith Lecture, 2005', *Labour Economics*, **13**(4): 423–43.

Böckerman, Petri and Roope Uusitalo (2009), 'Minimum Wages and Youth Employment: Evidence from the Finnish Retail Trade Sector', *British Journal of Industrial Relations*, **47**(2): 388–405.

Brewer, Mike, Alan Duncan, Andrew Shephard and María José Suarez (2006), 'Did Working Families' Tax Credit Work? The Impact of In-Work Support on Labour Supply in Great Britain', *Labour Economics*, **13**(6): 699–720.

Brink, Anna, Katarina Nordblom and Roger Wahlberg (2007), 'Maximum Fee versus Child Benefit: a Welfare Analysis of Swedish Child-Care Fee Reform', *International Tax and Public Finance*, **14**(4): 457–80.

Bub, Kristen L. and Kathleen McCartney (2004), 'On Childcare as a Support for Maternal Employment Wages and Hours', *Journal of Social Issues*, **60**(4): 819–34.

Burkhauser, Richard V. and Joseph J. Sabia (2007), 'The Effectiveness of Minimum-Wage Increases in Reducing Poverty: Past, Present, and Future', *Contemporary Economic Policy*, **25**(2): 262–81.

Campolieti, Michele, Morley Gunderson and Chris Riddell (2006), 'Minimum Wage Impacts from a Prespecified Research Design: Canada 1981–1997', *Industrial Relations*, **45**(2): 195–216.

Cho, Yoonyoung (2006), 'An Analysis of Women's Fertility and Labour Supply: Implications for Family Policies', International Conference on Declining Fertility in East and Southern Asian Countries, 14–15 December, Hitotsubashi Collaboration Center, Tokyo, Japan.

Del Boca, Daniela, Silvia Pasqua and Chiara Pronzato (2009), 'Motherhood and Market Work Decisions in Institutional Context: A European Perspective', *Oxford Economic Papers – New Series*, **61**: I147–71.

Del Boca, Daniela and Daniela Vuri (2007), 'The Mismatch Between Employment and Child Care in Italy: the Impact of Rationing', *Journal of Population Economics*, **20**(4): 805–32.

Doucouliagos, Hristos and T. D. Stanley (2009), 'Publication Selection Bias in Minimum-Wage Research? A Meta-Regression Analysis', *British Journal of Industrial Relations*, **47**(2): 406–28.

Eamon, Mary K., Chi-Fang Wu and Saijun Zhang (2009), 'Effectiveness and Limitations of the Earned Income Tax Credit for Reducing Child Poverty in the United States', *Children and Youth Services Review*, **31**(8): 919–26.

Eissa, Nada and Hilary W. Hoynes (2004), 'Taxes and the Labor Market Participation of Married Couples: the Earned Income Tax Credit', *Journal of Public Economics*, **88**(9–10): 1931–58.

Ellwood, David T. (2000), 'The Impact of the Earned Income Tax Credit and Social Policy Reforms on Work, Marriage, and Living Arrangements', *National Tax Journal*, **53**(4; Part 2): 1063–106.

Ernst Stähli, Michèle, Jean-Marie Le Goff, René Levy and Eric Widmer (2009), 'Wishes or Constraints? Mothers' Labour Force Participation and its Motivation in Switzerland', *European Sociological Review*, **25**(3): 333–48.

Fang, Tony and Morley Gunderson (2009), 'Minimum Wage Impacts on Older Workers: Longitudinal Estimates from Canada', *British Journal of Industrial Relations*, **47**(2): 371–87.

Feldmann, Horst (2009), 'The Unemployment Effects of Labor Regulation around the World', *Journal of Comparative Economics*, **37**(1): 76–90.

Fitzpatrick, Maria D. (2010), 'Preschoolers Enrolled and Mothers at Work? The Effects of Universal Prekindergarten', *Journal of Labor Economics*, **28**(1): 51–85.

Francesconi, Marco, Helmut Rainer and Wilbert van der Klaauw (2009), 'The Effects of in-Work Benefit Reform in Britain on Couples: Theory and Evidence', *Economic Journal*, **119**(535): F66–100.

Frick, Joachim R. (2007), 'Family Related Transfers and Child Poverty across Europe', in Schwarze, J., J. Räbiger and R. Thiede (eds), *Arbeitsmarkt-und Sozialpolitikforschung im Wandel-Festschrift für Christof Helberger zum 65. Geburtstag*, Hamburg: Kovac.

Gerfin, Michael, Robert E. Leu, Stephan Brun and Andreas Tschöpe (2002), *Steuergutschriften, Mindestlöhne und Armut unter den Erwerbstätigen in der Schweiz*, Bern: Staatssekretariat für Wirtschaft.

Giannarelli, Linda, Joyce Morton and Laura Wheaton (2007), 'Estimating the Anti-Poverty Effects of Changes in Taxes and Benefits with the TRIM3 Microsimulation Model', Urban Institute Technical Report, The Urban Institute.

Gregg, Paul, Susan Harkness and Sarah Smith (2009), 'Welfare Reform and Lone Parents in the UK', *Economic Journal*, **119**(535): F38–65.

Grogger, Jeffrey (2003), 'The Effects of Time Limits, the EITC, and Other Policy Changes on Welfare Use, Work, and Income among Female-Headed Families', *The Review of Economics and Statistics*, **85**(2): 394–408.

Gundersen, Craig and James P. Ziliak (2004), 'Poverty and Macroeconomic Performance across Space, Race, and Family Structure', *Demography*, **41**(1): 61–86.

Haan, Peter and Michal Myck (2007), 'Apply With Caution: Introducing UK-Style In-Work Support in Germany', *Fiscal Studies*, **28**(1): 43–72.

Heller Clain, Suzanne (2008), 'How Living Wage Legislation Affects US Poverty Rates', *Journal of Labor Research*, **29**(3): 205–18.

Herbst, Chris M. (2008), 'Do Social Policy Reforms have Different Impacts on Employment and Welfare use as Economic Conditions Change?', *Journal of Policy Analysis and Management*, **27**(4): 867–94.

Hotz, V. Joseph and John K. Scholz (2003), 'The Earned Income Tax Credit', in Moffit Robert A. (ed.), *Means-Tested Transfer Programs in the United States*, Chicago: University of Chicago Press.

Hyslop, Dean and Steven Stillman (2007), 'Youth Minimum Wage Reform and the Labour Market in New Zealand', *Labour Economics*, **14**(2): 201–30.

Jaeger, Ulrike (2010), 'Working or Stay-at-Home Mum? The Influence of Family Benefits and Religiosity', IFO Working Paper University of Munich, Institut für Wirtschaftsforschung (IFO).

Joassart-Marcelli, Pascale (2005), 'Working Poverty in Southern California: Towards an Operational Measure', *Social Science Research*, **34**(1): 20–43.

Kalb, Guyonne (2009), 'Children, Labour Supply and Child Care: Challenges for Empirical Analysis', *Australian Economic Review*, **42**(3): 276–99.

Kalb, Guyonne and Wang Sheng Lee (2008), 'Childcare Use and Parents' Labour Supply in Australia', *Australian Economic Papers*, **47**(3): 272–95.

Kalenkoski, Charlene M. and Donald J. Lacombe (2008), 'Effects of Minimum Wages on Youth Employment: the Importance of Accounting for Spatial Correlation', *Journal of Labor Research*, **29**(4): 303–17.

Kawaguchi, Daiji and Yuko Mori (2009), 'Is Minimum Wage an Effective Anti-Poverty Policy in Japan?', *Pacific Economic Review*, **14**(4): 532–54.

Kawaguchi, Daiji and Ken Yamada (2007), 'The Impact of the Minimum Wage on Female Employment in Japan', *Contemporary Economic Policy*, **25**(1): 107–18.

Kornstad, Tom and Thor O. Thoresen (2006), 'Effects of Family Policy Reforms in Norway: Results from a Joint Labour Supply and Childcare Choice Microsimulation Analysis', *Fiscal Studies*, **27**(3): 339–71.

Kreyenfeld, Michaela, Katharina C. Spiess and Gert G. Wagner (2000), 'A Forgotten Issue: Distributional Effects of Day Care Subsidies in Germany', IZA Discussion Paper No. 198, Forschungsinstitut zur Zukunft der Arbeit (IZA).

Lefebvre, Pierre and Philip Merrigan (2008), 'Child-Care Policy and the Labor Supply of Mothers with Young Children: A Natural Experiment from Canada', *Journal of Labor Economics*, **26**(3): 519–48.

Lefebvre, Pierre, Philip Merrigan and Matthieu Verstraete (2009), 'Dynamic Labour Supply Effects of Childcare Subsidies: Evidence from a Canadian Natural Experiment on Low-Fee Universal Child Care', *Labour Economics*, **16**(5): 490–502.

Leigh, Andrew (2007), 'Does Raising the Minimum Wage Help the Poor?', *Economic Record*, **83**(263): 432–45.

Lundin, Daniela, Eva Mörk and Björn Öckert (2008), 'How Far Can Reduced Childcare Prices Push Female Labour Supply?', *Labour Economics*, **15**: 647–59.

Matsaganis, Manos, Horacio Levy, Magda Mercader-Prats, Stefano Toso, Cathal O'Donoghue, Manuela Coromaldi, Carlos Farinha Rodrigues and Panos Tsakloglu (2005), 'Child Poverty and Family Transfers in Southern Europe', IZA Discussion Paper No. 1509, Forschungsinstitut zur Zukunft der Arbeit (IZA).

Meyer, Bruce D. and Dan T. Rosenbaum (2001), 'Welfare, the Earned Income Tax Credits, and the Labor Supply of Single Mothers', *The Quarterly Journal of Economics*, **116**(3): 1063–114.

Milligan, Kevin and Mark Stabile (2007), 'The Integration of Child Tax Credits and Welfare: Evidence from the Canadian National Child Benefit Program', *Journal of Public Economics*, **91**(1–2): 305–26.

Misra, Joya, Stephanie Moller and Michelle J. Budig (2007), 'Work-Family Policies and Poverty for Partnered and Single Women in Europe and North America', *Gender and Society*, **21**(6): 804–27.

Morgan, David R. and Kenneth Kickham (2001), 'Children in Poverty: Do State Policies Matter?', *Social Science Quarterly*, **82**(3): 478–93.

Müller, Kai-Uwe and Viktor Steiner (2008), 'Would a Legal Minimum Wage Reduce Poverty? A Microsimulation Study for Germany', IZA Discussion Paper No. 3491, Forschungsinstitut zur Zukunft der Arbeit (IZA).

Naz, Ghazala (2004), 'The Impact of Cash-Benefit Reform on Parents' Labour Force Participation', *Journal of Population Economics*, **17**(2): 369–83.

Neumark, David and Scott Adams (2003), 'Do Living Wage Ordinances Reduce Urban Poverty?', *Journal of Human Resources*, **38**(3): 490–521.

Neumark, David, Mark Schweitzer and William Wascher (2005), 'The Effects of Minimum Wages on the Distribution of Family Incomes – A Nonparametric Analysis', *Journal of Human Resources*, **40**(4): 867–94.

Neumark, David and William Wascher (2001), 'Using the EITC to Help Poor Families: New Evidence and a Comparison with the Minimum Wage', *National Tax Journal*, **54**(2): 281–317.

Neumark, David and William Wascher (2002), 'Do Minimum Wages Fight Poverty?', *Economic Inquiry*, **40**(3): 315–33.

Neumark, David and William Wascher (2006), 'Minimum Wages and Employment: A Review of Evidence from the New Minimum Wage Research', NBER working paper, National Bureau of Economic Research.

Noonan, Mary C., Sandra S. Smith and Mary E. Corcoran (2007), 'Examining the Impact of Welfare Reform, Labor Market Conditions, and the Earned Income Tax Credit on the Employment of Black and White Single Mothers', *Social Science Research*, **36**(1): 95–130.

Orrenius, Pia M. and Madeline Zavodny (2008), 'The Effect of Minimum Wages on Immigrants' Employment and Earnings', *Industrial and Labor Relations Review*, **61**(4): 544–63.

Pettit, Becky and Jennifer Hook (2005), 'The Structure of Women's Employment in Comparative Perspective', *Social Forces*, **84**(2): 779–801.

Portugal, Pedro and Ana Rute Cardoso (2006), 'Disentangling the Minimum Wage Puzzle: An Analysis of Worker Accessions and Separations', *Journal of the European Economic Association*, **4**(5): 988–1013.

Ragacs, Christian (2008), 'On the Empirics of Minimum Wages and Employment: Evidence for the Austrian Industry', *Applied Economics Letters*, **15**(1): 61–4.

Rammohan, Anu and Stephen Whelan (2007), 'The Impact of Childcare Costs on the Full-Time/Part-Time Employment Decisions of Australian Mothers', *Australian Economic Papers*, **46**(2): 152–69.

Sabia, Joseph J. (2008), 'Minimum Wages and the Economic Well-Being of Single Mothers', *Journal of Policy Analysis and Management*, **27**(4): 848–66.

Sabia, Joseph J. (2009a), 'The Effects of Minimum Wage Increases on Retail Employment and Hours: New Evidence from Monthly CPS Data', *Journal of Labor Research*, **30**(1): 75–97.

Sabia, Joseph J. (2009b), 'Identifying Minimum Wage Effects: New Evidence from Monthly CPS Data', *Industrial Relations*, **48**(2): 311–28.

Sánchez-Mangas, Rocio and Virginia Sánchez-Marcos (2008), 'Balancing Family and Work: The Effect of Cash Benefits for Working Mothers', *Labour Economics*, **15**(6): 1127–42.

Scarth, William and Lei Tang (2008), 'An Evaluation of the Working Income Tax Benefit', *Canadian Public Policy*, **34**(1): 25–36.

Shannon, Michael (2009), 'Canadian Lone Mother Employment Rates, Policy Change and the US Welfare Reform Literature', *Applied Economics*, **41**(19): 2463–81.

Skedinger, Per (2006), 'Minimum Wages and Employment in Swedish Hotels and Restaurants', *Labour Economics*, **13**(2): 259–90.

Stancanelli, Elena G.F. (2008), 'Evaluating the Impact of the French Tax Credit on the Employment Rate of Women', *Journal of Public Economics*, **92**(10–11): 2036–47.

Sutherland, Holly (2004), 'The National Minimum Wage and In-Work Poverty', Department of Applied Economics Working Papers MU0102, University of Cambridge.

Tekin, Erdal (2007), 'Childcare Subsidies, Wages, and Employment of Single Mothers', *Journal of Human Resources*, **42**(2): 453–87.

Thompson, Jeffrey P. (2009), 'Using Local Labor Market Data to Re-Examine the Employment Effects of the Minimum Wage', *Industrial and Labor Relations Review*, **62**(3): 343–66.

Trampe, Paul (2007), 'The EITC Disincentive: The Effects on Hours Worked from the Phase-Out of the Earned Income Tax Credit', *Econ Journal Watch*, **4**(3): 308–20.

Uunk, Wilfred, Matthijs Kalmijn and Ruud Muffels (2005), 'The Impact of Young Children on Women's Labour Supply – A Reassessment of Institutional Effects in Europe', *Acta Sociologica*, **48**(1): 41–62.

van Damme, Maike, Matthijs Kalmijn and Wilfred Uunk (2009), 'The Employment of Separated Women in Europe: Individual and Institutional Determinants', *European Sociological Review*, **25**(2): 183–97.

Van Ham, Maarten and Clara H. Mulder (2005), 'Geographical Access to Childcare and Mothers Labour-Force Participation', *Tijdschrift Voor Economische En Sociale Geografie*, **96**(1): 63–74.

Vedder, Richard and Lowell Gallaway (2002), 'The Minimum Wage and Poverty among Full-Time Workers', *Journal of Labor Research*, **23**(1): 41–9.

Vedder, Richard K. and Lowell E. Gallaway (2001), 'Does the Minimum Wage Reduce Poverty?', Employment Policies Institute, June.

Watson, Duncan (2000), 'UK Wage Underpayment: Implications for the Minimum Wage', *Applied Economics*, **32**(4): 429–40.

Wessels, Walter J. (2007), 'A Reexamination of Card and Krueger's State-Level Study of the Minimum Wage', *Journal of Labor Research*, **28**(1): 135–46.

Index

expected antipoverty effects 43–6, 122

employment effects 121–2, 123–6, 149–50

expected employment effects 41–3, low labour force attachment 3

meta-analysis *see under* meta-analytical approach

see also under individual countries

Moller, Stephanie 203

Netherlands 209
childcare 64–5, 207
employment-conditional benefits 51
family cash benefits 57
productivity 29
social security contributions 88

Neumark, David 118–19, 122, 125

'New Minimum Wage Research' (Card and Krueger) 118

New Zealand
childcare 63–5
family cash benefits 57
minimum wages 40, 126
tax credits 51

Nielsen, François 31

no such thing as 'the working poor' or a one-size-fits-all solution 189–212
different welfare regimes generate different types of working poverty 196–9
different social policy instruments and working poverty types 200–205
trade-off between jobs' quality/quantity dealt with in different ways 205–7
there is no such thing as 'the working poor' 189–91
each country must find its own combination of policies 200–207
economic/sociodemographic/policy factors' impact 192–6
there are three basic types of working poverty 189–91
where do we go now? challenges for working poverty research 207–12

dynamic aspects and longitudinal analyses 210–211

empirical challenges 210–212

meta-regressions 211–12

role of social norms and cultural values 208

specific context in which a model was implemented 209

theoretical developments 207–10

Nolan, Brian 45

Nordic countries *see under* individual countries

Norway
childcare 62–5
family cash benefits 57

Notten, Geranda 79, 85, 94

OECD countries 47
childcare 63, 67
family cash benefits 57
minimum wages and unemployment 40, 43, 70
poverty rates 49
tax credits 51
trade 32, 192

parental leave 60, 183, 197, 202
Germany 90, 159
Scandinavia 60
Sweden 77, 90, 159, 179

Paugam, Serge 13

Pearson, Karl 104

Portugal
childcare 63–5
employment protection 198
social security contributions 88

potential solutions *see* minimum wages, social transfers; childcare services
see also no such thing as 'the working poor' or a one-size-fits-all solution

poverty
absolute versus relative poverty 12–14, 28
child poverty *see under* individual countries
childcare services, antipoverty effect of 144–5, 148
expected antipoverty effect 67
see also childcare services